COSTS IN ARBITRATION PROCEEDINGS
SECOND EDITION

Other titles in this series are:

COSTS IN ARBITRATION PROCEEDINGS

BY

MICHAEL O'REILLY

BEng, LLB, PhD, CEng, MICE, FCIArb
of Gray's Inn, Barrister
Professor and Head of Civil Engineering at Kingston University

Second edition

LONDON   HONG KONG
1997

LLP Limited
Legal Publishing Division
69–77 Paul Street
London EC2A 4LQ
Great Britain

SOUTH-EAST ASIA
LLP Asia Limited
Room 1101, Hollywood Centre
233 Hollywood Road
Hong Kong

British Library Cataloguing in Publication Data

A catalogue record
for this book is available
from the British Library

ISBN 1–85978–146–2

Text set in Plantin by
Selwood Systems,
Midsomer Norton
Printed by WBC Limited, Bridgend, Mid-Glamorgan

PREFACE

No one involved in arbitration can doubt the importance of costs. Every final award deals with costs. And the amount of costs involved often forms a significant proportion of the overall sums in issue. This book aims to set out the relevant law and practice of this important subject in a manner which I hope is of use to practising arbitrators and advocates alike.

Since the first edition of this book was published, the Arbitration Act 1996 has been enacted and been brought into force for arbitrations commenced after 31 January 1997. This has resulted in a number of significant changes in the law. Nowhere will the changes have greater impact than in the question of costs. Arbitrators are now under a duty to manage arbitrations with cost-effectiveness in mind. They are given additional powers to do this, including exclusive powers to order security for costs, the power to limit the recoverable costs of the arbitration and the power to appoint experts, assessors, etc. to assist them. Furthermore, the new Act presumes that the arbitrator will determine the recoverable costs, although the court may still do so; this is a change in emphasis, but an important one nevertheless. And new mechanisms have been introduced to allow the parties to challenge the arbitrator's fees and expenses.

I would like to thank the many arbitrators and lawyers with whom I have discussed the new Act and other related topics. I wish especially to thank Ian Menzies, Mark Cato and Geoffrey Hawker for having brought unreported cases and other materials to my attention. It goes without saying that I, and I alone, bear full responsibility for everything in the text.

For reasons of economy I have used the masculine form throughout to include the feminine unless the context requires otherwise. The term "arbitrator" is used to mean "arbitrator or umpire" save where the context otherwise demands.

I have endeavoured to state the law as at 1 February 1997.

London   MICHAEL O'REILLY

CONTENTS

Contents

TABLE OF CASES

Table of Cases

Table of Cases

TABLE OF LEGISLATION

[Paragraph numbers printed in **bold** indicate where text is quoted]

Table of Legislation

CHAPTER 1

INTRODUCTION TO COSTS IN ARBITRATION PROCEEDINGS

1.1 THE STATUTORY REGIME

The Arbitration Act 1996 came into force on 31 January 1997.[1] It applies[2] to all arbitrations commenced[3] after that date which are conducted pursuant to a written agreement to arbitrate[4] and which have a seat in England, Wales or Northern Ireland.[5]

Arbitrations commenced before the date on which the Arbitration Act 1996 came into force are governed by the Arbitration Acts 1950, 1975 and 1979. Some arbitrations have a duration of several years and so the two statutory regimes will operate in parallel for some time.

In this book, it is assumed that the Arbitration Act 1996 applies to the arbitration.[6]

1.2 THE COSTS OF THE ARBITRATION

1.2.1 The costs of the arbitration and the recoverable costs

Section 59 of the Arbitration Act 1996 defines the "costs of the arbitration" as:

> (a) the arbitrators' fees and expenses,

1. The Arbitration Act (Commencement No. 1) Order 1996, S.I. No. 3146.
2. Section 84 of the Arbitration Act 1996.
3. Section 14 of the Arbitration Act 1996 defines the commencement date.
4. Section 5(1) of the Arbitration Act 1996 provides: "The provisions of this Part apply only where the arbitration agreement is in writing . . .". The meaning of "agreement in writing" is very wide: see section 5(2) to (6) of the Arbitration Act 1996. See also section 6(2) of the Arbitration Act 1996 which relates to arbitration agreements incorporated by reference.
5. Section 2 of the Arbitration Act 1996. As to the meaning of "the seat" see §1.3. Some provisions of the Act may apply to arbitrations with a seat outside England, Wales and Northern Ireland. These provisions are supporting provisions such as the stay of legal proceedings, enforcement of awards, securing the attendance of witnesses and court powers exercisable in support of arbitral proceedings or where intervention is required to support an arbitration where no seat has been designated or determined.
6. For arbitrations under the Arbitration Acts 1950 to 1979, readers should consult the first edition of this book.

>   (b) the fees and expenses of any arbitral institution concerned, and
>   (c) the legal or other costs of the parties.

The costs of the arbitration also include the costs of or incidental to any proceedings to determine the amount of the recoverable costs of the arbitration.

The arbitrator's fees and expenses not only covers the arbitrator's personal fees and expenses but includes any expense properly incurred by him in the conduct of the proceedings, including the fees and expenses of arbitrator-appointed experts, legal advisers and/or assessors.[7] The legal and other costs of the parties are the costs incurred by the parties in developing and presenting their cases, including the costs of legal advice and representation, the costs of evidence, both factual and expert, as well as accommodation and administrative support in connection with the arbitration.

The "recoverable costs of the arbitration" are those costs of the arbitration which may be recovered under an award as to costs. Subject to the right of the parties to agree otherwise,[8] the recoverable costs are determined by the arbitrator[9] or the court.[10] The recoverable costs are ordinarily determined on the basis that: "there shall be allowed a reasonable amount in respect of all costs reasonably incurred; and any doubt as to whether costs were reasonably incurred or were reasonable in amount shall be resolved in favour of the paying party."[11] The arbitrator may, however, limit the recoverable costs by direction.[12]

1.2.2 Liability for recoverable costs

In English law, the liability for the recoverable costs of an arbitration is in the discretion of the arbitrator. An arbitrator exercising this discretion must do so judicially, having primary regard to the principle that the successful party is prima facie entitled to have his reasonable costs paid by the unsuccessful party.[13] The unsuccessful party will also be prima facie liable for the arbitrator's fees and expenses.

These principles are designed to promote justice. The rationale is that a person who is forced to pursue an action in order to seek just redress should not have to pay the costs of that action; nor should anyone be required to pay to defend himself against unjust litigation.[14] "A great principle, which underlies the administration of the English law, is that the courts are open to everyone

---

7. Section 37(2) of the Arbitration Act 1996.
8. Section 63(1) of the Arbitration Act 1996.
9. Section 63(3) of the Arbitration Act 1996.
10. Section 63(4) of the Arbitration Act 1996.
11. Section 63(5) of the Arbitration Act 1996.
12. Section 65 of the Arbitration Act 1996. See Chapter 8.
13. See Chapter 3 where the exercise of the arbitrator's discretion is considered in detail.
14. Although the "protection" offered by costs has frequently had the opposite effect to that intended; the risk of having to foot a large costs bill prevents many with good claims from pursuing them and causes many with good defences to compromise when strictly they need not. The innovations of the Arbitration Act 1996 are designed to create a proper balance between protection and access.

and that no complaint can be entertained of trouble and anxiety caused by an action begun maliciously and without reasonable or probable cause; but as a guard against unjust litigation costs are rendered recoverable from an unsuccessful opponent."[15]

1.3 THE APPLICABILITY OF THE ENGLISH LAW OF COSTS IN ARBITRATION

The principle that the unsuccessful party is prima facie liable to pay the costs of the arbitration is not recognised by all legal systems.[16] It is often a matter of importance in proceedings with an international element, therefore, to determine whether or not the English rules apply.

Where the matter being arbitrated is purely domestic to England, the English law of costs clearly applies.[17] Where there is a foreign element, the English law of costs applies whenever England is the "seat of the arbitration".[18] The seat is a juridical concept[19] and is distinct from the place where the arbitration proceedings may actually take place. It is determined by the agreement of the parties, or where there is no agreement or designation, having regard to all the relevant circumstances.[20] For reasons of convenience, the seat is normally the place where the arbitration has its principal geographical focus, and/or where the majority of meetings and hearings will take place. Once designated the seat of the arbitration is fixed unless the parties agree to designate a new seat.

1.4 THE COSTS PROVISIONS OF THE ARBITRATION ACT 1996

The Arbitration Act 1996, unlike previous legislation, sets out the law on costs in some detail. The core provisions are set out under the heading "Costs of the Arbitration" in sections 59 to 65 of the Arbitration Act 1996. These, however, only deal with the recoverable costs under an award. Issues such as

15. *London Scottish Benefit Society* v. *Chorley* (1884) 13 Q.B.D. 873 *per* Bowen L.J. at 876.
16. "The English rules regarding costs, whilst not unique, are certainly a distinctive feature of English arbitration proceedings" *per* Evans L.J. in *The Maria* [1993] 2 Lloyd's Rep. 168 at 183. A useful summary of the position in international arbitrations under a range of institutional rules in a range of jurisdictions is given in N. C. Ulmer, "Notes on the allocation of costs in international arbitrations", Presented to the A.S.A. Conference on Costs and their Allocation, 31 January 1997, Zurich.
17. Unless, apparently, where the parties otherwise agree: see section 3(a) of the Arbitration Act 1996. Even where there can be no question, the seat must be stated in the award: section 52 of the Arbitration Act 1996.
18. Section 2(1) of the Arbitration Act 1996: "The provisions of this Part apply where the seat of the arbitration is England and Wales or Northern Ireland." Note there are some exceptions where the Act may apply even though there is a different seat; these relate to stays, enforcement of arbitral proceedings, securing the attendance of witnesses and court powers exercisable in support of arbitral proceedings.
19. Section 3 of the Arbitration Act 1996.
20. Section 3 of the Arbitration Act 1996.

the arbitrator's entitlement to fees and orders for security for costs are dealt with elsewhere in the Act.[21]

The most significant innovations of the Arbitration Act 1996 include:

(1) It focuses on cost-effectiveness in so far as this is consistent with the prime objective, namely the "fair resolution of the dispute". This is enshrined in sections 1(a) and 33 of the Act which enjoin the arbitrator to adopt procedures which ensure this.

(2) It provides that parties may, by agreement, define the recoverable costs of the arbitration[22] and the event which triggers the award as to costs.[23]

(3) The arbitrator may limit the recoverable costs by direction.[24]

(4) The arbitrator's fees and expenses are subject to review by the court.[25]

(5) Much of the old legalistic terminology is replaced by straightforward language. For instance the expression "tax or settle costs" has been replaced by the expression "determine the recoverable costs".[26] The expression "the costs of the award and reference" has been replaced by a defined list of costs which are included in the costs of the arbitration.[27]

1.5 AGREEMENTS AS TO COSTS

Section 1(b) of the Arbitration Act 1996 provides that: "the parties should be free to agree how their disputes are resolved, subject only to such safeguards as are necessary in the public interest". However, some provisions of the Act are mandatory[28] and have effect notwithstanding any agreement to the contrary. Many sections of importance in the context of costs are designated as mandatory.[29]

21. These include: section 24(4): order of the court as to fees and expenses upon removal of the arbitrator; section 25: fees and expenses of an arbitrator who resigns; section 28: joint and several liability of parties to arbitrators for fees and expenses, and adjustment by the court of the arbitrator's fees; section 37(2): fees of experts, advisers and assessors appointed by the tribunal; section 38(3): security for costs; section 39(2)(b): example of a provisional award dealing with costs; section 41(6): peremptory order in respect of security for costs; section 49(4): interest on an award as to costs; section 51(5): costs where parties have made a settlement; section 56: power to withhold award in the case of non-payment; section 57: power to make an additional award in respect of a claim for costs which was not dealt with in the award; section 70(5), (6): costs associated with challenging the award; section 75: charge to secure payment of solicitor's costs.

22. Section 63(1) of the Arbitration Act 1996.

23. Implied by section 61(2) of the Arbitration Act 1996.

24. Section 65 of the Arbitration Act 1996.

25. Sections 28(2) and 56(2) of the Arbitration Act 1996.

26. Section 63(3) of the Arbitration Act 1996.

27. Section 59 of the Arbitration Act 1996.

28. Section 4 of the Arbitration Act 1996. The mandatory provisions are listed in Schedule 1 to the Arbitration Act 1996. Note that these provisions are only mandatory where the Arbitration Act 1996 applies. Thus, where a seat other than England, Wales or Northern Ireland is designated, the provisions do not apply.

29. Especially sections 28, 33, 37(2), 56 and 60 of the Arbitration Act 1996.

Where provisions in the Arbitration Act 1996 are non-mandatory,[30] the parties may make their own arrangements by agreement. Any such agreement should, however, state whether matters which have been agreed are designed to exclude existing non-mandatory powers in the Act or to supplement them. For example, section 65 of the Arbitration Act 1996 provides: "Unless otherwise agreed by the parties, the tribunal may direct that the recoverable costs ... shall be limited ...". An agreement by the parties that "the recoverable costs of the arbitration shall not exceed £x" may thus be construed either as replacing the arbitrator's power under section 65 of the Arbitration Act 1996 or as a constraint upon it.[31]

Note that only agreements in writing are effective for the purpose of the Arbitration Act 1996.[32]

Arrangements which may be made under the Arbitration Act 1996 include agreements as to:

(1) The amount of recoverable costs.[33] Such agreements are valid, subject to the provisions of section 60 of the Arbitration Act 1996[34] which provides that: "An agreement which has the effect that a party is to pay the whole or part of the costs of the arbitration in any event is only valid if made after the dispute in question has arisen." The scope of the restriction imposed is not clear.[35] It is submitted that a prior agreement to allocate liability for recoverable costs which is clearly designed to deter a party from seeking proper legal representation contravenes section 60 and is invalid; on the other hand an agreement which promotes cost-effective dispute resolution with potential benefits for both parties is valid and enforceable.[36] Whether or not any agreement passes this test is no doubt a matter of impression rather than analysis.

(2) The types of expenses which shall be considered recoverable.

---

30. Section 4(2) of the Arbitration Act 1996.

31. If the limit agreed is too low, it may even be invalid as contrary to section 60 of the Arbitration Act 1996.

32. Section 5(1) of the Arbitration Act 1996 provides: "... any ... agreement between the parties as to any matter is effective for the purposes of this Part only if in writing." However, section 5(2) to (6) provide a wide definition of "agreement in writing" which includes agreements evidenced in writing or recorded "by any means".

33. Section 63(1) provides: "The parties are free to agree what costs of the arbitration are recoverable".

34. This derives from section 18(3) of the Arbitration Act 1950.

35. The only reported case on the earlier section 18(3) of the Arbitration Act 1950 appears to be *Windvale Ltd.* v. *Darlington Insulation Co. Ltd.* (1983), *The Times*, 22 December 1983. Here one party agreed in advance to pay the costs of the arbitration and this was held to be invalid within the terms of the section.

36. Professor John Uff Q.C. in an article in *Commercial Dispute Resolution*, 1996, edited by Odams and Higgins, Construction Law Press, writes of the forerunner to section 60: "Contrary to appearances, [the section]'s purpose is not to bar any restriction on payment of lawyer's fees but rather to avoid arbitration agreements which would have the effect of preventing or discouraging a less pecunious party from employing proper legal representation."

(3) The event which triggers costs liability.[37] The "event" is the success of the party, which is often difficult to define. Section 61(2) of the Arbitration Act 1996 suggests that parties are free also to depart from the traditional concept of "the event" and write in their arbitration clause a narrowly drawn definition which lends additional certainty.

---

37. Section 61(2) of the Arbitration Act 1996 provides: "Unless the parties otherwise agree, the tribunal shall award costs on the general principle that costs should follow the event . . .".

CHAPTER 2

THE ARBITRATOR'S FEES AND EXPENSES

2.1 HISTORICAL INTRODUCTION

That an arbitrator may recover his fees under an express agreement between him and the parties has been established for centuries. Since the end of the nineteenth century it has also been clear that an arbitrator in a commercial dispute is entitled to be paid for his services and to recover his reasonable expenses under an implied term in the agreement between him and the parties.[1]

The pre-1996 legislation did not deal with the question of the arbitrator's fees in detail. Where the matter was dealt with, the terminology was unhelpful[2] and provisions for the protection of the parties against excessive fees were only partly effective.[3] Decisions of the court clarified the position to some degree. It was understood that an arbitrator's entitlement to fees and expenses could be defined principally in contractual terms,[4] but that his status as arbitrator would influence the terms which might be implied into the contract.[5] An arbitrator was entitled to a reasonable fee for his work; but it was "misconduct" for him to charge excessive fees.[6] An arbitrator was not able to insist on a commitment fee for reserving time for hearings unless this had been expressly agreed prior to his appointment.[7] However, a number of questions relating to the arbitrator's fees and expenses remained unclear. For example, it was not certain whether the parties were jointly and severally liable for the arbitrator's

---

1. See the cases cited in *Crampton and Holt* v. *Ridley & Co.* (1887) 20 Q.B.D. 48 at 52 *et seq.*

2. For example, the arbitrator's fees and expenses were described as the "costs of the award" in section 18(1) of the Arbitration Act 1950: see *Government of Ceylon* v. *Chandris* [1963] 1 Lloyd's Rep. 214.

3. For the shortcomings in relation to section 19 of the Arbitration Act 1950 see, for example, *Government of Ceylon* v. *Chandris* [1963] 1 Lloyd's Rep. 214 at 227 and *Rolimpex Centrala Handlu Zagranicznego* v. *Haji E. Dossa & Sons Ltd.* [1971] 1 Lloyd's Rep. 380 at 385.

4. *Compagnie Européene de Cereals* v. *Tradax Export S.A.* [1986] 2 Lloyd's Rep. 301 *per* Hobhouse J. at 306.

5. "I find it impossible to divorce the contractual and status considerations: in truth the arbitrator's rights and duties flow from the conjunction of those two elements." *K/S Norjarl A/S* v. *Hyundai Heavy Industries Co. Ltd.* [1992] 1 Q.B. 863: *per* Sir Nicolas Browne-Wilkinson V.-C. at 884.

6. *Appleton* v. *Norwich Union Fire Insurance Society Ltd.* (1922) 13 Lloyd's Rep. 345; *Government of Ceylon* v. *Chandris* [1963] 1 Lloyd's Rep. 214 at 227.

7. *K/S Norjarl A/S* v. *Hyundai Heavy Industries Co. Ltd.* [1992] 1 Q.B. 863: *per* Leggatt L.J. at 877.

fees; and the extent to which an arbitrator could engage advisers and assessors at the parties' expense was not settled.

The Arbitration Act 1996 has clarified the law significantly. The result is a code which establishes the arbitrator's entitlement to fees and expenses in simple terms and tightens up the procedures to ensure that the level of fees claimed by arbitrators can be properly reviewed.

2.2 AN OVERVIEW OF THE PROVISIONS OF THE ARBITRATION ACT 1996 AS TO THE ARBITRATOR'S FEES AND EXPENSES

2.2.1 General principles

The Arbitration Act 1996 deals with a number of questions concerning the fees and expenses of the arbitrator.

It distinguishes between two concepts which, under the earlier law, were often confused:

    (a) the arbitrator's right to look to the parties for his fees and expenses; and

    (b) the liability of a party to pay the arbitrator's fees and expenses under an award.

It is now clear that an arbitrator is entitled to reasonable fees and expenses and the parties are jointly and severally liable for them[8]; where, however, any party has made an agreement with the arbitrator as to fees, that party will be liable to the arbitrator for the amount of those fees.[9] Where the arbitrator directs a party to pay his fees and expenses in an award, this relates only to the arbitrator's reasonable fees and expenses[10]; where the arbitrator is entitled, by virtue of an agreement, to a greater level of fees, he must recover the difference under the agreement.

Consider an arbitration between X and Y, where both parties appoint an arbitrator. If X appoints arbitrator A and agrees with him a fee $£q$ which exceeds the reasonable fee $£r$; and if Y loses the arbitration and is required by the award to pay A's fees, Y will only have to pay $£r$. X will be obliged to pay A the difference $£(q-r)$.

The Arbitration Act 1996 preserves the right of an arbitrator to insist on payment before he releases an award.[11] It also clarifies a number of issues and

---

8. Section 28(1) of the Arbitration Act 1996.

9. Section 28(5) of the Arbitration Act 1996.

10. Section 64(1) of the Arbitration Act 1996: the expression is "such reasonable fees and expenses as are appropriate in the circumstances." It is submitted that where both parties freely agree a higher fee than that which would otherwise be considered "reasonable", that higher fee may nevertheless be "appropriate in the circumstances" and recoverable under an award.

11. Section 56(1) of the Arbitration Act 1996.

institutes a number of procedures relating to the arbitrator's entitlement to fees following his removal,[12] resignation[13] etc.

2.2.2 Review of the arbitrator's fees and expenses by the court

The Arbitration Act 1996 makes provision for an arbitrator's fees and expenses to be reviewed; again, the distinction is maintained between the concepts (a) the arbitrator's right to look to the parties for his fees and expenses; and (b) the liability of a party to pay the arbitrator's fees and expenses under an award. There is a general right to have the matter of the arbitrator's entitlement to fees from the parties considered by the court at any time.[14] There is also a right to have reviewed by the court the question of what amounts to a reasonable fee recoverable under an award.[15] These matters are dealt with briefly in Chapter 9.

2.3 THE ARBITRATOR'S ENTITLEMENT TO FEES AND EXPENSES

2.3.1 General

Upon his appointment, the arbitrator enters into an agreement with the parties.[16] Subject to express terms, he agrees to undertake the role of arbitrator and the parties agree to pay him a reasonable amount plus expenses.[17] The parties may expressly agree terms with the arbitrator.

The arbitrator's basic contractual entitlement to fees is reinforced by a statutory entitlement. Section 28(1) of the Arbitration Act 1996 provides: "The parties are jointly and severally liable to pay to the arbitrators such reasonable fees and expenses (if any) as are appropriate in the circumstances." This does not affect any express contractual entitlement.[18]

12. Section 24 of the Arbitration Act 1996.
13. Section 25 of the Arbitration Act 1996.
14. Section 28(2) of the Arbitration Act 1996. It may be that the final time in practice is when the award which determines those fees and expenses becomes unappealable, unless there has been some duplicity which renders it reasonable to make a later challenge.
15. Section 64(2) of the Arbitration Act 1996.
16. Paragraph 128 of the DAC Report (see Appendix C) suggests: "... since Clause [now section] 28(1) gives a statutory right there remains no good reason for any implied contractual right." It is submitted, however, that the contractual model remains valid. It is important, for example, where the arbitrator resigns; here it is submitted that a wrongful resignation is a breach of contract—as indeed is suggested by the DAC Report itself at Paragraph 135.
17. *K/S Norjarl A/S* v. *Hyundai Heavy Industries Co. Ltd.* [1992] 1 Q.B. 863: "The arbitration agreement is a bilateral contract between the parties to the main contract. On appointment, the arbitrator becomes a third party to that arbitration agreement ... the arbitrator undertakes his quasi-judicial functions in consideration of the parties agreeing to pay him remuneration" *per* Sir Nicolas Browne-Wilkinson V.-C. at 885.
18. Section 28(5) of the Arbitration Act 1996.

2.3 The arbitrator's fees and expenses

2.3.2 Where more than one arbitrator is appointed

All arbitrators (and umpires[19]) properly appointed are contractually entitled to fees and expenses and are covered by the statutory provisions. This includes an arbitrator who has ceased to act and /or an umpire who has not yet replaced the other arbitrators.[20] Where the arbitration agreement provides that each party should appoint an arbitrator, each appointee becomes a party to the agreement for the duration of his time as arbitrator. If the agreement provides that, upon disagreement, these arbitrators become advocates for the parties who appointed them, they withdraw from the agreement. Accordingly, they may recover their fees while acting as impartial arbitrators from either or both parties[21]; but their fees as advocates (even if still called "arbitrators") are recoverable only from those by whom they were appointed.[22]

2.3.3 Express agreements as to fees and expenses: general

The arbitrator's entitlement to fees and expenses may be agreed between the parties and the arbitrator.[23]

Many arbitrators are appointed by or through professional or trade institutions before they have an opportunity to raise the question of fees. "Once appointed an arbitrator cannot unilaterally change the terms of his appointment ...".[24] Where an arbitrator has been appointed and then finds that the parties or any of them do not wish to agree his proposed terms it is submitted that he is obliged to continue and to recover reasonable fees[25] unless the commitment required is materially in excess of what could reasonably be expected at the time of the appointment.

The arbitrator's entitlement to fees may be varied as may the term of any other contract. It is entirely proper for an arbitrator to raise the question of his fees at any stage. He must, however, be assiduous in avoiding any impression that he is imposing terms upon the parties or that his continued participation in the arbitration is conditional upon the parties' acceptance of his proposed fees or charges. If the arbitrator is insistent, his continuing breach may amount to a serious irregularity and provide sufficient reason for removing the arbi-

---

19. Section 82(1) of the Arbitration Act 1996.
20. Section 28(6) of the Arbitration Act 1996.
21. *Brown* v. *Llandovery Terra Cotta Company Ltd.* (1888) 25 T.L.R. 625.
22. *Government of Ceylon* v. *Chandris* [1963] 1 Lloyd's Rep. 214.
23. Section 28(5) provides: "Nothing in this section [which deals with the arbitrator's general entitlement to fees] affects ... any contractual right of an arbitrator to payment of his fees and expenses." Some associations of arbitrators produce standard forms of appointment, which members are encouraged to use. For example the Society of Construction Arbitrators' Terms includes for cancellation fees on a sliding scale, with a stated percentage of fees to be paid for the days vacated.
24. *K/S Norjarl A/S* v. *Hyundai Heavy Industries Co. Ltd.* [1992] 1 Q.B. 863, *per* Stuart-Smith L.J. at 882.
25. In practice an arbitrator may resign. But he will not be immune from liability unless the resignation is reasonable within section 25(4) of the Arbitration Act 1996.

trator.[26] The arbitrator should be alive to the parties' real, though often unexpressed, concerns that resistance to the proposed fees or charges may put them at a disadvantage. Where one party indicates that he would prefer to continue with the implied or previously-agreed terms, the arbitrator should not then negotiate with the other party as this may reasonably give rise to a suspicion of partiality.[27] In short, when raising the question of fees and/or charges the arbitrator has an obligation to have proper regard to the interests of the parties as well as his own.[28]

2.3.4 Security, commitment fees and stage payments

Arbitration proceedings may last a considerable period of time and the arbitrator may be required to commit extended periods of his time for hearings etc. In addition, the arbitrator may, in pursuit of his obligations, engage experts, advisers and assessors for whose fees he becomes responsible.[29]

It is clear that, in the absence of an express agreement, an arbitrator may not claim a fee for committing his time.[30] However, he is not obliged to keep an unreasonable time free at the request of the parties. "Arbitrators are under no absolute obligation to make particular dates available: their obligation is to sit on such dates as may reasonably be required of them having regard to all the circumstances including the exigencies of their own practices."[31]

An arbitrator who has set aside a period of time and learns at a late stage that he will not be required, as where a late adjournment is allowed or a late settlement is agreed, may, it is submitted, claim a moderate cancellation charge even in the absence of an express agreement[32] provided that the arbitrator has

26. *K/S Norjarl A/S* v. *Hyundai Heavy Industries Co. Ltd.* [1992] 1 Q.B. 863 *per* Leggatt L.J. at 877. The application will be under section 24(1)(d) of the Arbitration Act 1996 "that he [the arbitrator] has refused or failed properly to conduct the proceedings or to use all reasonable despatch . . .". See also *Turner* v. *Stevenage Borough Council* [1996] 1 E.G.L.R 23.

27. *K/S Norjarl A/S* v. *Hyundai Heavy Industries Co. Ltd.* [1992] 1 Q.B. 863; *Turner* v. *Stevenage Borough Council* [1996] 1 E.G.L.R 23. In an extreme case, the arbitrator may be removed under section 24(1)(a) of the Arbitration Act 1996 on the grounds that circumstances exist which give rise to justifiable doubts as to his impartiality; where no such application is made, the irregularity may be sufficiently serious to have the award challenged under the procedure in section 68 of the Arbitration Act 1996.

28. *Government of Ceylon* v. *Chandris* [1963] 1 Lloyd's Rep. 214 at 228.

29. Section 37(2) of the Arbitration Act 1996.

30. *K/S Norjarl A/S* v. *Hyundai Heavy Industries Co. Ltd.* [1992] 1 Q.B. 863 *per* Leggatt L.J. at 877: "once an arbitrator has accepted an appointment, no term can be implied that entitles him to a commitment fee."

31. *K/S Norjarl A/S* v. *Hyundai Heavy Industries Co. Ltd.* [1992] 1 Q.B. 863 *per* Leggatt L.J. at 879.

32. In *K/S Norjarl A/S* v. *Hyundai Heavy Industries Co. Ltd.* [1991] 1 Lloyd's Rep. 260, Phillips J. suggested that cancellation charges would not ordinarily be recoverable under an implied term because such a term would conflict with the more readily implied term "that the parties may, at any stage, withdraw their request for the arbitrator's services as a result, for instance, of settling their dispute." It is submitted, however, that the parties' undoubted right to settle the proceedings does not conflict with a term by which the arbitrator is entitled to a reasonable fee, including moderate compensation for holding time free at the request of the parties which is then vacated at very short notice.

2.3 The arbitrator's fees and expenses

suffered a real loss.[33] Section 28(1) of the Arbitration Act 1996 entitles an arbitrator to fees which are reasonable and appropriate and these may, it is submitted, include cancellation charges where these are reasonable and appropriate.

An arbitrator may not, it is submitted, require payment before the conclusions of the arbitration without an express agreement. He must not insist on any advance fee backed by a threat to cease participation if it is not paid and he should not accept stage payments or commitment fees from one party if the other objects.[34] Where an agreement entitling the arbitrator to interim payments is being drawn up, the arbitrator should consider what is to happen if the respondent were to refuse to pay his share. It will rarely be appropriate to close the respondent out from submitting a defence or to accept payment from one party alone.

While, an arbitrator may order a claimant to provide security for his fees and expenses,[35] this device should only be used for purposes associated with security and not to accelerate payments to the arbitrator.

2.3.5 Changes in circumstances

"Once appointed an arbitrator cannot unilaterally change the terms of his appointment . . . any more than any other party to a contract can change the terms of the contract, unless there is a significant and substantial change in the commitment required of him such as to justify the payment of further consideration."[36] If, subsequent to his appointment, it appears that the level of commitment required is materially greater than could reasonably have been expected at the time of appointment, the arbitrator may indicate his intention to charge a reasonable sum in the event of cancellation,[37] commensurate with the additional degree of commitment required. If his proposed cancellation fees are reasonable, the arbitrator will simply charge them in appropriate circumstances and, if necessary, the court will take a view on whether they are "reasonable fees . . . as are appropriate in the circumstances".[38]

33. Note, however, Leggatt L.J.'s caution in *K/S Norjarl A/S* v. *Hyundai Heavy Industries Co. Ltd.* [1992] 1 Q.B. 863 at 878. He recognised that if actual loss were the test this would be "a fruitful source of discord, which might involve proof of the arbitrator's actual earnings during the relevant period as well as the reasons why they had not availed themselves of particular opportunities of work."

34. *Turner* v. *Stevenage Borough Council* [1996] 1 E.G.L.R 23.

35. Section 38(3) of the Arbitration Act 1996.

36. *K/S Norjarl A/S* v. *Hyundai Heavy Industries Co. Ltd.* [1992] 1 Q.B. 863 *per* Stuart-Smith L.J. at 882.

37. It is submitted that the provisions of section 28(1) of the Arbitration Act 1996 entitle an arbitrator to fees which are reasonable and appropriate, including cancellation charges. But see *K/S Norjarl A/S* v. *Hyundai Heavy Industries Co. Ltd.* [1991] 1 Lloyd's Rep. 260, *per* Phillips J. at 266.

38. Section 28(1) of the Arbitration Act 1996.

2.3.6 Recovering fees

Arbitrators normally recover their fees without difficulty. Arbitrators frequently make delivery of their awards conditional upon payment of their fees[39]; at least one party is usually eager to collect the award. Where, however, the parties do not pay, the arbitrator may recover due fees and expenses by action on the agreement and/or under the statutory entitlement under section 28(1) of the Arbitration Act 1996. His statutory entitlement is against the parties jointly and severally.[40] An arbitrator who acts in good faith is immune from liability[41]; it seems, therefore, that a party may not set off the consequences of the arbitrator's alleged negligence against his fees.

Illustrations

K/S Norjarl A/S v. Hyundai Heavy Industries Co. Ltd. [1991] 1 Lloyd's Rep 260, per **Phillips J. at 268** "The scale and complexity of many arbitrations today are such as to render desirable a more detailed agreement between the arbitrators and the parties than one which merely requires the arbitrators to conduct the reference with due diligence in exchange for reasonable remuneration for their services. The parties are likely to wish to have a firm fixture for a continuous hearing, so that they can make appropriate arrangements for witnesses and for legal representation. They may have specific requirements in relation to venue or other matters. The arbitrators, for their part, may be reluctant to commit themselves to refusing other offers of employment for a lengthy period in which, if the arbitration settles, they may find themselves idle. They may, accordingly, wish to specify precisely the terms upon which they are to be remunerated and, in particular, to be compensated for the risk of idle time."

K/S Norjarl A/S v. Hyundai Heavy Industries Co. Ltd. [1992] 1 Q.B. 863 H were Korean shipbuilders engaged by N to build a drilling rig. N refused to take delivery of the rig. The question of whether or not they were entitled to reject the rig was referred to three arbitrators. The arbitrators accepted their appointments without reference to fees. The parties then invited the arbitrators to reserve a 12-week period some two years in advance. The arbitrators, thereupon, asked for a substantial commitment fee as security against cancellation. H refused to agree to any advance fees, although N were willing to provide a more modest advance. Before accepting N's proposal, the arbitrators asked H whether they were willing for N to undertake such advance payment. H replied that such a bilateral agreement may raise a suspicion of partiality. The arbitrators then purported to resign. N applied for a declaration that the arbitrators might accept N's undertaking to pay an advance. H made a cross-application for their removal. At first instance Phillips J. refused to grant the declaration as he felt it inappropriate that an arbitrator should make an agreement with one party. But he was content that they should not be removed as they had not made such an agreement. This decision was affirmed by the Court of Appeal. Held, that arbitrators are not entitled to insist upon a commitment fee unless the parties have agreed to provide one at the time of their appointment. Neither were they obliged to commit themselves to

39. Section 56(1) of the Arbitration Act 1996.

40. Section 28(1) of the Arbitration Act 1996. The arbitrator's contractual entitlement will depend upon the true construction of the agreement.

41. Section 29(1) of the Arbitration Act 1996. "An arbitrator is not liable for anything done or omitted in the discharge or purported discharge of his functions as arbitrator unless the act or omission is shown to have been in bad faith."

hold hearings at the convenience of the parties if the proposed dates and durations were unreasonable.

Turner v. Stevenage Borough Council [1996] 1 E.G.L.R 23 An arbitrator was appointed on a rent review arbitration. He agreed an hourly charging rate with the parties. The proceedings became considerably more complicated than was apparent at the time of the appointment. The arbitrator then wrote to both parties asking them to pay his interim account in equal shares pending the final decision on costs. The letter did not state that he would refuse to continue with the arbitration if the account was not paid. It set out details of the work done and it included fees due to a legal adviser who was retained with the agreement of both parties. The council paid half of the account. The tenant refused to do so and applied to the court to have the arbitrator removed on the grounds (1) that a request for payment had been made; and (2) that the arbitrator has received payment from one party which must raise the question of bias. The arbitrator then repaid the council. "On behalf of the council it is said that given the unexpected delays and the fact that the costs had escalated out of all proportion the interim payment request was eminently reasonable. It is, however, plain from the *Hyundai* case [*supra*] that for an arbitrator to request a payment from both parties which is not in terms covered in their contractual arrangement is not in any way improper. In particular, it is worth bearing in mind that the arbitrators in that case were seeking a commitment fee which was a brand new element in the relationship whereas, here, [the arbitrator] was seeking agreement to an interim payment at a contractual rate which had already been agreed. In any event the mere making of the request for payment was, in my view, wholly unobjectionable ... [T]he mere fact that the arbitrator has learnt that one of the parties may be willing to pay his interim account but that the other is not so willing cannot, in my view, amount to misconduct on the part of the arbitrator. Nor does it, I think, provide any foundation for a reasonable or justifiable concern that the arbitrator either will be biased in favour of the more generous party or against the less generous one" *per* Anthony Grabiner Q.C. sitting as a deputy judge of the Chancery Division at 25–26.

2.4 ELEMENTS OF THE ARBITRATOR'S FEES AND EXPENSES

2.4.1 Proper level of fees chargeable

If the arbitrator makes an express agreement as to fees with the parties then this agreement will govern his entitlement. Where his entitlement is to reasonable fees, the question of the proper level of such fees arises. "The fees which are fair and appropriate depend on many factors, and generalisations would be unsatisfactory and dangerous. Nevertheless I think I can properly say this: it would be desirable that an umpire or arbitrator, in fixing his fees, should do so by reference to considerations which he can put forward and expect to justify as being reasonable, should a taxation be called for under section 19 of the [1950] Act."[42]

The relevant factors may include:

42. *Government of Ceylon* v. *Chandris* [1963] 1 Lloyd's Rep. 214 *per* Megaw J. at 228. The relevant provision is now section 56(2), (3) of the Arbitration Act 1996.

(1) The standing of the arbitrator in his primary profession.[43] If the arbitrator is appointed by a professional or trade body, the fees should reflect the expectations of the parties about the likely level of fees at the time when they agreed to delegate the appointment to the body in question.

(2) The skill and experience of the arbitrator.

(3) The location and duration of the arbitration hearings and viewings etc. For instance, if the arbitrator spends a significant time away from home, this seems a proper factor to be taken into account.

(4) The means of the parties. While the ancient tradition that the arbitrator acts in an honorary capacity without remuneration for his services[44] is not appropriate to the modern commercial world, it is submitted that the vestiges of that spirit remain[45] and that it is the responsibility of arbitrators to ensure that parties have proper access to justice.

2.4.2 Personal expenses

An arbitrator is entitled to recover for reasonable travel, hotel accommodation and other expenses incurred in connection with the arbitration. Personal secretarial expenses and other general overheads will normally not be recoverable; they will be included as an element in the reasonable charging rate unless there is an express agreement to the contrary.

2.4.3 Professional expenses

Subject to the agreement of the parties, the arbitrator may appoint experts or legal advisers to report to him and the parties, or appoint assessors to assist him on technical matters, and may allow such expert, legal adviser or assessor to attend the proceedings.[46] The fees and expenses of such experts, legal advisers or assessors appointed by the arbitrator become expenses of the arbitrator,[47] provided they are reasonably incurred and appropriate.[48] The level of fees which experts, advisers and assessors may charge will depend upon their standing in their professions, their experience, etc. The arbitrator is under

43. *Appleton v. Norwich Union Fire Insurance Ltd.* (1922) 13 Lloyd's Rep. 345 at 346 and 347: *Llandridod Wells Water Co. v. Hawksley* (1904) 20 T.L.R. 241.

44. See the cases cited in *Crampton and Holt v. Ridley & Co.* (1887) 20 Q.B.D. 48 at 52 *et seq.*

45. But see the observations of Megaw J. in *Government of Ceylon v. Chandris* [1963] 1 Lloyd's Rep. 214 at 228 where he categorised as not altogether realistic a submission by counsel that commercial arbitrators should consider their work as "a kind of public service for the general good of the trade".

46. Section 37(1)(a) of the Arbitration Act 1996.

47. Section 37(2) of the Arbitration Act 1996.

48. Section 28(1) of the Arbitration Act 1996. There should also be compliance with the requirement that the parties should be given a reasonable opportunity to comment on information, opinion or advice offered by the expert, legal adviser or assessor: section 37(1)(b) of the Arbitration Act 1996.

a duty to ensure that appointees have a standing and charging rate which is appropriate. Where the arbitration claim is small, the arbitrator should not appoint people in the most illustrious or most expensive bracket unless the parties agree or there is some overriding factor which make this appropriate. Where an arbitrator does so, he may not be able to pass the full account on to the parties.

The costs of a separate note of the proceedings will not normally be recoverable[49] unless otherwise agreed by the parties or where the arbitrator directs that a note be taken when adopting procedures suitable to the circumstances pursuant to his duty under section 33 of the Arbitration Act 1996.[50] Summary notes are usually taken by the arbitrator during the proceedings and more detailed notes are invariably taken by the parties. In the event that a dispute arises as to what was said or done, reference may be made to the notes made by the parties.

2.5 THE ARBITRATOR'S AWARD AS TO HIS OWN RECOVERABLE FEES AND EXPENSES

2.5.1 Allocation of liability for the arbitrator's fees and expenses

The arbitrator is obliged to make an award as to the costs of the arbitration.[51] The costs of the arbitration include his own fees and expenses[52]; he should therefore make an award as to these and direct which party is to bear them or in which proportions they are to be borne by each.[53]

Following the principle that the unsuccessful party is prima facie liable for the costs of the arbitration, the arbitrator's fees and expenses are normally paid by the unsuccessful party. However, he has a discretion as to who should pay them.[54]

2.5.2 Determination of the arbitrator's recoverable fees and expenses

The arbitrator is not obliged to determine his own recoverable fees and expenses but he may do so.[55] It is usual for an arbitrator to decide what fees

49. Costs of a note seem to have been allowed in some cases, but it is not clear whether this was agreed by the parties in advance: see e.g. *Re Becker Shillan & Co. and Barry Brothers* [1921] 1 K.B. 391.

50. A judge can require a copy of the transcript of the proceedings, *Griffith* v. *Howard* [1939] 3 All E.R. 56.

51. Section 61 of the Arbitration Act 1996.

52. Section 59 of the Arbitration Act 1996.

53. Unless, of course, the arbitrator wishes to forego his fees and expenses.

54. Section 61(2) of the Arbitration Act 1996 provides the arbitrator with a discretion as to who should pay his fees. This discretion must be exercised judicially—see Chapter 3 for a detailed discussion of this matter.

55. Section 63(3) of the Arbitration Act 1996. If he does not do so, either party may apply to the court which will either determine them or order that they shall be determined by such means and upon such terms as it specifies: section 63(4) of the Arbitration Act 1996.

he is owed by the parties and to include this sum in his award. The arbitrator must bear in mind the distinction between what he is entitled to recover from the parties[56] and what fees and expenses are recoverable under an award.[57] These may be the same amount, but they need not be. For example, where the tribunal comprises three arbitrators, two of whom were appointed by the parties on payment terms agreed in each case by the appointing party only, and the third was appointed by the first two arbitrators, the tribunal must determine what are reasonable fees for each of the arbitrators to be included in the award as recoverable costs of the arbitration. This determination will not affect the right of the two party-appointed arbitrators to recover any additional fee from their appointing party.

While the Arbitration Act 1996 does not make it entirely clear, it is thought, strictly speaking, that an arbitrator must determine the fee which is to form part of the recoverable costs of the arbitration even though he has agreed a rate (or even a fixed fee) with the parties. For instance, where both parties have agreed a fee of £q with the arbitrator, it is thought that he must consider whether that fee is reasonable and appropriate; he may consider that a lesser fee £r is reasonable and appropriate. He will then recover £r from the paying party under the award and half the difference between £q and £r from each party on the agreement. In practice, however, there is likely to be little or no difference between what the parties have agreed and what will be the "reasonable fees . . . as are appropriate in the circumstances" since the most important circumstance is the agreement itself.

An arbitrator must recognise that despite the safeguards now available to the parties,[58] his determination is likely to be accepted by the parties. Applications to the court are expensive and tiresome. Accordingly, the arbitrator must determine the fees and expenses which are to become recoverable costs of the arbitration "conscientiously and with a proper regard to the interests of the parties".[59] "It has to be realised that a serious responsibility rests upon one who is put in a position to assess his own reward; particularly since his self-allotted remuneration may fall to be paid by someone who had no part in his appointment; for example, in the case of an arbitrator appointed by the opposite party, or the umpire appointed, not by either party, but by the two arbitrators . . . an umpire or arbitrator, in fixing his own fees, must consider, not only his own interest, but also the interest of the party or parties who will ultimately be required to pay those fees."[60]

If the arbitrator's expenses include sums claimed by experts, legal advisers, assessors or others appointed by the arbitrator,[61] he must determine the amount

56. Section 28(1) of the Arbitration Act 1996.
57. Section 64(1) of the Arbitration Act 1996.
58. Section 28(2) of the Arbitration Act 1996; section 64(2) of the Arbitration Act 1996.
59. *Appleton* v. *Norwich Union Fire Insurance Society Ltd.* (1922) 13 Lloyd's Rep. 345 *per* Salter J. at 347.
60. *Government of Ceylon* v. *Chandris* [1963] 1 Lloyd's Rep. 214 *per* Megaw J. at 228.
61. Section 37(1) of the Arbitration Act 1996 entitles the arbitrator to appoint experts, legal advisers and assessors. Subsection 37(2) provides: "The fees and expenses of an expert, legal

payable in the interests of the parties rather than simply assuming that the accounts submitted are proper.[62] An umpire who has taken over the reference must be particularly careful where he receives accounts from the erstwhile arbitrators. He must exercise proper discretion in determining their recoverable fees and must not simply accept their accounts as binding on him. There are judicial dicta suggesting that an arbitrator who considers himself embarrassed in determining the fees of former arbitrators etc. should leave the matter to be determined by the court.[63]

2.6 THE ARBITRATOR'S RIGHT TO WITHHOLD AN AWARD UNLESS HIS FEES AND EXPENSES ARE PAID

The arbitrator may refuse to deliver up any award except upon full payment of his fees and expenses.[64] The fees and expenses include his personal fees, his personal expenses, the fees and expenses of experts, legal advisers and assessors properly appointed by the arbitrator[65] and the fees and expenses of erstwhile arbitrators in their capacity as arbitrators.

Normally the refusal to deliver an award except upon payment is an effective method for ensuring payment and it is a practice adopted by most arbitrators. One party is usually eager to collect the award either to discover the result or to review the award with a view to challenging it[66] if, for instance, it contains serious errors of law. If the award is not collected, the arbitrator may recover his fees and expenses by action.

Where a party considers the fees and expenses demanded to be excessive, he may pay into court the amount demanded, or such lesser amount as the court may specify.[67] The court will order that the award be delivered.[68] Out of the money paid in, the arbitrator will be paid the "fees and expenses properly payable".[69] This means "the amount the applicant is liable to pay under Section

adviser or assessor appointed by the tribunal for which the arbitrators are liable are expenses of the arbitrators."

62. *S.N. Kurkjian (Commodity Brokers)* v. *Marketing Exchange for Africa (No. 2)* [1986] 2 Lloyd's Rep. 618.

63. *Government of Ceylon* v. *Chandris* [1963] 1 Lloyd's Rep. 214; *Rolimpex Centrala Handlu Zagranicznego* v. *Haji E. Dossa & Sons Ltd.* [1971] 1 Lloyd's Rep. 380.

64. Section 56(1) of the Arbitration Act 1996. This right has been recognised in the decided cases since the nineteenth century and it was implied by the pre-1996 legislation: see section 19 of the Arbitration Act 1950.

65. Section 37(2) of the Arbitration Act 1996.

66. The parties must make their application within 28 days of the date of the award: section 70(3) of the Arbitration Act 1996. This date will be stated in the award: sections 52 and 54 of the Arbitration Act 1996. It will ordinarily coincide with the date when the arbitrator notifies the parties that the award is available for collection. The court has a discretion to extend this time if good reasons are shown, but a failure to collect an award will not usually be such a reason: see *The Faith* [1993] 2 Lloyd's Rep. 408.

67. Section 56(2)(a) of the Arbitration Act 1996.

68. Section 56(2)(a) of the Arbitration Act 1996.

69. Section 56(2)(b) of the Arbitration Act 1996.

28 or any agreement relating to the payment of the arbitrators.".[70] Thus in an arbitration between X and Y, where X has appointed arbitrator A and agreed with him a fee £q which exceeds a reasonable fee £r, then if X is the applicant the fee properly payable in respect of A's fees will be £q; but if Y is the applicant the fee properly payable will be £r because Y is not liable to pay the higher fee £q, and arbitrator A must then look to X to make up the difference £(q − r).

The balance between the money paid into court and the fees and expenses properly payable will be repaid to the applicant.[71]

The parties right to make an application under section 28(2) of the Arbitration Act 1996 is not lost where a party pays the arbitrator in order to obtain the award.[72] This is extremely valuable as time is often short if there is a need to challenge the award. Furthermore, the parties may understandably wish to avoid confrontation with the arbitrator part way through an arbitration.

2.7 THE ARBITRATOR'S FEES WHERE THE ARBITRATION IS TERMINATED PRIOR TO AN AWARD DISPOSING OF ALL ISSUES

2.7.1 Where the arbitrator's authority is revoked

The authority of an arbitrator may be revoked by the parties.[73] An arbitrator is entitled to be paid a reasonable sum for his time as arbitrator. The mere fact that his authority has been revoked because the parties perceive the arbitrator to be unsuitable, does not entitle them to reduce the payment provided his appointment was proper.[74]

2.7.2 Where the court removes the arbitrator

The court may remove the arbitrator[75] if there are justifiable doubts as to his impartiality, if he does not possess the requisite qualifications or is incapable of conducting the proceedings or has failed properly to conduct them. "Where the court removes an arbitrator, it may make such order as it thinks fit with respect to his entitlement (if any) to fees or expenses, or the repayment of fees and expenses already paid."[76]

The order which the court will make as to the arbitrator's fees and expenses will depend largely on the personal culpability of the arbitrator (e.g. where the arbitrator becomes mentally incapable of conducting the proceedings, he is

---

70. Section 56(3) of the Arbitration Act 1996.
71. Section 56(2)(c) of the Arbitration Act 1996.
72. Section 56(8) of the Arbitration Act 1996.
73. Section 23 of the Arbitration Act 1996. The revocation need not be in writing where the parties agree to terminate the arbitration agreement.
74. Where, however, the arbitrator obtains his appointment by misleading the parties as to some aspect affecting his suitability or independence, this is different.
75. Section 24 of the Arbitration Act 1996.
76. Section 24(4) of the Arbitration Act 1996.

not personally culpable); or any excusing factors (e.g. where the advocates are overbearing and lead him to indecision, so that he fails to conduct the proceedings with all reasonable despatch).

It is thought that an arbitrator who has been culpable or reckless and has thereby substantially contributed to his removal shall not be entitled to any fees or expenses unless he can show that the parties have received a real net benefit from his time as arbitrator. The parties will have to recommence proceedings and it seems unreasonable for the arbitrator to claim his fees in such circumstances. His expenses may, however, be paid, especially where experts etc. were appointed at the request of the parties.

2.7.3 Where the arbitrator resigns

An arbitrator's immunity does not extend to "any liability incurred by an arbitrator by reason of his resigning …".[77] A wrongful resignation is clearly a breach of contract and, in accordance with normal principles, the arbitrator may be liable for the parties' losses consequent upon that breach. The damages may include wasted legal and other costs, although credit must be given for any benefits which have permanently accrued to the parties. Where the arbitrator resigns at a late stage in the proceedings the damages which flow may be considerable.

Where the resignation is reasonable in all the circumstances, however, the arbitrator may apply to the court for an order granting him relief from liability and declaring his entitlement to (or obligation to repay) fees and expenses.[78]

2.7.4 Where the arbitrator dies

An arbitrator's appointment is personal.[79] The parties take the risk of the death of the arbitrator and may insure against it.

2.7.5 Where the parties settle the proceedings

The parties may settle the arbitration at any time. The arbitrator shall then terminate the substantive proceedings.[80] The arbitrator is entitled to his reasonable fees and expenses without deduction, and may, it is thought charge a reasonable cancellation fee if the settlement is made immediately before time which had been reserved for the proceedings. Where there is an agreement as to fees, the arbitrator is entitled to payment in accordance with that agreement. Unless the parties have settled the matter of the payment of costs, the arbitrator may determine by award the recoverable fees and expenses.[81]

77. Section 29(3) of the Arbitration Act 1996.
78. Section 25(3) of the Arbitration Act 1996.
79. Section 26 of the Arbitration Act 1996.
80. Section 51(2) of the Arbitration Act 1996.
81. Sections 51(5) and 63(3) of the Arbitration Act 1996.

2.7.6 Where the court determines that the arbitrator has no jurisdiction

Where the respondent claims that the arbitrator has no jurisdiction and successfully raises the arbitrator's lack of jurisdiction as a defence to the award, it is thought that an arbitrator will normally be entitled to be paid by the claimant. By prosecuting the arbitration, the claimant has represented that the "arbitrator" has jurisdiction or, alternatively, has requested him to act as arbitrator and must pay a reasonable amount for that service.[82]

Where, however, it was reasonably obvious that the arbitrator had no jurisdiction, he may not be able to claim any fee. This may be the case especially where the parties are not represented by lawyers and the arbitrator cannot be said to rely upon the parties.

2.7.7 Where the court sets the award aside or declares it to be of no effect

Where the award is set aside or declared to be of no effect, the arbitrator's entitlement to fees and expenses will depend upon the terms on which it is set aside or so declared. If the arbitrator remains appointed in the arbitration and is required to continue as arbitrator, the position will be much as if the award had been remitted to him.[83] If the effect of setting the award aside is that the arbitrator is removed, his entitlement to fees and expenses will be much as if he had been removed under section 24 of the Arbitration Act 1996.

2.8 THE ARBITRATOR'S FEES IN RESPECT OF APPLICATIONS TO OR REMISSIONS FROM THE COURT

2.8.1 The arbitrator's costs and fees for his involvement in applications to the court

Where an arbitrator properly participates in court proceedings arising out of the arbitration, he is entitled to reasonable (or agreed) fees for that participation.

Where an arbitrator makes an application for an order following his resignation,[84] he will necessarily be a party to the proceedings and may be subject to or entitled under an order for costs.

Where an application is made to remove the arbitrator,[85] to consider his

---

82. *James Bruce Humphrey* v. *Dua Contractors & Co. Ltd.* [1996] A.D.R.L.J. 339 (Supreme Court of Hong Kong).
83. See §2.8.2 below.
84. Section 25(3) of the Arbitration Act 1996.
85. Section 24(5) of the Arbitration Act 1996.

2.8 The arbitrator's fees and expenses

fees[86] or in relation to his refusal to deliver his award unless his fees are paid,[87] the arbitrator is to be made a respondent.[88] He is therefore entitled to appear and to be heard and may become subject to or entitled under an order for costs of the application.

Where an application is made under sections 67, 68 or 69 of the Arbitration Act 1996, the arbitrator is to be notified.[89] It may be appropriate for the arbitrator to attend before the court or to put in an affidavit for the assistance of the court,[90] particularly where the substance of the application relates to the conduct of the arbitrator or the proceedings, rather than a point of law or jurisdiction. Where an arbitrator attends and is heard by the court following the submission of an affidavit, it will normally be for the court to give directions as to the arbitrator's costs in respect of the application, although the terms of the judgment may make it plain that the arbitrator might reasonably claim fees for his attendance. Normally, however, an arbitrator who attends proceedings arising out of his award or appointment does so as a private individual, and will not be entitled to any fees or expenses for his attendance.

If, upon an application, it appears to the court that the award does not contain reasons in sufficient detail, the court may order the arbitrator to state the reasons and may make an order with respect to any additional costs of the arbitration resulting from the order.[91] This order as to costs may allow the arbitrator an additional fee for stating the reasons, but need not do so.

There may be other cases where an arbitrator properly participates in an application to the court. For instance, upon a non-urgent application to the court for the preservation of evidence etc. an arbitrator is to be notified[92] and may properly make materials available to the court.

2.8.2 The arbitrator's fees for correcting an award which is remitted to him

The remission of an award to an arbitrator for his reconsideration does not

---

86. Section 28(2) of the Arbitration Act 1996. Note that an arbitrator's fees and expenses recoverable under an award may be considered under sections 64(2) of the Arbitration Act 1996. The latter section does not require that the arbitrator be notified. This is because such an application does not (in theory) affect the arbitrator's entitlement. Nevertheless, for reasons discussed in §2.5.2 the distinction between what the arbitrator is entitled to recover from the parties and what amounts to reasonable fees and expenses recoverable under an award may be slight; and any determination under section 64(2) is likely to constrain a court when a subsequent application is made under section 28(2) of the Act. Therefore, it is suggested that it is proper that the arbitrator be notified of any application under section 64(2) of the Arbitration Act 1996.

87. Section 56(2) of the Arbitration Act 1996.

88. Rules of the Supreme Court, Order 73 rule 10(2).

89. Sections 67(1), 68(1) and 69(1) of the Arbitration Act 1996.

90. Rules of the Supreme Court, Order 73 rule 12(2). See also *The Chiechocinek (No. 2)* [1980] 1 Lloyd's Rep. 97 *per* Robert Goff J. at 102: "... it is certainly proper that notice should be given to arbitrators in these circumstances ... so that they can, if they think fit, make an affidavit for the assistance of the court."

91. Section 70(5) of the Arbitration Act 1996.

92. Section 44(4) of the Arbitration Act 1996.

create any presumption that the arbitrator has failed to exercise proper skill or care. Simple misinterpretations of law or mistakes over procedure will not disentitle an arbitrator to a fee for reconsidering the award. If, however, the remission is based on a serious failure of skill and care it is thought that the arbitrator will not be entitled to charge for putting the award into the condition in which it ought reasonably to have been in the first place. The court may helpfully give an indication as to whether a fee for correcting an award on remission is appropriate.

2.9 THE FEES OF ARBITRAL INSTITUTIONS

The fees and expenses of any arbitral institution concerned are part of the costs of the arbitration.[93] Such fees and expenses may range from the fees payable to a professional body for the appointment of an arbitrator through to a full arbitration administration service.

The Arbitration Act 1996 does not provide any mechanism for reviewing the fees and expenses charged by such an institution. It is submitted that where an institution represents that it provides an arbitration service, it may not unconscionably increase its charges to parties who, in reliance upon that representation make an agreement, the operation of which depends upon the service of that institution. Normally, of course, such bodies act reasonably and the fees and expenses which they claim are reasonable.

An arbitral institution vested with powers in relation to the delivery of an award may operate the provisions in section 56 of the Arbitration Act 1996 to withhold an award except on full payment of its own fees and expenses as well as those of the arbitrator.[94]

2.10 JUDGE-ARBITRATORS

Where a judge of the Commercial Court or an official referee is appointed as arbitrator, special rules come into effect. Schedule 2 to the Arbitration Act 1996 provides that the power of the court under section 28(2) to order consideration and adjustment of the liability for "the fees"[95] of the arbitrator may be exercised by the judge-arbitrator.[96] A new version of section 56 provides for the judge-arbitrator to deliver up an award and to order how his fees and

93. Section 59(1)(b) of the Arbitration Act 1996.
94. Section 56(6) of the Arbitration Act 1996.
95. Presumably the omission of "and expenses" is a slip.
96. Paragraph 3 of Schedule 2.

2.10 The arbitrator's fees and expenses

expenses properly payable are to be determined.[97] The power of the court to determine the arbitrator's reasonable fees and expenses under section 64(2) may be exercised by the judge-arbitrator.[98]

97. Paragraphs 6 and 7 of Schedule 2.
98. Paragraph 10 of Schedule 2.

CHAPTER 3

THE AWARD AS TO LIABILITY FOR COSTS

3.1 THE ARBITRATOR'S POWER AND DUTY TO AWARD COSTS

Section 61 of the Arbitration Act 1996 provides the arbitrator's power and duty to make an award as to costs.

61 Award of costs

(1) The tribunal may make an award allocating the costs of the arbitration as between the parties, subject to any agreement of the parties.
(2) Unless the parties otherwise agree, the tribunal shall award costs on the general principle that costs should follow the event except where it appears to the tribunal that in the circumstances this is not appropriate in relation to the whole or part of the costs.

This is a non-mandatory provision and is subject to an enforceable[1] agreement of the parties. This chapter proceeds on the assumption that no such agreement has been made.

3.1.1 The obligation to make an award as to costs

Section 61(1) of the Arbitration Act 1996 does not explicitly state that the arbitrator must make an award as to costs. Nevertheless where a discretion is given, it must be exercised in line with principle. Section 61(2) of the Arbitration Act 1996 not only sets out the general principle ("costs should follow the event") but requires its application ("the tribunal shall award . . .") unless the general principle is inapplicable. The effect of section 61 of the Arbitration Act 1996, therefore, is, it is submitted, to oblige the arbitrator to make an award as to costs and to oblige him to award those costs in line with the general principle unless there is a proper reason for making a different award.

The position under the Arbitration Act 1996 remains broadly as under

---

1. See §1.5 which deals with the enforceability of agreements as to costs in the light of section 60 of the Arbitration Act 1996. Such agreements must be in writing in accordance with section 5 of the Arbitration Act 1996.

section 18(1) of the Arbitration Act 1950.[2] There the arbitrator's discretion as to an award of costs carried with it a duty to consider what order was appropriate and to make an award; it was his "bounden duty".[3] The existence of a discretion on costs "does not mean that it is in [the arbitrator]'s discretion whether he will deal with them or not, but that he must deal with them by exercising his discretion upon them. If he chooses he can say that he leaves them to be borne by the parties that incur them and make no order that either party pays the costs of the other. But he must exercise his discretion upon them".[4] The arbitration is incomplete without an award on costs. If an arbitrator purports to make a final award without dealing with costs, he may, on his own initiative or upon the application of either party, make an additional award as to costs.[5] If he fails to do so then either party is free within the time limits to make an application to the court for a remission of the award to the arbitrator on the grounds that he has not dealt with all the issues.[6] If no such application is made, an irrebuttable presumption may arise that costs are to lie where they fall.

3.1.2 Awards determining the recoverable costs of the arbitration

An arbitrator is both empowered and obliged to make an award as to liability for costs. However, he is empowered but not obliged to determine the recoverable costs of the arbitration. Section 63 of the Arbitration Act 1996 provides: "(3) The tribunal may determine by award the recoverable costs of the arbitration . . . If it does so, it shall specify . . . (4) If the tribunal does not determine the recoverable costs of the arbitration, any party may apply to the court (upon notice to the other parties) which may—(a) determine the recoverable costs . . . (b) order that they shall be determined by such means and upon such terms as it may specify . . .". In strict legal terms, it is submitted that the position remains largely the same as it was under the Arbitration Act 1950. Nevertheless there are important changes in emphasis. Under the old legis-

---

2. "Unless a contrary intention is expressed therein, every arbitration agreement shall be deemed to include a provision that the costs of the reference and award shall be in the discretion of the arbitrator . . ., who may direct to and by whom and in what manner those costs or any part thereof shall be paid . . .". These words had the effect that the arbitrator was obliged to make an award as to costs.

3. *The Aghios Nicolaos* [1980] 1 Lloyd's Rep. 17, *per* Ormrod L.J. at 21.

4. *Re Becker, Shillan & Co. and Barry Bros.* [1921] 1 K.B. 391 *per* Rowlatt J. at 395.

5. Section 57(3) of the Arbitration Act 1996 provides: "The tribunal may on its own initiative or on the application of a party—. . . (b) make an additional award in respect of any claim (including a claim for interest or costs) which was presented to the tribunal but was not dealt with in the award." It is submitted that the expression "presented to the tribunal" does not deprive the arbitrator of the right to deal with costs simply because no express presentation of a claim for costs was made; a claim for costs will be impliedly presented in every case.

6. It is submitted that the question of costs is one which is put to the arbitrator, either expressly or impliedly by the parties and/or by the terms of the Arbitration Act 1996; accordingly, a failure to deal with costs on an award amounts, if not corrected by a subsequent award, to a serious irregularity within section 68(2)(d).

lation, the arbitrator was empowered to "tax or settle" the amount of costs[7]; but there was also a presumption that an arbitrator would ordinarily leave this to the court.[8] Furthermore, the use of the term "tax" created an impression that the complex rules and procedures of taxation used in court were applicable, at least to some extent. Under the new legislation it is clearly supposed that the arbitrator will ordinarily determine the recoverable costs[9] and that he will do so using the simple tests set out in section 63 of the Arbitration Act 1996 rather than in accordance with any established procedure of the court.

3.1.3 The terms of the award as to costs

The award as to costs should deal with all the recoverable costs of the arbitration. These include[10] (a) the arbitrators' fees and expenses; (b) the fees and expenses of any arbitral institution concerned; and (c) the legal and other costs of the parties.

3.1.4 The award may only allocate liability for costs as between parties

The arbitrator's jurisdiction derives from the agreement of the parties to the arbitration; hence the arbitrator has no jurisdiction to order a non-party to pay costs.[11]

Where two or more connected arbitrations are heard at the same time by the same arbitrator without being formally consolidated,[12] the arbitrator must deal with costs in each arbitration separately.[13] However, the arbitrator is entitled to award costs in those arbitrations with an eye to the realities of the successes and failures in the proceedings as a whole.[14] Where there is no consolidation, the only "exception" to the rule that the costs of each arbitration are to be treated separately is where the costs of Arbitration A can properly be claimed as damages or an entitlement in Arbitration B.[15]

7. Section 18(1) of the Arbitration Act 1950.

8. Section 18(2) of the Arbitration Act 1950 provided: "Any costs directed by an award to be paid shall, unless the award otherwise directs, be taxable in the High Court."

9. Section 63(4) of the Arbitration Act 1996: "If the tribunal does not determine . . .".

10. Section 59 of the Arbitration Act 1996.

11. For example, *Forbes-Smith* v. *Forbes-Smith & Chadwick* [1901] P. 258 at 271; this was a divorce case in which Collins L.J. held that the co-respondent could not be obliged to pay the costs of the proceedings to which he was not a party. The court may now, by virtue of section 51 of the Supreme Court Act 1981, order a non-party to pay costs in exceptional circumstances: see *Symphony Group plc* v. *Hodgson* [1994] Q.B. 179 for the situations in which such an order may be made. Also see *The Vimeira* [1986] 2 Lloyd's Rep. 117 where a third party costs order was made by the court in relation to arbitration proceedings. An arbitrator has no such power.

12. Consolidation may only be effected where the parties to the various arbitrations agree that the proceedings are to be dealt with as a single set of proceedings, with a single award to bind all the parties. See section 35 of the Arbitration Act 1996.

13. *The Antaios* [1981] 2 Lloyd's Rep. 284; *The Takamine* [1980] 2 Lloyd's Rep. 204; *The Catherine L.* [1982] 1 Lloyd's Rep. 484.

14. *The Catherine L.* [1982] 1 Lloyd's Rep. 484 at 489.

15. *Hammond* v. *Bussey* (1888) 20 Q.B.D. 79; *Suzuki & Co. Ltd.* v. *Burgett and Newsam* (1922) 10 Lloyd's Rep. 223. *The Antaios* [1981] 2 Lloyd's Rep. 284: the tests of causation and remoteness must both be satisfied, *per* Robert Goff J. at 299.

3.1 The award as to liability for costs

Where two or more arbitrations are formally consolidated, so that one award binds all the parties, the award as to costs may require that any party to those consolidated proceedings pays the costs of any other party to those proceedings.[16]

If a party believes that he is entitled to a contribution from a non-party, including his own representatives, he must commence a separate action to recover such entitlement.

Illustration

The Catherine L [1982] 1 Lloyd's Rep. 484 The Catherine L's owners, CH, let her to G, who let her to CT, who in turn let her to U. It was alleged that she had taken the ground at Karachi with resulting damage valued at $100,000. CH claimed against G, G claimed an indemnity against CT and CT claimed an indemnity against U. A sole arbitrator heard all three arbitrations in one hearing, but they were not formally consolidated so that three separate awards were made. The main issues were between CH and U as the ultimate claimant and respondent. The arbitrator found that the damage did not occur at Karachi and dismissed CH's claim against G. But he then proceeded to find that the claims for an indemnity succeeded in the other two arbitrations. He made separate awards of costs in three arbitrations as he had to do. But as a result of his finding that the claims for indemnities succeeded he made a complex series of awards with the result that U, who had been cleared of wrongdoing, was made liable for a significant element of the overall costs. U made an application to the court. Bingham J. said at 489–490: "the formal independence of the arbitrations did not require him [the arbitrator] to turn a blind eye to the realities of the litigation as a whole ... The arbitrator here faced a situation in which perfect justice could not be achieved. He could not (as he would, I think have wished, and as would have been usual in legal proceedings) make an order which would have laid the costs of all the parties at the door of CH, whose resort to arbitration had initiated the whole process. In this dilemma the question which ultimately falls to be answered in the third arbitration, as between CT and U, is in my judgment this: what order for costs is in all the circumstances most fair and just to reflect the relative success and failure of each party as a matter of substance in the context of the three arbitrations, bearing in mind the responsibility (if any) of each party for the litigation, their conduct in the course of it, the litigious burden each has borne, the end result of any order in either of the other arbitrations and any other circumstances relevant to the litigation?"

3.2 THE EVENT

3.2.1 The general principle: costs follow the event

Section 61(2) of the Arbitration Act 1996 provides: "Unless the parties otherwise agree, the tribunal shall award costs on the general principle that costs should follow the event except where it appears to the tribunal that in the circumstances this is not appropriate in relation to the whole or part of the

---

16. This is the practice of the courts where proceedings are frequently consolidated. See also *The Catherine L*. [1982] 1 Lloyd's Rep. 484 at 486 where an indication to this effect is given for consolidated arbitrations.

costs." This sets up the following scheme, in line with the long-standing principle that costs should ordinarily follow the event.[17]

(1) Where the parties have made an enforceable agreement[18] as to the allocation of costs as between the parties, this prevails.

(2) In the absence of such agreement, the arbitrator should ordinarily award costs to "follow the event". The Arbitration Act 1996 does not define "the event". The event will therefore be "the event" as considered in the decided cases, unless the parties have agreed a different definition.

(3) Despite the general principle that costs follow the event, the arbitrator has a discretion to make a different award "where it appears ... that in the circumstances this is not appropriate ...".

3.2.2 Defining "the event"

The expression "the event" has the ring of a term of art. A review of the cases reveals, however, that it simply relates to "success".[19] "Success" cannot always be defined precisely and the identity of the successful party may, in many cases, ultimately be a matter of impression. This is especially likely in cases where each party contends for a different position (e.g. disputes over share valuations, rent reviews, etc.) or where the substance of the dispute is not monetary (e.g. disputes over the location of land boundaries). In such cases, as elsewhere, the arbitrator must decide what the event is and who has been successful. Where appropriate, he may adopt the concept of partial success.

3.2.3 The basic case: a single claim for money

Where a single claim for money is advanced and the claimant recovers a small amount relative to the sum claimed, there may be a question as to whether or not the claimant has been successful. If the sum recovered was "nominal"[20] or "trifling" the arbitrator may consider the respondent to have been successful and to award him his costs.[21] But where the sum is merely a small proportion of the sum claimed and cannot be considered "trifling", the identification of

17. *The Erich Schroeder* [1974] 1 Lloyd's Rep. 192: "In exercising his discretion judicially an umpire/arbitrator must have regard in the first place to the primary principle guiding courts and arbitral tribunals in the exercise of their discretion in relation to costs, namely, that costs follow the event", *per* Mocatta J. at 194.

18. See §1.5.

19. In the cases, the term "the event" is used as an identifier for the "winning party" or the "successful party". For example in *Messers Ltd.* v. *Heidner & Co.* [1961] 1 Lloyd's Rep. 107, Winn J. said at 115: "The arbitrators were ... making an award as to costs without having, as their formal award shows, applied their minds to the most important consideration relevant to the exercise of their discretion, namely who had won—who had been successful in the proceedings."

20. *Alltrans Express Ltd.* v. *C.V.A. Holdings Ltd.* [1984] 1 W.L.R. 394.

21. *Harris* v. *Petherick* (1879) 4 Q.B.D. 611, restated in *Tramountana Armadora S.A.* v. *Atlantic Shipping Co. S.A.* [1978] 1 Lloyd's Rep. 391 at 398.

success is not straightforward.[22] It is submitted that the key question is whether the claimant can be regarded as successful when what he actually recovered is compared with what he set out to prove.[23] If the claimant recovers a substantial proportion of what he claims (so that an objective observer would consider that he had "won"), he may reasonably be considered to have been successful. If the claimant recovers an insubstantial amount (so that the objective observer would have considered that he had "lost"), he can reasonably be considered to have been unsuccessful. There will be an intermediate region, where there has been a degree of success, but insufficient to be able to regard the claimant as the "only winner"; here the arbitrator will, it is submitted, be entitled to treat the claimant as partially successful and make an order as to costs which reflects this, normally by depriving the partially successful claimant of a proportion of his costs.

An arbitrator must not use the logic that the respondent should have made an offer of settlement to protect himself[24]; it is for the claimant to prove his claim and a claimant who substantially fails to do so cannot be regarded as successful.

3.2.4 Multiple heads of claim

Where a series of claims are advanced which arise substantially out of the same body of facts and one minor claim is successfully defended[25] the claimant will ordinarily expect to be considered successful and to receive all his costs. Where, however, two distinct and substantial[26] claims are advanced, and each party is successful on one,[27] the respondent may expect to be considered partially successful and anticipate a costs order which does not give the claimant all his costs; indeed a hopeful respondent who has succeeded on the more substantial issue may even expect to receive a proportion of his costs.[28]

3.2.5 The effect of amendments to a party's case during the proceedings

The question of success is usually determined by comparing the position of the parties after the award with their positions at the commencement of the

22. See *Perry* v. *Stopher* [1959] 1 All E.R. 713 where a rather liberal definition of "success" was allowed.

23. *Anglo-Cyprian Trade Agencies Ltd.* v. *Paphos Wine Industries Ltd.* [1951] 1 All E.R. 873; *Alltrans Express Ltd.* v. *C.V.A. Holdings Ltd.* [1984] 1 W.L.R. 394; *Lipkin Gorman* v. *Karpnale Ltd.* [1989] 1 W.L.R. 1340; *Beoco Ltd.* v. *Alfa Laval Co. Ltd.* [1994] 3 W.L.R. 1179.

24. *Alltrans Express Ltd.* v. *C.V.A. Holdings Ltd.* [1984] 1 W.L.R. 394. See Chapter 7 where such offers are discussed.

25. For example *The Rozel* [1994] 2 Lloyd's Rep. 161.

26. But not as in *Harris* v. *Petherick* (1879) 4 Q.B.D. 611 where two distinct claims were advanced, one for £85 and one for £0–00–6d; only the 6d claim succeeded.

27. For example *Thyssen (Great Britain) Ltd.* v. *Borough Council of Afan* (1978) 15 Build. L.R. 98.

28. This was the contention of the applicant in *Thyssen (Great Britain) Ltd.* v. *Borough Council of Afan* (1978) 15 Build. L.R. 98.

proceedings. However, this simple comparison may produce injustice where the case being advanced by one of the parties is amended during the proceedings. In such situations, the courts will normally apply the following test: "As a general rule, where a plaintiff makes a late amendment ... which substantially alters the case the defendant has to meet and without which the action will fail, the defendant is entitled to the costs of the action down to the date of the amendment."[29] Thus the respondent may be "successful" before the amendment, and "unsuccessful" after it. Where a claim as originally pleaded fails, but is saved by an amendment which is so late that it is impracticable for the respondent to protect himself by making an offer of settlement, the respondent will not only have his costs down to the date of the amendment but he will also recover a substantial proportion of the costs incurred afterwards as though he were the successful party, notwithstanding the claimant's apparent success.[30] Defensive amendments are treated in a more liberal manner, since it is for the claimant to prove his case.[31]

3.2.6 Offers of settlement[32]

When an offer of settlement has been made, success for a claimant generally means that his recovery exceeds any proper offer made. There are clear indications in the reported cases that once an offer is made, the arbitrator's discretion is significantly constrained. The rationale for this is that once a party makes an offer, he notifies the other party that he intends to put the definition of "success" on a win/lose basis, to be determined by comparing the eventual recovery to the value of the offer. When a proper offer is made, the primary question to be asked is: "Has the claimant achieved more by rejecting the offer and going on with the arbitration than he would have achieved if he had accepted the offer?"[33] But even where an offer is made, the arbitrator retains a discretion and may award costs against the "successful" party, providing he does so for a proper reason.

3.2.7 Counterclaims and set-offs

The question of success is frequently complicated by the fact that both parties advance connected claims.

If the counterclaim is, in substance, a defence by way of set-off or is based on substantially the same facts as the claim, it may be appropriate to treat the party who is successful on aggregate as being the successful party and entitled

29. *Beoco Ltd.* v. *Alfa Laval Co. Ltd.* [1994] 3 W.L.R. 1179, *per* Stuart Smith L.J. at 1193.

30. *Anglo-Cyprian Trade Agencies Ltd.* v. *Paphos Wine Industries Ltd.* [1951] 1 All E.R. 873; *Alltrans Express Ltd.* v. *C.V.A. Holdings Ltd.* [1984] 1 W.L.R. 394; *Lipkin Gorman* v. *Karpnale Ltd.* [1989] 1 W.L.R. 1340; *Beoco Ltd.* v. *Alfa Laval Co. Ltd.* [1994] 3 W.L.R. 1179.

31. *Beoco Ltd.* v. *Alfa Laval Co. Ltd.* [1994] 3 W.L.R. 1179, *per* Stuart Smith L.J. at 1193.

32. See generally Chapter 7.

33. *Tramountana Armadora S.A.* v. *Atlantic Shipping Co. S.A.* [1978] 1 Lloyd's Rep. 391 *per* Donaldson J. at 397–8.

to his costs.[34] Most counterclaims in arbitration proceedings will rank as set-offs since they arise out of the same contract as the claim.[35]

If the counterclaim is substantially different in nature from the claim, it may be appropriate to award costs to reflect the success of each. This result is often most conveniently achieved by the making of a proportionate award of costs to the party who is successful on aggregate.[36]

Where the arbitrator awards costs to both claimant and counterclaimant (e.g. where both are successful or where both are unsuccessful) he should make clear which costs he proposes to go to each party. Otherwise, the received rule of taxation will be applied, namely that the costs of the counterclaim are those which are incurred only because of the counterclaim[37]; evidence etc. which relates to both the claim and the counterclaim will be allocated to the claim alone. This may cause injustice as where the description of the parties as claimant and counterclaimant is a matter of historical accident.[38]

Illustrations

Anglo-Cyprian Trade Agencies Ltd. v. Paphos Wine Industries Ltd. [1951] 1 All E.R. 873 The plaintiffs claimed £2,000 for defects in goods delivered. At the trial the defendants gave evidence that the defects could be remedied for a small expenditure of about £50. The plaintiffs then amended their claim to include the £50 claim as an alternative. They failed on the £2,000 claim, but succeeded on the £50 claim. Devlin J. decided that on the unamended claim, the plaintiffs would have recovered nominal damages only; on that basis they would not have established anything of value to them and the defendants should be regarded as successful. Devlin J. then dealt (at 875) with the head of claim on which the plaintiffs were successful: "If their original pleading had contained the amended claim, while I do not suppose that I could have given them the costs of the action since they recovered only £52 when their main claim was for a much larger sum, I do not think it would have been right to order them to pay all the costs of the defendants." But having taken the late amendment into account, the plaintiffs were ordered to pay all the defendants' costs.

Hanak v. Green [1958] 2 Q.B. 9 H engaged G to perform work to her house. H sued G for defects and incomplete work. G counterclaimed for work performed in addition to that agreed, disruption to his work and trespass to his tools. The technical matters were heard by a referee. The judge then awarded £75 to H and £85 to G, a net recovery of £10 by G. The judge ordered H to pay the costs of the counterclaim and G to pay

---

34. *Nicholson* v. *Little* [1956] 1 W.L.R. 829; *Hanak* v. *Green* [1958] 2 Q.B. 9; *Tramountana Armadora S.A.* v. *Atlantic Shipping Co. S.A.* [1978] 1 Lloyd's Rep. 391.

35. *Hanak* v. *Green* [1958] 2 Q.B. 9, e.g. *per* Sellers L.J. at 29.

36. *Archital Luxfer* v. *Henry Boot Construction Ltd.* [1981] 1 Lloyd's Rep. 642; *Chell Engineering Ltd.* v. *Unit Tool and Engineering Co. Ltd.* [1950] 1 All E.R. 378; *Childs* v. *Gibson* [1954] 1 W.L.R. 809.

37. *Medway Oil and Storage Co. Ltd* v. *Continental Contractors* [1929] A.C. 88. It is sometimes suggested that this case makes it a matter of law that the counterclaimant's costs can only be those necessarily incurred as a result of advancing the counterclaim. A reading of the judgments of the House of Lords indicates, however, that the point of the case was: what should a taxing officer understand by a judge's order that both claim and counterclaim succeed with costs (or fail with costs against)? In any event, the importance of this matter has diminished significantly since the decision in *Hanak* v. *Green* [1958] 2 Q.B. 9.

38. As was recognised in *Medway Oil and Storage Co. Ltd* v. *Continental Contractors* [1929] A.C. 88 by Lord Blaneburgh at 111–12.

the costs of the claim. The Court of Appeal revised this order on the grounds that it was unfair to G whose counterclaim was to be set off in equity against the claim. G was awarded all his costs in the court and both G and H were to pay one half of the costs before the referee. [Note: This case is frequently cited as authority for the proposition that where a counterclaim amounts to a set-off, the "winner" is the party who recovers a net payment in the arbitration and is therefore entitled at law to his costs. It is submitted that *Hanak* v. *Green* merely holds that where the counterclaim amounts to a set-off, a single costs order in favour of the party who receives a net recovery will normally be appropriate. It is submitted that the arbitrator must still decide whether, in all the circumstances, this is the fair and just order: indeed, even in *Hanak* v. *Green*, G did not receive all his costs. See, in this regard, Gibson J. in *Archital Luxfer* v. *Henry Boot* [1981] 1 Lloyd's Rep. 642 at 649. It is submitted that the less doctrinaire approach suggested in the following extracts from *Tramountana* v. *Atlantic* [1978] 1 Lloyd's Rep. 391 and *Archital Luxfer* v. *Henry Boot* represents the correct position at law.]

Perry v. Stopher [1959] 1 All E.R. 713 The claimant builder claimed £54 against the respondent building owner but recovered only £11. Costs were awarded to the respondent. The claimant sought to have the award on costs set aside. The Court of Appeal held that there were grounds upon which an arbitrator could have exercised his discretion to deprive the claimant of his costs. "One may well ask 'Who was the successful party in this case?' . . . the plaintiff may be said to have been successful so far as £11 is concerned, but equally it may be said that the defendant has been successful as far as some £40 is concerned. One wonders what the plaintiff would have said if, as he had just finished reading the award of the arbitrator, some friends of his had come up to him and warmly congratulated him on the 'success' he had achieved in his case. I apprehend that the plaintiff would have regarded himself as having substantially failed in his claim. If so, the plaintiff having substantially failed in his claim, but the defendant not having wholly succeeded in defeating the claim, it seems to me that it was open to the arbitrator to take almost any course with regard to the costs in the exercise of his discretion, and we have not got the information which would justify us, as I see it, in criticising the course which he did take", *per* Willmer L.J. at 720.

Thyssen (Great Britain) Ltd. v. Borough Council of Afan (1978) 15 Build. L.R. 98 BCA engaged T to construct a crematorium. Following completion of the works, T claimed under two separate heads, one based on a construction of the contract, the other for delay. The first claim was for £20,000, the second for £7,000. BCA successfully defended the first claim and T recovered about £3,000 in respect of the second. After written submissions, the arbitrator's final award ordered that each party should bear its own costs. BCA sought to have the order overturned. The arbitration hearing was very costly, lasting about 20 days and it was assumed by the Court of Appeal that the claim which BCA successfully defended occupied the substantial proportion of the hearing. Counsel for BCA contended that there were two "separate disputes" and that costs should be awarded for each separately. Held, the arbitrator was not required to treat the claims separately for the purposes of costs and the arbitrator had not acted unjudicially in making his order. Megaw L.J. (at 106) considered that there was no "overriding principle, in relation to a two-issue case such as this, as [counsel] contends for". Shaw L.J. (at 108) considered "that in deciding the question of costs the arbitrator was entitled to take an overall view. In my judgment he would be entitled to do so even if there was a true dichotomy between the different issues . . .". Waller L.J. emphasised the fact that since there was only one award, counsel's argument failed. He went on, at page 108, to describe the breadth of the discretion available: "If the whole of the costs had been awarded either way, I could see there would have been a strong argument for saying that the arbitrator was not acting judicially. It would then be possible to say, either that the arbitrator had ignored the findings in BCA's favour—

that is, if he had ordered BCA to pay all the costs—or that he had ignored the finding in T's favour if he had ordered T to pay all the costs. Once the award is somewhere in between those two extremes, for example, making no order as to costs, in my view it is impossible to say that the arbitrator was not acting judicially."

Tramountana Armadora S.A. v. Atlantic Shipping Co. S.A. [1978] 1 Lloyd's Rep 391 "The starting point is always the rule that costs follow the event. This at once gives rise to a difficulty when there is a claim and counterclaim, the one being set off against the other. On some occasions it is then appropriate to consider each separately and, for example, to give the claimant the costs of the claim and the respondents the costs of the counterclaim. This leaves it to the parties to agree, or to the taxing authority to determine, what proportion of the costs of each party is attributable to the claim and what to the counterclaim. On other occasions it may be clear to the judge or arbitrator that the claim and counterclaim have no independent existence, the counter-claim being really a defence to the claim or vice versa. In such a case it is inappropriate to make cross-orders for costs. One or other or neither party should be awarded all or some proportion or the costs of both claim and counterclaim", *per* Donaldson J. at 399.

The Aghios Nicolaos [1980] 1 Lloyd's Rep. *17* A ship was brought into Valparaíso and experienced damage during two separate storm events a week apart. The owner sought compensation from the charterer and the question of liability was referred to arbitration. The arbitrator found the charterer liable for one event only. His award on costs was that each party should bear its own costs and the costs of the award should be borne equally by the parties. The Court of Appeal suggested that on making an apportionment of costs, the arbitrator might have had explicit regard to such factors as the time taken to try each issue. Nevertheless, it upheld the award as a "perfectly intelligible" exercise of discretion since each party had succeeded on one issue, each of which would have similar costs.

Archital Luxfer Ltd. v. Henry Boot Construction Ltd. [1981] 1 Lloyd's Rep. 642 "In a case where a subcontractor is owed money on his final account and a claim by the main contractor is made against him vastly in excess of the amount so owed, a court or arbitrator might well in some circumstances conclude that if the main contractor's claims are eventually upheld in a sum less than the amount owing to the subcontractor, the subcontractor should have all the costs of the action. It is the experience of everyone who has to do with such cases that from time to time an inflated claim is put forward with the apparent purpose of frightening the subcontractor, by the fear of the costs of such proceedings, to accept much less than the sum due to him. It is to be hoped that when this is done the purpose will be discerned and an order for costs made which will reflect the justice of the situation ... The court may properly in such circumstances direct the main contractor to pay all the costs even though by the proceedings he has reduced in part what otherwise he would have had to pay. This is, however, merely to state, as is already well established, that a judge or an arbitrator has a wide discretion as to costs. There is of course no general principle that a main contractor, who owes money to a subcontractor, must necessarily pay all the costs of proving the extent of any damage done to him by breach of contract by the subcontractor, merely because the main contractor overestimated the amount due to him for such breach and retained, out of money due to the subcontractor more than is ultimately found due from the subcontractor for damages", *per* Gibson J. at 649.

Re Elgindata No. 2 [1992] 1 W.L.R. 1207 The petitioners were shareholders in a company. They claimed that the respondent, the majority shareholder, had acted in a way which prejudiced their shareholdings; they sought an order that the respondent should purchase their shares. They alleged a number of different items of wrongdoing.

The judge categorised these allegations into four sets of allegation and decided that they had succeeded in proving one set, but not the other three. Nevertheless, he made the order which they sought. When dealing with costs, he decided that since the petitioners had succeeded on only one out of the four sets of allegation, they should pay the respondent three-quarters of his costs and that he should pay one quarter of theirs. The result was that the petitioners who had reasonably brought the claim and obtained the order which they sought ended up with a far higher costs bill than the unsuccessful respondent. The Court of Appeal overturned the order; it decided that the successful party should not pay any part of the unsuccessful party's costs and it awarded the successful petitioners 50 per cent of their costs.

Metro-Cammell Hong Kong Ltd. v. F.K.I. Engineering plc [1996] A.D.R.L.N. 5 May 1996 "The successful party should be awarded his costs unless there was a good reason connected with the case why he should be deprived of them. Where a party recovered significantly less than claimed, this, of itself, provided no justification for not awarding that party all of its costs . . ." *per* Judge Lloyd Q.C.

3.3 THE DISCRETION TO MAKE AN AWARD WHICH DOES NOT FOLLOW THE EVENT

3.3.1 General

The arbitrator may make an award as to costs which does not follow the event "where it appears ... that in the circumstances this is not appropriate ...".[39] There are two distinct possibilities available. The arbitrator may deprive a successful party of his costs or part of them; while this is an unusual order, it may frequently be justified. Far more unusual is the award of costs to the unsuccessful party to be paid by the successful party.

Where an arbitrator departs from the general principle that costs follow the event, his award must be made with proper judicial discretion.[40] "Prima facie, a successful party is entitled to his costs. To deprive him of his costs or to require him to pay a part of the costs of the other side is an exceptional measure."[41] If the arbitrator decides to award costs which do not follow the event,[42] he "ought to bear in mind the principles as to costs which have

---

39. Section 61(2) of the Arbitration Act 1996.

40. See for the pre-1996 cases: *Smeaton Hanscomb & Co. Ltd. v. Sassoon I. Setty, Son & Co.* (No. 2) [1953] 1 W.L.R. 1481; *Lewis v. Haverfordwest Rural District Council* [1953] 2 All E.R. 1599; *Matheson & Co. Ltd. v. A. Tabah & Sons* [1963] 2 Lloyd's Rep. 270. It is submitted that the term "judicially" requires an arbitrator to base his discretion on reasons which are available to a judge, since both are confined to "proper" reasons. It may not be possible to define the term "proper" in any exhaustive or prescriptive way, but it is submitted that it bears an identical meaning whether used in the context of a judge's or of an arbitrator's discretion: see *The Rozel* [1994] 2 Lloyd's Rep. 161 *per* Phillips J. at 169.

41. *Smeaton Hanscomb & Co. Ltd. v. Sassoon I Setty, Son & Co.* (No. 2) [1953] 1 W.L.R. 1481 *per* Devlin J. at 1484; see also *Tramountana Armadora v. Atlantic Shipping Co.* [1978] 1 Lloyd's Rep. 391 at 394 "the prima facie rule of English law and practice [is] that costs should follow the event".

42. *The Erich Schroeder* [1974] 1 Lloyd's Rep. 192.

been worked out by the court".[43] Furthermore, "the arbitrator must not act capriciously and must, if he exercises his discretion to refuse the usual order [that the successful party should receive his costs], show a reason connected with the case which the court can see is proper".[44] An arbitrator will misdirect himself where he deprives the successful party of his costs and bases his discretion on no material[45]; or on irrelevant material[46]; or on a reason which the law considers an improper reason; or purports to apply a proper principle but seriously misunderstands the applicable law and hence misapplies the principle.[47]

A failure to use proper judicial discretion will be an error of law which may found an appeal under section 69 of the Arbitration Act 1996.

3.3.2 The importance of making predictable awards as to costs

While an arbitrator has a wide discretion on costs, it is also important that parties know how that discretion will be exercised in common situations. An arbitrator's principal task when exercising his discretion is to do justice, but this is not an untethered concept. It involves, among other things, a consideration of the expectations of the parties. An arbitrator's role is certainly not to experiment with the limits of his discretion, while ignoring these expectations. An arbitrator should, therefore, make his award on costs fully in line with established principles unless there are matters which require an unusual order.[48] On the other hand, certainty must give way when justice requires. Thus, while arbitrators, such as those who operate under institutional schemes may find it convenient to adopt a settled practice, they must not disable themselves from departing from this practice if justice demands it.[49]

---

43. *Smeaton Hanscomb & Co. Ltd.* v. *Sassoon I. Setty, Son & Co.* (No. 2) [1953] 1 W.L.R. 1481 *per* Devlin J. at 1485.

44. *Lewis* v. *Haverfordwest Rural District Council* [1953] 2 All E.R. 1599 *per* Lord Goddard C.J. at 1599.

45. *Civil Service Co-operative Society* v. *General Steam Navigation Company* [1903] 2 K.B. 756 at 765 *per* Lord Halsbury; *Ritter* v. *Godfrey* [1920] 2 K.B. 47: "[A] discretion exercised on no grounds cannot be judicial" *per* Lord Sterndale M.R. at 52, affirmed in *Perry* v. *Stopher* [1959] 1 All E.R. 713 at 715. See also *Rosen & Co.* v. *Dowley and Selby* [1943] 2 All E.R. 172; *The Erich Schroeder* [1974] 1 Lloyd's Rep. 192.

46. Material is irrelevant if it is (a) extraneous to the reference, e.g. *The Maria* [1993] 2 Lloyd's Rep.168 *per* Sir Thomas Bingham M.R. at 173; or (b) based on extra-legal considerations, e.g. *Rosen & Co.* v. *Dowley and Selby* [1943] 2 All E.R. 172.

47. *The Maria* [1993] 2 Lloyd's Rep.168.

48. *K/S A/S Bani* v. *Korea Shipbuilding and Engineering Corporation* [1987] 2 Lloyd's Rep. 445: "While the exercise of any discretion necessarily means that there is an area within which the judge's discretion is final and unchallengeable, it is highly desirable that the general lines on which a familiar discretion will be exercised should be generally known and broadly predictable", *per* Bingham L.J. at 448.

49. *James Allen (Liverpool) Ltd.* v. *London Export Corporation Ltd.* [1981] 2 Lloyd's Rep. 632, where the GAFTA Board of Appeal's practice of ordering both parties to pay their own costs was considered inconsistent with the discretion vested in them.

3.3.3 Defining judicial and unjudicial exercise of the discretion

There are no fixed formulae as to what awards may be considered unjudicial or in what circumstances the arbitrator may be said to have misdirected himself. The discretion is to be exercised by the particular arbitrator appointed by the parties (or on their behalf) and the fact that another arbitrator or the court would have exercised the discretion differently is largely irrelevant. The court will only interfere where there has been a manifest failure to act judicially or where the arbitrator has clearly misdirected himself.[50]

When awarding costs, the arbitrator is exercising a discretion rather than applying a rule of law. Consequently, the decided cases only define the limits of the discretion. They do not define the ordinary exercise of that discretion. Indeed, the courts have been cautious not to lay down any clear guidelines which may be interpreted as "rules of law".[51] Furthermore, when cases come before the courts, there is a presumption that the award as to costs, whether or not its terms may be criticised as being unusual or unexpected, is to be upheld.[52] While awards of costs have been overturned,[53] there are also many cases where the courts have clearly been uneasy about what had been awarded but nevertheless felt unable to interfere[54]; here the award is not judicially approved.

3.3.4 Reasons which amount to unjudicial exercise of discretion or misdirection

Where an arbitrator departs from the general principle that the successful party is entitled to his reasonable recoverable costs, he will generally misdirect himself if:

---

50. *Tramountana Armadora S.A.* v. *Atlantic Shipping Co. S.A.* [1978] 1 Lloyd's Rep. 391: "In reviewing an arbitrator's decision on costs, it is of the greatest importance to remember that the decision is within his discretion and not that of the courts. It is nothing to the point that I might have reached a different decision and that some other judge or arbitrator might have differed from both of us. I would neither wish, nor be entitled, to intervene, unless I was satisfied that the arbitrator had misdirected himself", *per* Donaldson J. at 396.

51. *Blexen Ltd.* v. *G Percy Trentham Ltd.* (1990) 54 Build. L.R. 37 at 47: "Where an unfettered discretion has been granted by Parliament it is never desirable to hedge it about with too much guidance, in case the guidance comes to be regarded as an inflexible rule of law or practice. It can be no such thing."

52. In *Centrala Morska Impotowo Eksportowa* v. *Companhia Nacional de Navegacao S.A.R.L.* [1975] 2 Lloyd's Rep. 69, Donaldson J. at 72 summarised the law and affirmed the principles laid down by Mocatta J. in *The Eric Schroeder* [1974] 1 Lloyd's Rep. 192: "There is a burden of proof upon the party seeking to set aside an award in relation to the decision of an umpire or arbitrator in relation to costs or seeking to have the award remitted so that the arbitrator or umpire may deal with the costs in a way other than that in which he originally dealt with them."

53. For example, *The Maria* [1993] 2 Lloyd's Rep. 168.

54. E.g. *Perry* v. *Stopher* [1959] 1 All E.R. 713; *P. Rosen & Co. Ltd.* v. *Dowley & Selby* [1943] 2 All E.R. 172; *Matheson & Co. Ltd.* v. *A. Tabah & Sons* [1963] 2 Lloyd's Rep. 270.

3.3 The award as to liability for costs

(1) he takes into account any matter which is not connected with the arbitration[55];

(2) he takes into account a matter which is not properly before him; for example if the arbitrator learns about "without prejudice" negotiations and uses this knowledge in making his award as to costs[56];

(3) he takes into account any matter which relates to extra-legal considerations, such as his disapproval of the morality of the claim[57];

(4) he takes into account the fact that a party has raised technical points or defences. A successful party may be required to pay any costs wasted as a result of unsuccessful and/or frivolous applications; but the fact that a party uses all legitimate force to protect his position is no reason to deduct costs generally, providing that he has not acted with "motives of malice or for some extravagance or self-aggrandisement"[58];

(5) he takes into account the fact that the sum recovered by the claimant is only marginally in excess of a proper offer made when there are no other supporting factors[59];

(6) he purports to apply any proper reason in the usual manner but in fact applies it in a manner inconsistent with the established law and practice.[60]

55. E.g. *The Maria* [1993] 2 Lloyd's Rep. 168 *per* Sir Thomas Bingham M.R. at 173; *Donald Campbell & Co. Ltd. v. Pollak* [1927] A.C. 732 *per* Viscount Cave at 811–12. But see *Bostock* v. *Ramsey U.D.C.* [1900] 2 Q.B. 616, *per* A.L. Smith L.J. at 622: "The judge is not confined to the consideration of the defendant's conduct in the actual litigation itself, but may also take into consideration matters which led up to and were the occasion of that litigation". Also, see *East* v. *Berkshire C.C.* (1911) 106 L.T. 65 where it was decided that a successful defendant who had made misstatements in circumstances where he had an obligation to be truthful and thereby brought the litigation about could be deprived of costs. But simple provocation to bring proceedings is insufficient; thus in *Hanak* v. *Green* [1958] 2 Q.B. 9, the judge at first instance refused to give the successful defendant his costs based partly upon the fact that the defendant's workman had been "loutish"—"This matter seems to have arisen in the evidence, but it had nothing to do with the defendant's conduct of the case", *per* Sellers L.J. at 27.

56. *Stotesbury* v. *Turner* [1943] 1 K.B. 370.

57. *Messers Ltd. Heidner & Co.* [1960] 1 Lloyd's Rep. 107; *Rosen & Co. Ltd.* v. *Dowley & Selby* [1943] 2 All E.R. 172; *Lloyd del Pacifico* v. *Board of Trade* (1930) 46 T.L.R. 476; *Andrew* v. *Grove* [1902] 1 K.B. 625.

58. *Messers Ltd.* v. *Heidner & Co.* [1961] 1 Lloyd's Rep. 107, *per* Winn J. at 116.

59. *The Maria* [1993] 2 Lloyd's Rep. 168, *per* Sir Thomas Bingham at 175 and Evans L.J. at 181. A discussion of this point is also to be found in *Archital Luxfer Ltd.* v. *Henry Boot Construction Ltd.* [1981] 1 Lloyd's Rep. 642 and *Tramountana Armadora S.A.* v. *Atlantic Shipping Co. S.A.* [1978] 1 Lloyd's Rep. 391.

60. *The Maria* [1993] 2 Lloyd's Rep. 168 (where the arbitrator purported to apply the established practice when an offer had been made but did so incorrectly); *Dineen* v. *Walpole* [1969] 1 Lloyd's Rep. 261 (where the arbitrator took undue account of the respondent's defence that he was prepared to put right the matters complained of).

3.3.5 Proper reasons for depriving a successful party of some or all of his reasonable recoverable costs

An arbitrator may, in general, properly deprive a successful party of some or, exceptionally, all of his costs in the following situations:

(1) where the successful party has conducted his part in the arbitration improperly[61];

(2) where the successful party has grossly exaggerated his claims, this may be a proper reason for depriving a successful claimant of "some of his costs"[62] where the exaggeration has contributed to the cost of the proceedings. Thus where leading counsel are instructed because of the exaggerated claims or a longer hearing is required to investigate what seem to be serious claims, an element of costs may be deducted;

(3) where the success is partial. Where a claimant has run a series of claims and has lost some of them, this, of itself, is no reason to deprive him of his costs in pursuing those lost claims.[63] However, "[w]here a claimant takes substantial time pursuing discrete issues of fact on which he is unsuccessful, this can constitute a legitimate reason for not awarding him all his costs, the more so if the arbitrator considers that his conduct has been unreasonable".[64] "Unreasonable" in this context may include where the claimant runs issues of no real merit, or has spent an inordinate amount of time on issues, or has run issues to gain an unfair advantage such as where the costs are wilfully inflated in an attempt to force a settlement.

3.3.6 Reasons for ordering the successful party to pay some or all of the unsuccessful party's costs

A successful party may be required to pay all or part of the costs of the unsuccessful party, but only in exceptional circumstances. In particular, it will rarely be proper to require a successful respondent[65] to pay any of the unsuccessful claimant's costs; the very fact that the respondent has been

---

61. *Matheson & Co. Ltd.* v. *A Tabah & Sons* [1963] 2 Lloyd's Rep. 270; *The Catherine L.* [1982] 1 Lloyd's Rep. 484; *Demolition & Construction Co. Ltd.* v. *Kent River Board* [1963] 2 Lloyd's Rep. 7 *per* McNair J. at 15; *Andrew* v. *Grove* [1902] 1 K.B. 625 *per* Channell J. at 628.

62. *The Rozel* [1994] 2 Lloyd's Rep. 161, *per* Phillips J. at 170; see also *Perry* v. *Stopher* [1959] 1 All E.R. 713 and *Dineen* v. *Walpole* [1969] 1 Lloyd's Rep. 261.

63. *The Rozel* [1994] 2 Lloyd's Rep. 161, *per* Phillips J. at 170–71. This report is notable for the fact that it includes a table setting out the various claims, the amount of each, the time spent on each and the degree of success on each. See also *Metro-Cammell Hong Kong Ltd* v. *F.K.I. Engineering plc* [1996] A.D.R.L.N. 5 May 1996.

64. *The Rozel* [1994] 2 Lloyd's Rep. 161 *per* Phillips J. at 170. See also *Re Elgindata No. 2* [1992] 1 W.L.R. 1207 *per* Nourse L.J. at 1214; see also *Emmanuel (Lewis) & Son* v. *Sammut* [1959] 2 Lloyd's Rep. 629 and *Matheson & Co. Ltd.* v. *A. Tabah & Sons* [1963] 2 Lloyd's Rep. 270.

65. The term "respondent" used here means the person (if any) who is reluctantly brought before the arbitrator to defend himself. In practice, both parties are often eager to have their own significant claims heard; here the distinction between claimant and respondent does not apply.

successful shows that the arbitration was wrongly brought against him and he should not, unless his conduct has been deliberately obstructive or misleading,[66] be required to pay the costs of the person who wrongly brought it.[67]

When minded to order the successful party to pay the costs of the unsuccessful party, the arbitrator should take care to ensure that he is exercising his discretion properly and should set out his reasoning so that the parties and the court can see why he has made this unusual award. The following grounds may, in exceptional circumstances, provide the arbitrator with sufficient reason for making such an award:

(1) where the successful party has been guilty of serious impropriety in the conduct of the proceedings;

(2) where the claimant's success is so trifling that it cannot reasonably be said that there was any real merit in prosecuting the arbitration.[68] Where an offer is made, however, an added element of precision seems to be required; normally an arbitrator will misdirect himself if he awards costs to the respondents on the sole basis that the award was only a marginal improvement on the respondent's offer[69];

(3) where issues are clearly distinct and the successful party on aggregate has failed on a number of distinct issues.[70] The courts generally disapprove of awards of costs to a party which is unsuccessful solely on the grounds that they have succeeded in their defence on specific issues.[71] "A successful party who neither improperly nor unreasonably raises issues or makes allegations on which he fails ought not to be ordered to pay any part of the unsuccessful party's costs"[72];

(4) where a combination of the above factors exists; where the "successful" party has received a small award and other complaints are made about the way he pursued the case, the arbitrator may be entitled to consider the cumulative effect and so award costs against him. This may be the case even though none of the individual complaints seem serious enough to form grounds for reaching that conclusion.[73]

Illustrations
Bostock v. Ramsey Urban District Council [1900] 2 Q.B. 616 R prosecuted B unsuccessfully; B then sued R for malicious prosecution. Notwithstanding the fact that

66. *Andrew* v. *Grove* [1902] 1 K.B. 625 *per* Channell J. at 628.
67. *Civil Service Co-operative Society* v. *General Steam Navigation Company* [1903] 2 K.B. 756.
68. *Harris* v. *Petherick* (1879) 4 Q.B.D. 611, restated in *Tramountana Armadora S.A.* v. *Atlantic Shipping Co. S.A.* [1978] 1 Lloyd's Rep. 391 at 398. See also dicta in *Anglo-Cyprian Trade Agencies Ltd.* v. *Paphos Wine Industries Ltd.* [1951] 1 All E.R. 873; *Alltrans Express Ltd.* v. *C.V.A. Holdings Ltd.* [1984] 1 W.L.R. 394; *Lipkin Gorman* v. *Karpnale Ltd.* [1989] 1 W.L.R. 1340; *Beoco Ltd.* v. *Alfa Laval Co. Ltd.* [1984] 3 W.L.R. 1179.
69. *The Maria* [1993] 2 Lloyd's Rep. 168.
70. *John Richardson Computers Ltd* v. *Flanders* (No. 2) [1994] F.S.R. 144.
71. If specific offers have been made in relation to these issues, the situation will be different: *The Rozel* [1994] 2 Lloyd's Rep. 161 at 169.
72. *Re Elgindata No. 2* [1992] 1 W.L.R. 1207 *per* Nourse L.J. at 1214.
73. See e.g. *The Emvar* [1984] 2 Lloyd's Rep. 581.

R successfully defended in this civil action, Lord Russell of Killowen C.J. deprived them of their costs on the grounds that the manner in which R had handled the prosecution had given B reasonable grounds for believing that R had acted with malice. The Court of Appeal unanimously upheld this decision. Romer L.J. at 627 considered what might be "good cause for depriving the defendant of costs ... It might, for example, in the case of a successful defendant, be founded on conduct of the defendant outside the action, if the conduct were such as to have led the plaintiff reasonably to suppose that he had a good cause of action, and thus induced him to bring the action ... Misconduct in no wise connected with the action could not be any ground for depriving a successful defendant of costs. Nor, I think, could conduct of the defendant outside the action constitute 'good cause', if it were not such as to induce the plaintiff reasonably to suppose that he had a good cause of action, and so to conduce the action."

Lloyd del Pacifico v. Board of Trade (1930) 46 T.L.R. 476 The Board sold L a ship. L claimed damages for late delivery and for the ship's poor condition. The arbitrator rejected L's claim for late delivery, but allowed its claim in respect of the ship's condition. He ordered the Board to pay its own costs, half of L's costs and two-thirds of his fees and expenses. The arbitrator then stated a special case for the opinion of the court on the question whether L was entitled in law to damages for poor condition. The court held that the arbitrator was wrong and that L should recover nothing. The award on costs was remitted to the arbitrator for his reconsideration. He repeated his original award on costs, stating that even if the Board's failure to supply a satisfactory ship was legal, it was, nevertheless, "immoral". The Board had, in his view, forced a helpless purchaser to accept an unsatisfactory ship and ought to be "penalised". Held, that the arbitrator had acted on grounds which were outside the reference and he had not exercised his discretion judicially; he had no jurisdiction to proceed on considerations of morality in a business transaction, nor was he entitled to penalise the Board for something which was not within the terms of the reference. The award as to costs was set aside.

P. Rosen & Co. Ltd. v. Dowley & Selby [1943] 2 All E.R. 172 The claimant's premises were converted into an air-raid shelter. He was entitled to compensation but a dispute arose and arbitration proceedings were commenced to recover the compensation. He recovered virtually the entire amount which he claimed, but was awarded a lump sum of £78 for costs, which was a small proportion of his actual costs, with no reasons given. The claimant sought a review of the award. Held, that the court could only interfere where it is shown that the arbitrator had done something which he has no power to do; the court was not satisfied on this point since there may have been excessive representation (apparently two counsel were instructed by the claimant) or excessive evidence (there were a number of witnesses of fact and more than one expert witness for the claimant) or other such matters which the arbitrator may have taken into account. The application was dismissed. Atkinson J. did, however, express an opinion (at 175) as to the most convenient order where the arbitrator considers that unnecessary costs have been incurred: "[The arbitrator] does not know what costs have been incurred. He does not know all the difficulties which may have arisen before the hearing. It may be it is wiser to give a proportion of the costs, if he thinks the case has been too extravagantly conducted."

Perry v. Stopher [1959] 1 All E.R. 713 The claimant builder claimed £54 against the respondent building owner but recovered only £11. Costs were awarded to the respondent. The claimant sought to have the award on costs set aside. The Court of Appeal held that the arbitrator was not obliged to state his reasons and that the small recovery by the claimant indicated that there were grounds upon which an arbitrator could have exercised his discretion to deprive the claimant of his costs. "It was clear on the face of the award that the claim was a much exaggerated claim in relation to the amount actually awarded, and it was also clear that the plaintiff [claimant] had failed on the important issues. So it is not a case in which, on the face of the award, nothing is shown which justifies the arbitrator exercising his discretion by making an order such as he made", *per* Hodson L.J. at 717.

Demolition & Construction Co. Ltd. v. Kent River Board [1963] 2 Lloyd's Rep. 7 D&C were engaged by KRB to build a sea wall. The project was delayed. D&C claimed £200,000, but were eventually awarded only £107,000. In addition they were awarded their costs. KRB claimed that the award as to costs failed to take account of the fact that the claim had been significantly reduced. Held, that the order for costs made was the usual one and no complaint could be made about it. "Where there has been no misconduct by the successful plaintiff in the preparation or conduct of the case ... if he recovers a substantial part of his claim, even though it is less than the whole of his claim, he would normally be expected to get the costs", *per* McNair J. at 15.

Matheson & Co. Ltd. v. A. Tabah & Sons]1963] 2 Lloyd's Rep. 270 "Where a party is successful, by which I understand to be meant that he obtains judgment for a sum of money, in the ordinary way, he is entitled to recover the costs which he has incurred in the proceedings which have been necessary for him to obtain an order for the payment of that sum to which he is entitled. But that is subject of course to exceptions and provisos in relation to particular cases. If, for example, the claim has been grossly exaggerated and the award is for a much smaller sum than the award claimed, that is a factor which the court is entitled to take into consideration in depriving a successful claimant of his costs or of part of them. There are all kinds of other matters which may also properly be considered in the exercise of the court's discretion. They would include the conduct of the parties in the course of the hearing, they would include questions whether one particular facet of the claim failed on which a large amount of time had been spent and so forth. The principles which an arbitrator is, by his legal duty, obliged to apply are the same", *per* Megaw J. at 273.

Dineen v. Walpole [1969] 1 Lloyd's Rep. 261 W built a bungalow for D. The agreement provided that W should return to rectify defects which appeared within six months, but this did not create a limitation on liability. Cracks and other defects occurred after the expiry of the six-month period. W sent tradesmen to execute remedial works but they were not properly performed and D refused further access to W. D issued arbitration proceedings against W for the cost of the defects, claiming about £60. W's defence was that he was at all times ready to return to remedy the defects. D was awarded £45 but was ordered to pay W's costs. Held, that the only conceivable reason to justify this drastic order was the statement that W was always ready to execute further remedial works; this did not constitute proper material upon which to make the order. The order was set aside. "There being ... a settled practice of the courts that in the absence of special circumstances a successful litigant will receive his costs, it is necessary to show some grounds for depriving him of them. If, without more, one finds that an arbitrator not only deprives a successful party of costs but awards them to the unsuccessful party, there is in my judgment a prima facie indication of misconduct by the arbitrator", *per* Edmund Davies L.J. at 265.

Tramountana Armadora S.A. v. Atlantic Shipping Co. S.A. [1978] 1 Lloyd's Rep. 391 "If the sum recovered was trifling and did not justify the proceedings, it may well be right not only to deprive the claimant of his costs, but to order him to pay the respondent's costs: see *Harris v. Petherick* (1879) 4 Q.B.D. 611. But this would be a wholly exceptional case ..." *per* Donaldson J. at 398.

The Emvar [1984] 2 Lloyd's Rep. 581 The Emvar had been let to a charterer. Some 15 months after her redelivery, the owner claimed that damage had been caused to the vessel and claimed compensation in two sums, namely 40,000 D.fl. and $5,000. Three years after this notification, the owner commenced arbitration proceedings to recover the sums which it alleged were due. The arbitrator awarded the owner 2,000 D.fl. (about £600) and ordered the owner to pay the charterer's costs because of (i) the small award in favour of the owner; (ii) the owner's failure on the $5,000 claim; (iii) the successful contentions of the charterers; and (iv) the unsatisfactory way in which the claim was progressed. "It is quite plain from the language of the award that the arbitrator recognised that he had a discretion and, moreover, that he exercised it … My decision [to dismiss the application to have the award as to costs set aside] is based solely on the fact that I detect no misconduct whatever—technical or otherwise—in the way this very experienced arbitrator exercised his discretion as to costs", *per* Leggatt J. at 585.

CHAPTER 4

ORDERS AND AWARDS AS TO COSTS: PRACTICAL CONSIDERATIONS

4.1 COSTS ORDERS AND AWARDS AS TO COSTS

4.1.1 Costs orders

An arbitrator may make orders as to costs during the arbitration. He may, for instance, order that the costs of a preliminary meeting are to be "costs in the arbitration" and/or "fit for counsel". This is useful practice. It enables the parties more readily to appreciate their liability as to costs; and assists where the court determines the recoverable costs of the arbitration.

An order for costs, however, is not strictly enforceable until it forms part of an award.[1] Indeed, in some situations, the arbitrator may rescind earlier costs orders where there are proper reasons for so doing.[2] Where an arbitrator makes interlocutory orders as to costs he should incorporate them into his full award on costs at the conclusion of the arbitration. This may be done either by restating the terms of the orders or by reference to the orders and appending them to the award.

4.1.2 Awards as to costs made during the proceedings

The award as to costs is ordinarily made at the end of the proceedings. However, the arbitrator may make a partial award as to costs during the proceedings.[3] Unlike an order, an award may never be reopened by the arbitrator except where the court remits it to him.[4]

Where the arbitrator intends that the payee under an order as to costs should recover interest on those costs as from the date of the order, that order must be converted into an award.[5] Where the arbitrator intends that costs be payable

1. *Re Prebble and Robinson* [1892] 2 Q.B. 602.
2. *Hawkins* v. *C.G. Franklin Building Ltd.* (1994) Q.B.D, 6 October 1994.
3. The arbitrator is entitled to "make more than one award at different times on different aspects of the matters to be determined"—section 47(1) of the Arbitration Act 1996.
4. Unless the parties have given the arbitrator authority to make a "provisional award" under section 39 of the Arbitration Act 1996.
5. There is no liability for costs until an award is made: *Hunt* v. *R.M. Douglas (Roofing) Ltd.* [1988] 1 A.C. 398. Hence interest is not payable.

immediately, he must direct in the award that those costs be determined and paid forthwith.[6]

Illustration
Hawkins v. C.G. Franklin Building Ltd. (1994) Q.B.D, 6 October 1994 "I am prepared to assume for present purposes that in litigation, in proceedings before a court, this alteration—a change from costs in any event to costs to be taxed and paid forthwith—would . . . not be one which a court will have jurisdiction to make. However . . . it is not necessarily appropriate to an arbitrator from whom there is no appeal in any ordinary sense. If he makes errors, unless he can correct them or, even if they were not erroneous when first made, he comes to the conclusion that a different provision should now be made, then there will be no way of dealing with the matter. So it is not at all clear to me that the same dichotomy [between orders which may be changed by the tribunal which makes them and those which cannot] applies in arbitration as in litigation", *per* Judge Hicks Q.C.

4.2 PROCEDURE WHEN MAKING AN AWARD AS TO COSTS: SUBMISSIONS

In the past, some arbitrators have proceeded to make a combined award, including costs, without hearing submissions on costs.[7] It is submitted that this is not good practice; it is widely recognised that the right to make submissions on costs is a valuable and a desirable one.[8] The arbitrator should allow the parties an opportunity to address him on such matters as may be properly brought to bear upon his discretion. There may be an offer or other factors which might properly be taken into account; unless the arbitrator asks for submissions he may be unaware of them.

It is suggested that an arbitrator should, as a matter of course:

(1) advise the parties that he shall (unless both parties invite him to proceed directly to a final award) make an award dealing with the substantive issues only; then

(2) upon the publication of the award which deals with all substantive issues, he should request such submissions on costs as the parties wish to make; then

(3) upon receiving those submissions, he should proceed to make an award as to costs.

Some arbitrators adopt an "award nisi" procedure, where the arbitrator

---

6. There are practical difficulties with making costs payable forthwith. No money can be paid until the recoverable costs are determined. This requires a document to be submitted which sets out the costs claimed for that part of the proceedings. This is not always convenient at an intermediate stage.

7. See for example, *The Aghios Nicolaos* [1980] 1 Lloyd's Rep. 17 *per* Ormrod L.J. at 21 and Eveleigh L.J. at 22.

8. *Harrison* v. *Thompson* [1989] 1 W.L.R. 1325, *per* Knox. J. at 1335; *Centrala Morska Importowo Eksportowa* v. *Companhia Nacional de Navegacao S.A.R.L.* [1975] 2 Lloyd's Rep. 69, *per* Donaldson J. at 72.

indicates provisionally how he is minded to award costs, asking for submission if the parties object. It is submitted that this is not an appropriate device, except for very small disputes; not only does it appear to prejudice the arbitrator but such a provisional award may require the advocates to make delicate submissions that the arbitrator was wrong in law in his initial decision.

Where an arbitrator proceeds to an award as to costs without providing the parties with an opportunity to make submissions, and this has led to substantial injustice, it is submitted that the court may remit the award to the arbitrator.[9]

Illustrations
Harrison v. Thompson [1989] 1 W.L.R. 1325 A dispute over the value of two bundles of shares was referred to arbitration. Both parties made Calderbank offers stating a value at which they would be prepared to settle. Although both parties expected the arbitrator to provide an opportunity to make submissions on costs, the arbitrator proceeded to make a final award dealing with costs. Held, that if the decision not to request an opportunity to make submissions on costs had been a deliberate choice, there would be no remission; but here there had been a procedural mishap and there was jurisdiction to remit. The award on costs was remitted.

King v. Thomas McKenna Ltd. [1991] 2 Q.B. 480 TMcK commenced arbitration proceedings against K. K made an offer of £5,000. The offer was rejected and the proceedings continued. At the end of the hearing, K's counsel failed to make it clear to the arbitrator that he should refrain from making his decision on costs until after he had made his substantive award. The arbitrator proceeded directly to make a final award, awarding TMcK £4,700 plus costs. The Court of Appeal remitted the award as to costs to the arbitrator for his reconsideration in the light of the offer made on the grounds that there had been a "procedural mishap".

4.3 THE PROVISION OF REASONS FOR AN AWARD AS TO COSTS

4.3.1 The requirement for reasons

An award as to costs requires the same formalities as any other award. These are set out in section 52 of the Arbitration Act 1996. The award should contain reasons unless it is an agreed award[10] or the parties have agreed to dispense with reasons.[11] A failure to supply reasons may amount to a serious irregularity.[12]

9. Section 68 of the Arbitration Act 1996, grounds (a) failure to comply with section 33; and/or, where applicable, (i) irregularity admitted by the tribunal. The court may also vary the award.

10. Section 52(4) of the Arbitration Act 1996.

11. Under the pre-1996 legislation an arbitrator was not obliged to give reasons for his award. Nevertheless, arbitrators who made awards as to costs which were "unusual" were encouraged to do so. See, for example: *Smeaton Hanscomb & Co. Ltd.* v. *Sassoon I. Setty, Son & Co.* (No. 2) [1953] 1 W.L.R. 1481 *per* Devlin J. at 1485; *The Erich Schroeder* [1974] 1 Lloyd's Rep. 192 *per* Mocatta J. at 193; *Pepys* v. *London Transport Executive* [1975] 1 W.L.R. 234 *per* Lord Denning M.R. at 238; *King* v. *Thomas McKenna Ltd.* [1991] 2 Q.B. 480 *per* Lord Donaldson at 495.

12. Section 68(2): "Serious irregularity means an irregularity of one or more of the following kinds which the court considers has caused or will cause substantial injustice to the applicant— ... (h) failure to comply with the requirements as to the form of the award". Note that a serious irregularity is not created by the mere fact of failure to comply with the requirements as to form; it is also necessary that the court considers that it will lead to a substantial injustice.

Nevertheless, it is submitted that an award which is defective only as to form will be enforceable[13] and sets time running.[14]

4.3.2 Sufficient reasons

Where the case is straightforward and the award as to costs clearly follows the general principle that costs follow the event, there is no need to give reasons beyond stating that principle. Where, however, the award is unusual or there are additional factors, such as offers of settlement, the arbitrator should explain his reasoning. The explanation need not be detailed or contain legal authorities. It should, however, enable the parties and the court to see how the decision was arrived at.[15]

Illustration
President of India v. Jadranska Slobodna Plovidba [1992] 2 Lloyd's Rep. 274
"The reasons given by an arbitrator should be sufficient to justify every award that he is making, or declining to make, in his published award, including any award on costs. In most cases the award will simply reflect the principle that costs should follow the event and no further reasons or explanation need be given. It will only be where some more complicated situation exists or where some special award is being made on costs that the arbitrator will need to give more specific reasons . . .", *per* Hobhouse J. at 279–80.

4.4   SPECIAL COSTS ORDERS IN RELATION TO ISSUES WHICH ARISE DURING THE PROCEEDINGS

It is frequently appropriate to make costs orders in relation to specific meetings, hearings or applications as the arbitration proceeds. The arbitrator may make such orders, for instance: (1) at the conclusion of a preliminary meeting; (2)

---

13. This is consistent with the language of the Act, which uses the following words: (a) "failure to comply with the requirements as to form of the award"—section 68(2)(h) of the Arbitration Act 1996; and (b) "if it appears to the court that the award . . . does not contain the tribunal's reasons"—section 70(4) of the Arbitration Act 1996. In each instance the Act describes the defective document as an award.

14. Section 70(3) of the Arbitration Act 1996. If no appeal is made within the time, the award, including the award on costs becomes "final, valid and unassailable": *Cohen v. Baram* [1994] 2 Lloyd's Rep. 138, *per* Hirst L.J. at 143.

15. In *The Nimenia* [1986] Q.B. 802 Sir John Donaldson M.R. said at 807 that a reasoned award is one which "states the reasons for the award in sufficient detail for the court to consider any question of law arising therefrom". In *Bremer Handelsgesellschaft m.b.H.* v. *Westzucker G.m.b.H.* [1981] 2 Lloyd's Rep. 130 Donaldson L.J. said at 133 that: "arbitrators will not be expected to analyse the law. It will be quite sufficient that they should explain how they reached their conclusion". In *Universal Petroleum Co. Ltd.* v. *Handels und Transportgesellschaft m.b.H.* [1987] 2 All E.R. 737 Kerr L.J. said at 748: "A reasoned award is usually requested in order to lay the foundation for a possible application for leave to appeal. An arbitrator should therefore remember to deal in his reasoned award with all issues which may be described as having a 'conclusive' nature, in the sense that he should give reasons for his decisions on all issues which lead to conclusions on liability or other major matters in dispute on which leave to appeal may subsequently be sought."

at the conclusion of a hearing dealing with a preliminary point; (3) at the conclusion of an application to the arbitrator for security for costs; or (4) upon an application to amend a pleading or a statement of case.

An order as to costs is not enforceable unless and until it is incorporated into an award; however, once made, it should not be changed unless there are exceptional circumstances, such as concealment of relevant documents or information at the time the order was originally made.

4.4.1 Interaction of costs orders with limit on recoverable costs

The arbitrator may direct a limit on recoverable costs.[16] Where he does so and also makes an order for costs during the proceedings, he should indicate how the two are to interact. For example, where the recoverable costs are limited to £x and an interlocutory costs order is subsequently made, the arbitrator should state clearly whether the liability for the costs of the application is to be separate from, or included within, the overall limit of £x.

4.4.2 Costs orders following preliminary meetings or proceedings

At the conclusion of interlocutory proceedings or an application for some special procedure, the arbitrator may, on his own initiative or at the invitation of one of the parties, consider it appropriate to make an order as to costs. He should not, of course, do so without providing the parties with an opportunity to make submissions on the form of order which is appropriate. The arbitrator may make one of the following orders[17]:

(1) Costs to be costs in the cause/arbitration: here the costs occasioned by the interlocutory proceedings are to be included in the overall costs of the arbitration.

(2) Costs to be reserved: here the arbitrator reserves his judgment on who is to pay the costs of the interlocutory proceedings until a later stage.

(3) Claimant's/Respondent's costs in any event: here the named party is to receive his costs relating to the interlocutory procedure whatever the outcome of the arbitration. This is the order which provides the greatest degree of security to the named party.

(4) Claimant's/Respondent's costs in the cause/arbitration: here the named party will receive his costs of the preliminary procedure if he is successful overall; but if he is unsuccessful overall, he will not be required to meet the other party's costs relating to the procedure.

(5) No order for costs: here each party is to pay his own costs in relation

16. Section 65 of the Arbitration Act 1996.
17. See *Surrey Heath Borough Council* v. *Lovell Construction Ltd.* (1990) 48 Build. L.R. 108 for the general principles upon which an arbitrator may award costs following the hearing of preliminary issues.

to the preliminary procedure. Such an order must be made expressly, as a simple omission to make an order will ordinarily have the effect that costs are to be costs in the arbitration.[18]

It may be appropriate in some cases to make an order which is a combination of the above. For example, where excessive documentation is produced in support of, or to resist, an interlocutory application, a general costs order may be made, combined with a special order to the effect that the party who has incurred the excessive costs is to bear them in any event[19]; in many such cases a proportionate order for the costs of the interlocutory procedure is frequently a more convenient means of achieving the same result.

4.4.3 Costs orders following procedural applications

Where a procedural application is made, the arbitrator must decide whether or not to allow it.[20] Where he does so, there will normally be some costs consequences. Ordinarily the other party will be entitled to an order for his consequential costs in any event. Common examples of procedural applications relate to:

(1) Amendment to pleadings or statements of case: Parties often wish to amend their pleadings or statement of case. Providing this can be done without causing unacceptable prejudice to the other party, such an amendment should normally be allowed.[21] An amendment frequently requires the opposing party to amend his pleadings to suit and may also require other alterations or time to consider the effect of the amendment. If an amendment is made during the hearing, an adjournment may be allowed to the other party if it is reasonable for them to take time to consider their position in the light of the amendment or to call new evidence to deal with it. A party who seeks to amend his case will normally be allowed to do so "on the usual terms", namely that the costs incurred and thrown away by the amendment and the costs of any consequential amendment are to be the other party's in any event. In some situations, however, the arbitrator may adjudge that the amendment was made necessary by some action on

18. *Friis* v. *Paramount Bagwash Co. Ltd.* (No. 2) [1940] 2 K.B. 654.
19. Professional arbitrators frequently report that excessive documents and evidence are produced on interlocutory applications.
20. In accordance with his general duty under section 33 of the Arbitration Act 1996 to "act fairly and impartially ... giving each party a reasonable opportunity of putting his case and dealing with that of his opponent, and ... avoiding unnecessary delay or expense, so as to provide a fair means for the resolution of the matters falling to be determined."
21. *Tildesley* v. *Harper* (1878) 10 Ch.D. 393 *per* Bramwell L.J. at 396. Arguments based on prejudice to the other party must not prevail save in exceptional cases since if the applicant is not allowed to make his amendment his opportunity to advance his amended case may be lost forever: see *Talbot* v. *Berkshire County Council* [1994] Q.B. 290 and *Beoco Ltd.* v. *Alfa Laval Co. Ltd.* [1994] 3 W.L.R. 1179.

the part of the opposing party, in which case a different costs order may be made.

(2) Adjournments and other delays: If a party requests an adjournment, the arbitrator should consider whether such an adjournment is appropriate, in view of the length of adjournment requested, the reasons given for the adjournment, the likely effect on the timetable and the prejudice which it may cause to the other party. An adjournment is usually granted on the basis that all costs incurred as a result are to be borne by the party seeking it. Where, however, an adjournment is requested because of some unreasonable act or unexpected revelation by the other party, some other order as to costs may be appropriate.

(3) Extensions of time: When a party applies for an extension to a deadline for service of pleadings or other documents or materials, such extension may generate costs. If so, the extension may be granted on the understanding that resulting costs are to be borne by the applicant.

Illustration
Surrey Heath Borough Council v. Lovell Construction Ltd. (1990) 48 Build. L.R. 108 SH engaged L to construct a building by a specified date. Due to a fire on site, L completed the works late. SH sued L for breach of contract and an indemnity. A trial of preliminary issues was heard. The judge's decision was substantially, though by no means wholly, favourable to L; nor was it conclusive of the final outcome at the main trial. The judge nevertheless ordered SH to pay two-thirds of L's costs of the trial of preliminary issues. On appeal it was contended by SH that the order as to costs was wrong in principle. SH argued that since it had succeeded on some of the issues, it should not be required to bear any of L's costs. While some disquiet about the order for costs is evident in the Court of Appeal's judgment, they upheld it as being within the judge's discretion. Dillon L.J. considered (at 121–5) the general position as to orders for costs on the trial of preliminary issues. "It is not in dispute on this appeal that a judge who has decided preliminary issues has (unless he is going to make no order as to costs) three possible courses before him in relation to the costs of the trial of the preliminary issues, viz: (i) he may make those costs costs in the cause; or (ii) he may reserve the costs to the trial; or (iii) ... he may award the costs, or a proportion of the costs, to one or other party. To make the costs costs in the cause is not, however, satisfactory to a defendant if as a result of the defendant's success on certain of the preliminary issues, very important parts of the claim will go out and will not be pursued to trial. To reserve the costs to the trial may be necessary in some cases, e.g. if there has already been a payment into court. But it can have its disadvantages, particularly if ... the judge who tried the preliminary issues may not himself be the trial judge. It is not mandatory that the costs of preliminary issues be reserved to the trial judge. ... Moreover if the judge who has tried preliminary issues wants to make an immediate award of costs instead of reserving the costs to the trial or making them costs in the cause, he should be entitled, in my judgment, to regard the trial of the preliminary issues as being a separate "event" on its own. ... The alternative propounded by [counsel for SH] gives any plaintiff an unfair built-in advantage over the defendant, even though the procedure of the trial of preliminary issues is intended for the equal benefit of both ... Although the partial success of the plaintiffs was neither trivial nor de minimis, [the judge] was entitled to take the view that the defendants were the substantive victors, and to order the plaintiffs to pay a part of the defendant's costs of the hearing of the preliminary issues."

4.5 NOTICES TO ADMIT

In litigation proceedings, the parties are encouraged to admit facts and the authenticity of documents. Where a party unreasonably denies some relevant matter, the rules of court allow the other party to serve a "notice to admit" upon him. The recipient may insist that the matter is proved in court, but where he does so, he will have to pay the costs of that proof unless his original denial was justified. This principle is readily adapted for use in arbitrations. A notice to admit need not be in any particular form. Where the recipient fails to admit the matters in the notice, the arbitrator shall exercise his discretion when considering what effect any such notice is to have on costs. In particular, he should consider whether or not it was reasonable, in all the circumstances, for the recipient to admit the matters in the notice.

Illustrations
The Catherine L [1982] 1 Lloyd's Rep. 484 "an order [for costs] may quite properly reflect sustainable criticisms of a party's conduct in the litigation: for example . . . if he has obstinately and unreasonably refused to admit the obvious, so increasing the costs overall", *per* Bingham J. at 489.

Higgs & Hill Building Ltd. v. University of London (1983) 24 Build. L.R. 139
An application was made for an order that an award on costs be remitted. Parker J. said at 153: "Each case must depend on its own facts and circumstances and there may be other factors to be taken into account such as the amount, date and nature of a sealed offer, notices to admit and so on, all of which will be known to the arbitrator."

4.6 THE AWARD AS TO COSTS: TERMS SPECIFYING THE BASIS ON WHICH COSTS ARE TO BE COMPUTED

4.6.1 Certificates for the level of representation

In interlocutory proceedings in court there is a readily displaced presumption that counsel need not appear. If either party in litigation appears by counsel the master or judge is usually invited to certify that the matter was "fit for counsel"; in other words that it was reasonable for counsel to appear given the nature of the proceedings. If such a certificate is made, it requires the taxing officer to allow a reasonable fee for counsel's appearance. In interlocutory arbitration proceedings, the arbitrator is often requested to make an equivalent certificate, stating whether or not the matter is fit for counsel. The arbitrator may, upon such an application, consider whether the proceedings warranted such a level of representation, and exercise his discretion either to make or to withhold such certificate.

4.6.2 The basis upon which costs will be determined

Section 63(5) of the Arbitration Act 1996 provides:

(5) Unless the tribunal or court determines otherwise—
   (a) the recoverable costs of the arbitration shall be determined on the basis that there shall be allowed a reasonable amount in respect of all costs reasonably incurred, and
   (b) any doubt as to whether costs were reasonably incurred or were reasonable in amount shall be resolved in favour of the paying party.

This is commonly referred to as the "standard basis". Where the arbitrator considers that a different basis is appropriate, this should be stated in the award. For example, where the arbitrator considers that the benefit of the doubt when determining costs should be given to the receiving party (the "indemnity basis") this should be clearly stated. Costs should only be awarded on an indemnity basis in exceptional circumstances, where the conduct of the party paying those costs is somehow oppressive or unreasonable.[22] If the arbitration agreement provides that costs are to be awarded on an indemnity basis, the arbitrator's discretion should be exercised to correspond with the contractual entitlement.[23]

Arbitrators frequently use the expression "commercial basis". There seems to be no fixed meaning for this expression and an arbitrator should explain in his award precisely what is meant so that the parties can see the calculation they should employ in order to settle costs, or so that the court can see what the arbitrator envisages.[24]

4.7 APPORTIONMENT OF COSTS

Where an arbitrator decides that each party should receive a portion of his costs, the most convenient method of achieving this objective is to award one party a proportion of his costs.[25] This has the practical advantage that only one party's recoverable costs need to be determined. Thus, for instance, if the

22. *Johnson Matthey plc* v. *Eros Castings Ltd.*, *The Times* 7 December 1993. In *Burgess* v. *Stafford Hotel Ltd.* [1990] 1 W.L.R. 1215 costs were not allowed on an indemnity basis against a tenant who "played the system" and had taken advantage of a statutory right of appeal to extend his tenancy as far as he could.

23. *Gomba Holdings Ltd.* v. *Minories Finance* [1992] 3 W.L.R. 723. Here, in proceedings in court, the Court of Appeal allowed costs on an indemnity basis where a mortgage deed provided for this.

24. Under the pre-1996 legislation, the taxing officer was the delegate of the arbitrator and where the arbitrator laid down guidelines for the determination of costs he was constrained to tax costs on that basis. The 1996 Act, however, states that where the arbitrator does not determine the costs himself, the court may determine them "on such basis as it thinks fit"—section 63(4)(a). It is thought that a court would give significant weight to what the arbitrator had directed.

25. *Cinema Press Ltd.* v. *Picture and Pleasures Ltd.* [1945] 1 K.B. 356; *Archital Luxfer* v. *Henry Boot Construction Ltd.* [1981] 1 Lloyd's Rep. 642.

arbitrator decides that both parties are successful, and both have required a similar amount of time to prove their cases, an appropriate order may be that each party should bear his own costs, rather than making a cross-order for costs which will require the consideration of all costs in the proceedings. If different amounts of time are spent on each, or there are other factors which the arbitrator considers relevant, the appropriate order may be that one party should pay the other a proportion of his recoverable costs.[26]

Illustration
Archital Luxfer v. Henry Boot Construction Ltd. [1981] 1 Lloyd's Rep. 642
Following expensive arbitration proceedings, the arbitrator considered that both parties had been successful to a degree. He awarded that both parties should recover a proportion of their costs. Upon an application to the court the award was remitted to the arbitrator for other reasons, but Gibson J. was critical of the award which required that the costs bills of both parties be taxed. He said at p. 651: "The order, with reference to costs after the commencement of the hearing would (if no agreement was reached) require taxation of the full bill of costs of both sides. It is well known that taxation of a large bill, such as will be required in litigation of this nature, is by itself an expensive item of costs. It cannot be said that an order for the respondent to recover all his taxed costs, coupled with an order that the claimant recover one-eighth of his taxed costs, should never be made—circumstances may conceivably require it. The submissions of [counsel for both parties] in this case have, however, united in saying that such an order should be avoided if the desired apportionment can be achieved by giving to one side a portion only of his costs. Taxation, of course, can be avoided if there is agreement. Nevertheless, in my judgment, [counsel] are right in their criticism of this aspect of the award and, in reconsidering it, the arbitrator will decide whether it can be avoided in his final award."

4.8 AWARD OF INTEREST ON COSTS

A party is not entitled to costs until an award as to costs is made.[27] While the Arbitration Act 1996 contains a wide provision empowering the arbitrator to award interest for periods up to the date of the award,[28] it is submitted that a necessary prerequisite is that the paying party is liable to pay the principal sum. This precludes an arbitrator awarding interest before the date of the award. The arbitrator may, however, award interest on costs from the date of the award.[29]

---

26. *The Aghios Nicolaos* [1980] 1 Lloyd's Rep. 17.
27. *Hunt* v. *R.M. Douglas (Roofing) Ltd.* [1988] 1 A.C. 398.
28. Section 49 of the Arbitration Act 1996 provides that: "(3) The tribunal may award simple or compound interest from such dates, at such rates and with such rests as it considers meets the justice of the case—(a) on the whole or part of any amount awarded by the tribunal, in respect of any period up to the date of the award."
29. Section 49(4) of the Arbitration Act 1996: "(4) The tribunal may award simple or compound interest from the date of the award (or any later date) until payment, at such rates and with such rests as it considers meets the justice of the case, on the outstanding amount of any award (including any award of interest under subsection (3) and any award as to costs)."

CHAPTER 5

DETERMINING THE RECOVERABLE COSTS OF THE ARBITRATION

The arbitrator is obliged to make an award as to liability for costs.[1] He is empowered to determine the amount of recoverable costs, but he is not obliged to do so.[2] In this chapter the principles used in determining the recoverable costs are discussed.

5.1 AN OVERVIEW

The costs of the arbitration are[3]: (a) the arbitrators' fees and expenses; (b) the fees and expenses of any arbitral institution concerned, and (c) the legal and other costs of the parties. In addition they include the costs of or incidental to any proceedings to determine the amount of the recoverable costs of the arbitration.

The purpose of determining the recoverable costs of the arbitration is to establish the amount of costs due to a party entitled to costs under an award. In practice, the parties to arbitration proceedings frequently reach agreement as to the receiving party's recoverable legal and other costs, so that there is no need for a formal determination.

The arbitrator may determine the recoverable costs[4] or he may allow them to be determined by the court.[5] In either case the basic process is the same:

(1) the party entitled to costs submits a list of claimed costs[6];
(2) the arbitrator/court considers the list and disallows and/or adjusts costs which were unnecessary or unreasonable;
(3) the arbitrator/court computes the aggregate amount properly payable and issues an award/certificate determining the entitlement.

Where any agreement as to costs is relevant[7] or where a direction limiting the

---

1. See §3.1.
2. Unless the arbitration agreement requires him to do so: see *Morgan* v. *Smith* (1842) 9 M. & W. 427.
3. Section 59 of the Arbitration Act 1996.
4. Section 63(3) of the Arbitration Act 1996.
5. Section 63(4) of the Arbitration Act 1996.
6. This list of costs is generally called a bill of costs.
7. Section 63(1) of the Arbitration Act 1996.

recoverable costs has been made,[8] the determination of the recoverable costs takes such agreement and/or direction into account.

Where the arbitrator determines the recoverable costs himself,[9] he must act fairly and with proper discretion; but he is not constrained by set procedures. Nevertheless, it is in the interests of justice that he has regard to the principles which have been established by the courts.

Where the arbitrator does not determine the recoverable costs, either party may apply to the court for them to be determined.

5.2 DETERMINATION IN THE COURT FOLLOWING ARBITRATION PROCEEDINGS

Where costs are determined in the court, the party entitled to costs must supply such documents in such format as are required by the court.[10] Ordinarily the court will pass the matter over to a taxing officer. The taxing officer is a delegate of the arbitrator[11] and, subject to any other direction of the court, is obliged to carry out the arbitrator's instructions, if any, as to how the costs are to be determined. The taxing officers will normally expect a bill of costs to be submitted in the same format as that which would be submitted following litigation proceedings. At the time of writing[12] such a bill:

(1) distinguishes between professional charges and disbursements as viewed from the solicitor's perspective. The solicitor's time taken on the case is counted as professional fees, while fees paid to counsel or expert witnesses etc. are disbursements;

(2) sets out the costs claimed in chronological order within the headings prescribed by the Rules of the Supreme Court;[13]

(3) claims for solicitors' time as two separate components. First, a basic charging rate is claimed; this reflects the typical charging rate of a solicitor in the same location, with the same experience and expertise. Second, there is an uplift (expressed as a percentage) for "care and

8. Section 65 of the Arbitration Act 1996. See Chapter 8.

9. In practice, an arbitrator should state in his award as to liability for costs whether or not he proposes to determine the recoverable costs himself. Historically, arbitrators have been reluctant to determine the legal and other costs of the parties, but in most cases, it is of benefit to the parties if the arbitrator does so. He is familiar with the proceedings and will be able to take a clear view on what costs were reasonably incurred, what rates might properly be charged for the type of work involved, etc.

10. Section 63(4) of the Arbitration Act 1996 provides that the court may order that the recoverable costs "shall be determined by such means and upon such terms as it may specify".

11. *Piper Double Glazing Ltd.* v. *D.C. Contracts* [1994] 1 W.L.R. 777.

12. There are proposals for a review of the civil litigation system following Lord Woolf's recommendations in "Access to Justice", H.M.S.O. 1996. It may be that procedures for taxation may change.

13. Order 62 of the Rules of the Supreme Court, Appendix 2, Part 2. The headings are: (1) Interlocutory attendances; (2) Conferences with counsel; (3) Attendances at trial or hearing; (4) Preparation; (5) Taxation.

conduct". This reflects the weight and complexity of the work involved; there is no uplift for travelling time, while for work requiring a high level of skill it may be as high as 100 per cent or more. Note that the actual charge which the solicitor makes to his client is not relevant; the purpose of the exercise is to determine the amount which it is reasonable for the losing party to pay;[14]

(4) is accompanied by those documents which are required to show what work was done (e.g. solicitor's correspondence, counsel's instructions) and the disbursements incurred (receipts and vouchers). If the taxing officer needs additional information, he may call for it;

(5) is signed by the solicitor who has the conduct of the case.

The amount of costs to be allowed is in the discretion of the taxing officer. He considers the bill, receives and considers objections, and decides whether activities claimed for are reasonable, what time is allowable for each and at what rate. At the conclusion of the taxation, the taxing officer issues a certificate for the costs allowed.

5.3 THE BASIS UPON WHICH RECOVERABLE COSTS ARE ASSESSED

If the arbitrator decides to determine costs himself, he shall specify "(a) the basis on which [he] has acted".[15] The "basis" is, in essence, the criterion for allowing or disallowing costs. The Arbitration Act 1996 provides: "Unless the tribunal or the court determines otherwise—(a) the recoverable costs of the arbitration shall be determined on the basis that there shall be allowed a reasonable amount in respect of all costs reasonably incurred, and (b) any doubt as to whether costs were reasonably incurred or were reasonable in amount shall be resolved in favour of the paying party".[16] This is commonly referred to as the "standard basis".

The arbitrator or court may determine that some other basis is applicable. He may specify that some elements of costs are to be determined on the "indemnity basis" where doubts are resolved in favour of the receiving party rather in favour of the paying party. This should only be done, however, where the behaviour of the paying party was unreasonable.

Arbitrators frequently assert that they determine costs on a "commercial basis" to indicate that they are not using the detailed technical court rules of "taxation". Here the arbitrator frequently calls for a schedule of the costs for

14. *Johnson* v. *Reed Corrugated Cases Ltd.* [1992] 1 All E.R. 169. Evans J. said at 183–4: "The court is not concerned with charges, only with costs ... Its function, as Order 62 requires, is to assess the reasonable amount of costs for work reasonably done; that, and nothing else."

15. Section 63(3)(a) of the Arbitration Act 1996. This applies as much to the fees and expenses of the arbitrator as to the legal and other costs of the parties as his fees and expenses are part of the costs of the arbitration.

16. Section 63(5) of the Arbitration Act 1996.

which the receiving party is actually liable as the basis of his determination, rather than the rather artificial rates (which are based on typical charging patterns) used for taxation in court. However, the expression "commercial basis" has no settled meaning and it is preferable for an arbitrator to state precisely how he arrived at his determination.

5.4 DETERMINING THE FEES AND EXPENSES OF THE ARBITRATOR

5.4.1 General

The fees and expenses of the arbitrator form part of the costs of the arbitration and must be determined. These fees and expenses include those of erstwhile arbitrators, arbitrator-appointed experts, advisers, assessors, etc. "Unless otherwise agreed by the parties, the recoverable costs of the arbitration shall include in respect of the fees and expenses of the arbitrators only such reasonable fees and expenses as are appropriate in the circumstances."[17] Any questions as to this may be resolved by the court.[18]

5.4.2 Costs of arbitrator-appointed experts, legal advisers and assessors

Section 37 of the Arbitration Act 1996 empowers the arbitrator to appoint experts, legal advisers or assessors to assist in technical matters and to allow such appointees to attend the proceedings. It provides also that: "(2) The fees and expenses of an expert, legal adviser or assessor appointed by the tribunal for which the arbitrators are liable are expenses of the arbitrators ...". The arbitrator must use proper discretion when considering the accounts which they submit.

5.5 DETERMINING THE PARTIES' RECOVERABLE COSTS

5.5.1 General

Where the arbitrator determines the recoverable costs of the parties, he should:

(1) identify the basis or bases upon which he will determine them[19];
(2) consider any relevant agreement between the parties as to the recov-

17. Section 64(1) of the Arbitration Act 1996. Section 64(4) makes it clear that the parties may not agree, among themselves, to deprive the arbitrator of his fees.
18. Section 64(2) of the Arbitration Act 1996. See also sections 28(2) and 56(2) of the Arbitration Act 1996.
19. See §5.3.

erable costs[20] and/or any direction which he has made limiting the recoverable costs[21];

(3) call for such supporting documents as he considers appropriate;
(4) call for the paying party to make objections and, if necessary, convene a meeting to consider issues raised;
(5) at the conclusion, consider the costs of determining the recoverable costs.

5.5.2 The relevance of court procedures and practice

An arbitrator is not bound by the procedural rules of the taxing officers, nor the calculation schemes which they employ; an arbitrator is not required to compute a solicitor's entitlement using reasonable basic charges with uplifts for "care and conduct".[22] The arbitrator may receive submissions in any convenient format and may accept any evidence that costs have been incurred; his only constraint is that he acts fairly and allows the parties a reasonable opportunity to put their cases.[23]

However, there are a number of matters to which the arbitrator should have regard. First, the indemnity principle must be observed[24]; a party who is entitled to costs cannot recover more than the proceedings have cost him. Second, the arbitrator should, notwithstanding that he has decided to use his own scheme of calculation, entertain reasonable submissions which the parties wish to make as to the practice of the taxing officers and consider properly whether or not such practice should affect his determination.[25] And third, the overall result should not be so dissimilar from what would be achieved by determination in court that the parties can be said to have a substantial interest in whether the matter is dealt with in court or by the arbitrator.

5.5.3 Documents to be submitted in support of a claim for the parties' legal costs

The arbitrator is entitled to call for such documents and supporting evidence as he considers appropriate in support of a claim for recoverable costs. He should specify what documents he wishes to see and the format in which he wishes them to be submitted. Typical documents which may be called for include a list of items of costs actually incurred supported by a set of invoices, receipts, etc. and/or a list of items of costs claimed, together with a brief explanation of when and why they were incurred. Where time is charged by

20. Section 63(1) of the Arbitration Act 1996.
21. Section 65 of the Arbitration Act 1996.
22. See §5.2 above.
23. Section 33 of the Arbitration Act 1996.
24. *Re Eastwood, deceased* [1975] Ch. 112 at 131.
25. This follows from (a) the requirement that parties be given an adequate opportunity to make representations and (b) the fact that the courts have laid down many sensible rules concerning taxation which a prudent arbitrator ought to consider when arriving at his decision.

solicitors or claims consultants he may require that time records be produced; the right to charge does not inherently depend on the existence of records, but claims for unrecorded time should be viewed with care.[26]

5.5.4 The costs of determining the amount of recoverable cost

The party who is entitled to his costs of the arbitration is also entitled, subject to the award of the arbitrator, to his reasonable costs of determining those costs. The party liable for these costs may make a written offer of costs "without prejudice save as to the costs of determining the recoverable costs".[27] An arbitrator may treat such an offer as having put the offeree at risk.

5.6 ALLOWABLE COSTS: GENERAL PRINCIPLES

The sections which follow are designed to be of assistance to arbitrators in determining the recoverable costs. The cases cited necessarily relate to the principles and practice of the taxing officers of the court. While an arbitrator is not bound by these "authorities", they are instructive in a number of ways. They indicate not only how the courts view the process of determining costs generally, but illustrate the nature of the discretion which it entails and the principles which are judicially approved.

The costs which are allowable are those which are reasonably incurred in or incidental to the arbitration.[28] As far as the arbitrator is concerned, these exclude the costs of applications to the court[29] which will be dealt with by the court itself. The arbitrator may disallow items in the bill which he considers unreasonable; if he considers the number of hours claimed for particular items of work to be excessive he may reduce the allowable time[30] and he may reduce the fees claimed by representatives and witnesses. The question of reasonableness is to be judged at the time when the decision to incur the costs was made and not in hindsight.[31]

The arbitrator when determining recoverable costs should take into account: (1) the complexity or difficulty of the issues; (2) the level of skill and responsibility required; (3) the number and importance of documents involved; (4)

---

26. *Brush* v. *Bower Cotton & Bower* [1993] 4 All E.R. 741.

27. *Platt* v. *G.K.N. Kwikform Ltd.* [1992] 1 W.L.R. 465; *Chrulew* v. *Borm-Reid & Co.* [1992] 1 All E.R. 953.

28. *Johnson* v. *Reed Corrugated Cases Ltd.* [1992] 1 All E.R. 169.

29. *Higham* v. *Havant and Waterloo U.D.C.* [1951] 2 T.L.R. 87 *per* Cohen L.J. at 90: "I should have doubted very much whether it was competent for the arbitrator to deal with costs which might be incurred before the Divisional Court. I think that those costs were necessarily in the discretion of the Divisional Court." In this case, the arbitration was statutory and questions of law were referable to the Divisional Court; it is submitted that the same principle applies to arbitrations under the Arbitration Acts when there is an application to the High Court.

30. *Re Gibson's Settlement Trusts* [1981] Ch. 179 at 189.

31. *Bartlett* v. *Higgins* [1901] 2 K.B. 230, where the costs of an examination of evidence was allowed, although it turned out to be unnecessary as the case unfolded.

the circumstances of meetings, hearings etc.; (5) the importance of the matter to the client and (6) the value of the claims.[32]

Illustrations

London, Chatham and Dover Railway v. South Eastern Railway Company (1889) 60 L.T. 753 Two railway companies were in dispute concerning the method of accounting for railway receipts. The sums in issue were very large. The plaintiff succeeded and was awarded its costs. The defendant objected to the magnitude of fees claimed for counsel and the plaintiff's principal expert witness. Kekewich J. said at 754: "... although it is impossible to lay down any general rule for the guidance of taxing masters or the court, and it is difficult to express in words what is known to all members of the profession, yet it is certainly true, and in my judgment is certainly right, that the money issue involved in a case, and the importance from the commercial point of view, should be taken into consideration in fixing the remuneration for the solicitor and other persons employed, including the fees to counsel. ... This was distinctly a large case, and large issues were involved, not only as regards the money claimed at the moment, but as regards the principle on which accounts were to be taken in the future between two large railway companies. It is to my mind certainly a case in which both the solicitor and counsel might reasonably expect to be remunerated on a liberal scale, giving, of course, as I am sure they all did, a liberal scale of labour and industry in exchange."

Bartlett v. Higgins [1901] 2 K.B. 230 "In my judgment, it is not correct to say that costs are not to be allowed simply because in the ultimate event they turn out to have been unnecessary. The taxing master must not consider whether they have been 'necessary' having regard to the event, but whether they 'have been necessary or proper for the attainment of justice'—that is (as I think) necessary or proper having regard to the state of things at the time the [items of work for which the costs were incurred] were ordered."

P. Rosen & Co. Ltd. v. Dowley & Selby [1943] 2 All E.R. 172 The claimant substantially recovered the amount claimed, but was awarded a lump sum of £78 for costs, which was a small proportion of his actual costs, with no reasons given. The claimant sought a review of the award. Atkinson J. at page 174 suggested a range of possible reasons why the arbitrator may have made such an award: "[The arbitrator] may think that it is altogether wrong to saddle the owner with the cost of two counsel: he may think that one counsel is ample. He may think that there was an unnecessary amount of evidence called—I do not know. A number of witnesses were called; their names are set out in the affidavit. He may have taken the view that one expert witness was enough; or, at any rate, that the whole thing could have been done much more cheaply than it was." He held that the court could only interfere where it is shown that the arbitrator has done something which he has no power to do; he was not satisfied on this point and dismissed the application. The judge did suggest, however, that where the arbitrator considers the successful party's case to have been conducted extravagantly it is generally more convenient to award him a proportion of his costs rather than a lump sum.

---

32. This list is derived from the criteria set out in the Rules of the Supreme Court, Order 62, Appendix 2, Part 1.

5.7 TIME FACTORS

5.7.1 Costs arising prior to or shortly after the commencement of arbitration proceedings

There is a general convention that a claimant must advise a respondent prior to initiating proceedings, ordinarily by a "letter before action". The respondent is to be alerted to the fact that costs will be incurred and that he should consider protecting himself with an offer. Where no such letter is sent, the claimant takes a risk in costs if the matter is settled shortly after the commencement of proceedings.

Nevertheless, some costs incurred before proceedings formally began[33] are allowable if they were made in contemplation of arbitration proceedings and were relevant to the dispute as ultimately constituted. "It would, indeed, be most unfortunate if the costs of obtaining evidence while it was fresh after an accident could not be allowed, even if litigation seemed probable, merely because no writ had then been issued."[34] A number of tests have been suggested as to the recoverability of such costs including "that of proving of use and service in the action, that of relevance to an issue, and that of attributability to the defendant's conduct".[35] Clearly, work properly and reasonably done by the respondent after the commencement of proceedings may be claimed by way of costs even if the matter does not proceed.[36]

5.7.2 Work prematurely done or instructions prematurely delivered

Where an arbitration proceeds to a full hearing and final award, the time at which work was actually performed matters little. The cost of items of work which were reasonably required for the proper conduct of the case will be allowable irrespective of when those items of work were performed. Where, however, the arbitration is terminated at some earlier stage and the recoverable costs have to be determined, the question may arise whether or not certain items of cost were incurred prematurely. For example, counsel's brief may be delivered some time before a hearing; if a compromise is reached between the date of delivery of brief and the commencement of the hearing, the question may arise whether or not it was reasonable for the brief to be delivered so early.[37] There are no fixed rules governing the time at which work is to be done or when the brief or other instructions are to be delivered. It is always a

---

33. See section 14 of the Arbitration Act 1996.

34. *Re Gibson's Settlement Trusts* [1981] Ch. 179, *per* Sir Robert Megarry V.-C. at 186.

35. *Re Gibson's Settlement Trusts* [1981] Ch. 179, *per* Sir Robert Megarry V.-C. at 186 following an analysis of *Pecheries Ostendaises (Soc. Anon.)* v. *Merchants' Marine Insurance Co.* [1928] 1 K.B. 750 and *Frankenburg* v. *Famous Lasky Film Service Ltd.* [1931] 1 Ch. 428.

36. *Scheff* v. *Columbia Pictures Corporation Ltd.* [1938] 4 All E.R. 318; here a writ for breach of copyright was issued and the defendant began to collect a wide range of evidence to refute this allegation. After three months the claim was dismissed for want of prosecution. Costs properly and reasonably incurred could be claimed even though no statement of claim was ever served.

37. As in *Thomas* v. *Palin* (1882) 21 Ch.D. 360.

question of reasonableness in every case, to be decided by the arbitrator.[38]

5.7.3 Financing of costs outstanding during lengthy proceedings

Arbitration proceedings may sometimes last many years. Items of cost may thus be incurred by the party who is ultimately successful a significant time before they are reimbursed by the unsuccessful party. However, no entitlement to costs arises until an award for those costs has been made by the arbitrator. Hence the ultimately successful party is not entitled to recover for the costs incurred in financing the proceedings[39] or for being out of pocket for the duration of the proceedings.[40] It seems also that the amount to be allowed for work done in the past is a reasonable rate for work at that time, not for the same work done at the date of the award as to costs.[41]

Illustrations

Harrison v. Leutner (1881) 16 Ch.D. 559 The plaintiff gave notice that he would apply for an injunction. The defendant commenced work on affidavits. The plaintiff then discontinued his action by notice and was ordered to pay the defendant's taxed costs. The costs of affidavits prepared by the defendant but which had not been filed at the date of abandonment were disputed. Sir George Jessel M.R. asked the Taxing Masters to indicate their practice. They certified: "That we have always acted upon the principle that the costs of all work in preparing, briefing, or otherwise relating to affidavits or pleadings, reasonably and properly and not prematurely done, down to the time of any notice which stops the work, is allowable; and that the Taxing Masters, having regard to the circumstances of each case, must decide whether the work was reasonable and proper and the time for doing it had arrived." The Master of the Rolls accepted that the correct test was being applied and dismissed the application.

In Re Gibson's Settlement Trusts [1981] 1 Ch. 179 Upon the taxation of a bill of costs, the party paying objected to the fact that the taxing officer had allowed items of costs which arose before the date on which proceedings were commenced. Sir Robert Megarry V.-C. said at 187: "If the proceedings are framed narrowly, then I cannot see how antecedent disputes which bear no real relation to the subject of the litigation could be regarded as being part of the costs of the proceedings. On the other hand, if these disputes are in some degree relevant to the proceedings as ultimately constituted, and the other party's attitude made it reasonable to apprehend that litigation would include them, then I cannot see why the taxing master should not be able to include these costs among those which he considers to have been 'reasonably incurred'."

38. *Harrison* v. *Leutner* (1881) 16 Ch.D. 559; *Thomas* v. *Palin* (1882) 21 Ch.D. 360.

39. *Mann* v. *Eccott*, 27 June 1994 (C.A.) Unreported: interest on money borrowed by a successful plaintiff to finance litigation is not part of the costs.

40. *Hunt* v. *R.M. Douglas (Roofing) Ltd.* [1988] 1 A.C. 398. Note, however, that section 49(3)(a) of the Arbitration Act 1996 provides that an arbitrator may award interest "on the whole or any part of any amount awarded by the tribunal . . .". Clearly costs may form part of such an amount. It is submitted, however, that interest should only be awarded in respect of any matter back to the date when the entitlement arose, and, unlike the substantive entitlements, no entitlement arises as to costs until the date of the award.

41. *R.* v. *Wilkinson* [1980] 1 W.L.R. 396. Reaffirmed in *Johnson* v. *Reed Corrugated Cases Ltd.* [1992] 1 All E.R. 169.

5.8 COSTS OF LEGAL REPRESENTATION

5.8.1 General principles

Parties are, subject to any agreement they make,[42] entitled to engage representatives who are skilled and experienced in the type of case being dealt with; the successful party is entitled to engage representatives who are able properly to enforce or defend his rights.[43] Subject to any direction of the arbitrator as to procedures,[44] or limiting the recoverable costs,[45] the reasonable costs of such representatives are recoverable.

In determining the recoverable costs, it is for the arbitrator to make a judgment as to what level of representation was reasonable in all the circumstances. If the arbitrator is of the view that the numbers of representatives or the fees claimed are in excess of what is reasonable, he may disallow some or all of the claims for costs made in respect of individual representatives.[46] Such judgments should, however, be viewed from the perspective of the time when the representatives were instructed and not with the benefit of hindsight.[47]

5.8.2 Counsel's fees

In High Court proceedings, representation is ordinarily by counsel instructed by a solicitor.[48] In arbitration proceedings there is no requirement that the parties be represented by lawyers[49]; notwithstanding this, counsel instructed by solicitor is the most common mode of representation. It is thought that, in arbitrations of any significant weight, a successful party will normally be "entitled" to recover the costs of one counsel instructed by a solicitor. If parties wish to displace this convention they should do so in their arbitration agreement[50] or they should make an application to the arbitrator for a direction limiting recoverable costs.[51]

In the early stages of proceedings, counsel receive instructions to perform certain items of work (e.g. settling pleadings/statements of case); the fee for this work is normally agreed by the instructing solicitor and counsel's clerk.

42. See, for example, *Ceval Alimentos S.A.* v. *Agrimpex Trading Co. Ltd.* [1995] 2 Lloyd's Rep. 380. Here the arbitration rules (GAFTA) provided that no lawyers in independent practice were to attend the hearing without the leave of the arbitrators. See also section 36 of the Arbitration Act 1996.

43. *Simpsons Motor Sales (London) Ltd.* v. *Hendon Borough Council* [1965] 1 W.L.R. 112.

44. Section 33 of the Arbitration Act 1996.

45. Section 65 of the Arbitration Act 1996.

46. *P. Rosen & Co. Ltd.* v. *Dowley & Selby* [1943] 2 All E.R. 172.

47. By analogy with *Bartlett* v. *Higgins* [1901] 2 K.B. 230.

48. There are exceptions. Solicitors frequently attend on interlocutory matters and some are entitled to appear in the higher courts. Counsel may be instructed by any professional entitled to Direct Professional Access.

49. Section 36 of the Arbitration Act 1996. Also see *Piper Double Glazing Ltd.* v. *D.C. Contracts* [1994] 1 W.L.R. 777.

50. See Section 63(1) of the Arbitration Act 1996.

51. Section 65 of the Arbitration Act 1996.

Traditionally, counsel's fees for attendance at the hearing have been paid in two parts. First, a brief fee becomes due upon the delivery of the brief (i.e. the instructions to appear at the hearing). This is a fee for reading through the documents, preparing speeches, considering how the evidence is to be adduced etc. The brief fee includes payment for the first day of the hearing and, if necessary, for being present to receive the award (although awards are normally dispatched in writing).[52] A discount to the brief fee may be agreed in the event that the matter is settled before the day of the hearing. Then a refresher fee is paid for the second and each subsequent day of the hearing.

In recent years, novel schemes of payment for the hearing have been developed. Counsel have been unhappy about keeping dates for long hearings clear without any commitment. Many counsel request that brief fees be paid in rising instalments. Portions of the brief fee may be paid a significant period before the start of the hearing. If the arbitration is settled, with costs to be determined, before the hearing but after the payment of some of the instalments, the question arises whether these early instalments are recoverable costs. The test is whether the instalments were reasonably paid at the date of the settlement; if so, a reasonable sum will be recoverable in respect of them.[53]

It is appropriate to instruct Queen's Counsel when the nature of the case, its importance for the client, the sums involved, or the need for special expertise suggest that it is reasonable, having regard to the principle that the successful party is entitled to representatives who are able properly to enforce or defend that party's rights.[54] Queen's Counsel should be accompanied by junior counsel where it is important for the conduct of the case. Proper considerations include whether a junior will be required to make representations, take a note, deal with the documentation, assist in negotiations or to deal with clients known to him through conferences etc.

The fees which eminent counsel may command are not automatically allowable. The arbitrator must consider whether the level of fees included in the bill of costs is reasonable by the standards of "an hypothetical counsel capable of conducting the particular case effectively but unable or unwilling to insist on the particular high fee sometimes demanded by counsel of pre-eminent reputation".[55] However, the fact that another lawyer of equal experience and competence would have done it for less is not usually to the point since such comparisons do not decide the question of whether the fees of the lawyer actually engaged were reasonable. The level of fees charged by counsel who

---

52. The brief fee and refreshers taken together include for all normal evening and weekend preparation and the drawing up of closing submissions: *Loveday* v. *Renton* (No. 2) [1992] 3 All E.R. 184.

53. *Thomas* v. *Palin* (1882) 21 Ch.D. 360. Sir George Jessel M.R. said at 364: "If . . . the Taxing Master thought that the moving party had delivered his briefs prematurely, he disallowed them as being delivered for the purpose of making costs, but if he thought they were fairly delivered he allowed them."

54. *Simpsons Motor Sales (London) Ltd.* v. *Hendon Borough Council* [1965] 1 W.L.R. 112.

55. *Simpsons Motor Sales (London) Ltd.* v. *Hendon Borough Council* [1965] 1 W.L.R. 112 *per* Pennycuick J. at 118.

represent the opposing party is generally not material in determining the proper level of recoverable costs.[56]

5.8.3 Solicitor's charges

In litigation proceedings, the bill submitted for taxation will be drawn up by or on behalf of the solicitors for the successful party. The bill divides the charges made by the solicitor into two parts: the basic charge and an element for "care and conduct".[57]

Because most parties in arbitration are represented by solicitors, many bills of costs will be presented in the same format as a bill in litigation unless the arbitrator directs otherwise. An arbitrator may, of course, award a proper basic charge and an appropriate care and conduct element. He is not, however, bound to determine costs in accordance with these rather artificial procedures and may require that the bill be submitted in a format which he directs.

5.8.4 Claims consultants

The general principles which apply to the determination of lawyers' costs are applicable when the party awarded costs is represented by claims consultants rather than solicitors and counsel.[58] A claims consultant will not charge a care and conduct element, but will claim a charging rate which is appropriate in all the circumstances.

5.8.5 Parties who represent themselves

A natural person may represent himself; a company may be represented by a director or other employee. The question arises as to the costs which may be recovered for such representation.

In the courts, litigants in person have traditionally not been entitled to a fee for representing themselves, except for reasonable expenses.[59] This rule was modified to some degree by the Litigants in Person (Costs and Expenses) Act 1975. This enables rules of court to be drawn up which allow costs to be recoverable by litigants in person. Rules of the Supreme Court now provide that litigants in person may recover their disbursements; in addition, for work on the case which causes them pecuniary loss, they may recover up to two-thirds the amount that may have been charged by a solicitor.[60]

Directors may now, where the court gives leave, represent their companies in court. It seems that where a company director represents his company, the

56. *Simpsons Motor Sales (London) Ltd.* v. *Hendon Borough Council* [1965] 1 W.L.R. 112.
57. See §5.2 above. As to the appropriate level of uplift see, for example: *Re Gibson's Settlement Trusts* [1981] Ch. 179 at 190; *Loveday* v. *Renton* (No. 2) [1992] 3 All E.R. 184.
58. *Piper Double Glazing Ltd.* v. *D.C. Contracts* [1994] 1 W.L.R. 777.
59. See *Buckland* v. *Watts* [1970] 1 Q.B. 27.
60. Rules of the Supreme Court, Order 62, rule 18.

company is not entitled to its costs under the 1975 Act unless the rules of court are amended specifically to allow this.[61]

Arbitration is a private and consensual procedure and there is no presumption that a party will be represented by lawyers.[62] Further, the discretion as to costs is conferred on the arbitrator and is not fettered by specific rules of court. Consequently, it is submitted that an arbitrator may allow a party-advocate's reasonable costs, as represent the reasonable value of the work done in all the circumstances. There are a number of factors which should be taken into account:

(1) A party-advocate without legal training will necessarily spend more time on the case than a lawyer and this must be reflected in any costs which are awarded, by reducing the charging rate.

(2) If a party-advocate presents his case in a way which causes delay or additional expense in the proceedings, thereby increasing the costs of the other party, this may be taken into account by awarding the successful party-advocate a proportion only of his costs.[63]

(3) The basic purpose of an award of costs is indemnity. The fact that a private individual will not have the significant overhead costs payable by professional lawyers should, where appropriate, be taken into account. Furthermore, while a reasonable rate may be paid for the time spent by the party-advocate, there should be no additional payments to represent the fees which might have been recovered had counsel been instructed.[64]

5.8.6 Contingency and conditional fees

Traditionally, an agreement between a lawyer (or other adviser) and a party whereby the fee payable to the lawyer depends on the outcome of the proceedings has not been enforceable.[65] The basis of the rule is to be found in the ancient laws of maintenance and champerty, which forbade the maintenance

---

61. *Jonathan Alexander Ltd.* v. *Procter* [1996] 2 All E.R. 334. While feeling himself bound to support the result, Hirst L.J. expressed his regret at 339: "... it seems to me that this case reveals a serious lacuna in the law, and results in a considerable injustice to the company, which properly incurred very substantial costs in defeating a grossly inflated counterclaim ...". On the other hand a successful party who employs in-house lawyers is entitled to recover his costs on the normal basis as if those lawyers were in independent private practice: *Re Eastwood, deceased* [1975] 1 Ch.D. 112.

62. Section 36 of the Arbitration Act 1996.

63. *Gupta* v. *Klito*, *The Times*, 23 November 1989. Here the successful litigant in person wasted so much time that the judge ordered him to pay the defendants' costs. The Court of Appeal ordered that each party should pay their own costs.

64. *Hart* v. *Aga Khan Foundation (UK)* [1984] 1 All E.R. 239: "... there is no reason why an unsuccessful defendant should get off more lightly just because the successful plaintiff has conducted his or her own litigation in person ... but ... the whole object of an award for costs is to indemnify the successful party ... He cannot recover what he has not incurred. To this general principle Parliament has provided a limited exception in the case of a litigant in person," *per* Lloyd J. at 241.

65. *Wallerstein* v. *Moir* (No. 2) [1975] 1 All E.R. 849.

of an action by a non-party.[66] It is now recognised that there are potential benefits in allowing conditional[67] and/or contingency[68] fees. Indeed, new regulations have been brought into force permitting the fees in certain classes of litigation to be agreed on a conditional fee basis.[69]

This shift in attitude and the private, consensual nature of arbitration suggests that conditional fee arrangements and even contingency fee arrangements are permissible in arbitration,[70] provided they are not oppressive or mischievous. Accordingly, it is suggested that a party who engages legal representatives on a conditional or contingency fee basis may recover a proper amount for costs expended. Clearly this amount should not exceed that payable to representatives working on a time charging basis and it is submitted that substantiated time records and disbursements should be called for, even though this is not the basis upon which payment as between the client and his advisers will ultimately be made. Furthermore, it is suggested that a party who enters into such an agreement with his advisers should indicate this to the arbitrator at an early opportunity so that such safeguards as the arbitrator deems necessary can be put in place.

Illustrations

Wallerstein v. Moir (No. 2) [1975] 1 All E.R. 849 "English law has never sanctioned an agreement by which a lawyer is remunerated on the basis of a 'contingency fee', that is that he gets paid the fee if he wins, but not if he loses. Such an agreement was illegal on the ground that it was the offence of champerty ... It was suggested to us [by counsel] that the only reason why 'contingency fees' were not allowed in England was because they offended against the criminal law as to champerty; and that now that criminal liability is abolished, the courts were free to hold that contingency fees were lawful. I cannot accept this contention. The reason why contingency fees are in general unlawful is that they are contrary to public policy", *per* Lord Denning at 860. Buckley L.J. stated the basic policy reasons at 867: "First, in litigation a professional lawyer's role is to advise his client with a clear eye and an unbiased judgment. Secondly, a solicitor retained to conduct litigation is not merely the agent and adviser to his client, but also an officer of the court ...."

Piper Double Glazing Ltd. v. D.C. Contracts [1994] 1 W.L.R. 777 Potter J. made

66. The offences of champerty and maintenance were abolished in 1967. In *Wallerstein* v. *Moir* (No. 2) [1975] 1 All E.R. 849 it was restated that the objection to contingency fees survived the abolition of the offences.

67. Where the fee depends on success.

68. Where the fee depends on the amount of proceeds.

69. Conditional Fee Agreements Order 1995, S.I. No. 1674; Conditional Fee Agreements Regulations 1995, No. S.I. 1675. The regulations only extend to proceedings for personal injuries, certain company law matters and human rights litigation.

70. See "Contingency fees in arbitration?" by T. Keevil, *Arbitration Journal* November 1995, pp 284–5. See the case of *Cannonway Consultants Ltd.* v. *Kenworth Engineering Ltd.*, High Court of Hong Kong, 25 November 1994, described there. This involved a contingency fee arrangement between a claims consultant (the plaintiff) and a building contractor (the defendant) whereby the contractor agreed to pay the consultant a percentage of the proceeds of an arbitration. When the plaintiff attempted to recover the agreed money by action, the defendant resisted on the grounds that the agreement was champertous. Kaplan J. decided that the law of champerty was the same in Hong Kong as in England. He indicated that its extension to arbitration was not warranted.

the following observations in relation to the taxation of bills submitted by claims consultants (at p. 787): "In so far as the taxing master may, in the case of a claims consultant, be considering a new and/or unconventional breed of litigator, it may be that the taxing master will consider that some difference of approach will be called for, not least to accommodate the extent to which, in relation to various items of work, it might be the case that the fee earner concerned has acted in a multi-disciplinary capacity. It may be, at least in theory, that in performing a particular task, the fee earner has in effect done two jobs at the same time and saved money for the client. On that basis, it may be, again at least in theory, that the taxing master would consider it appropriate to allow a charging rate for the single fee earner higher than the rate which might have been allowed in respect of two individual fee earners jointly rendering the same service. On the other hand, it may well be that a lower charging rate or fee will be considered appropriate in the case of an employee of a claims consultant who the master considers lacks the expertise of a conventional qualified fee earner or otherwise provides a less valuable service. If the employment of claims consultants becomes widespread in the arbitration field it may be that the taxation of their bills will become a developing science in relation to which taxing masters will consider that particular scales or methods of charge, different from those developed in relation to solicitors, are appropriate. Whether or not that is so, I have no doubt that taxing masters will and should be reluctant to develop or apply scales of charges, or indeed any approach to the taxation of the costs of claims consultants, which leads to an overall *increase* in the costs of arbitration."

KPMG Peat Marwick McLintock v. HLT Group Ltd. [1995] 2 All E.R. 180 The plaintiff accountants were engaged by the defendant in connection with share valuations. The defendants alleged professional negligence in doing the work and did not pay the plaintiffs' fees. The plaintiffs engaged City solicitors, took action to recover their fees and succeeded. The defendants then claimed that the costs claimed were excessive and that equally good advice and support could have been obtained from solicitors outside the City. Held, bearing in mind the plaintiffs' standing and location and the allegations of professional negligence it was reasonable for them to instruct City solicitors of high calibre. The charges being made were not out of line with what other solicitors in the City were charging and were reasonable.

5.9 WITNESSES AND EVIDENCE

5.9.1 Costs of evidence generally

The costs of evidence include:

(1) witness statements;
(2) attendance of witnesses at the hearing;
(3) preservation of physical evidence;
(4) charges associated with obtaining documents;
(5) tests, surveys and experiments designed to obtain details and/or to prove matters in dispute;
(6) expert reports;
(7) attendance of experts at the hearing.

The test to be applied in considering whether the costs of evidence are allowable is whether such costs were reasonably incurred in all the circumstances.[71] The costs of needless duplication and evidence to prove facts admitted in the pleadings will normally be disallowed.[72]

5.9.2 Witnesses of fact

Witnesses of fact are entitled to out-of-pocket expenses plus a moderate allowance for their time. The applicable principles are somewhat vague[73]; it is submitted that the arbitrator should form a judgment in the light of all the relevant circumstances as to the allowable witness fee. In the case of witnesses who are employees, the allowance will normally cover any loss of income and expense to which the witnesses have been put. In the case of self-employed professional witnesses, the allowance should have regard to the witnesses' normal fee rate in their primary professions. People who are not in gainful employment are entitled to a sensible fee if they have had to cancel other duties.[74]

5.9.3 Expert witnesses

The expense of experts' reports reasonably commissioned with a view to litigation or arbitration is a proper part of the costs of the arbitration, even if those costs are incurred before the submission to arbitration.[75] If, on the other hand, the report was produced solely in order to advise on how to ameliorate any defects in the goods or property provided by the contract, its cost will not be part of the costs of the arbitration, but may form an item of loss which can be claimed as damages for breach of contract. If the arbitrator is of the view that the cost of the report is properly an item of costs of the arbitration, it should not be dealt with as damages.[76]

The arbitrator is entitled to take a view as to whether there was excessive expert opinion,[77] particularly since it is clear that a technically qualified arbitrator is entitled to use his own knowledge and experience.[78] The arbitrator may disallow the costs of an expert who has given evidence which is not to the point, or allow only a proportion of the costs.[79] The fact that the arbitrator has

71. *L.C. & D. Railway* v. *S.E. Railway* (1889) 60 L.T. 753.
72. For example *Re Morris* [1912] 1 Ch. 730.
73. In former times, the witness's proper allowance depended on criteria such as the witness's "station in life" which seem inappropriate today, particularly in the context of commercial proceedings.
74. For example, *Reed* v. *Gray* [1952] 1 All E.R. 241, where a housewife witness was entitled to a fee for having her household duties disrupted.
75. *Pecheries Ostendaises (Soc. Anon.)* v. *Merchants' Marine Insurance Co.* [1928] 1 K.B. 750 *per* Atkin L.J. at 763; *Bolton* v. *Mahadeva* [1972] 1 W.L.R. 1009, *per* Cairns L.J. at 1014.
76. *Hutchinson* v. *Harris* (1978) 10 Build. L.R. 19, *per* Stephenson L.J. at 39–40.
77. *P. Rosen & Co. Ltd.* v. *Dowley & Selby* [1943] 2 All E.R. 172.
78. See for example *Navrom* v. *Callitsis Ship Management* [1988] 2 Lloyd's Rep. 416; *Fox* v. *Wellfair* [1981] 2 Lloyd's Rep. 514.
79. *Mitchell* v. *Mulholland* (1973) 117 S.J. 307.

issued an order for directions that no more than X experts may be called does not constrain him to find that the costs of X experts are to be allowed. The question remains whether those expert witnesses were reasonably called.[80]

The parties are entitled to engage experts of the appropriate seniority. Thus in an important case, involving large sums, a expert "of the highest education and intelligence in his profession" may be engaged.[81]

5.9.4 Witnesses' reasonable attendance at the hearing

Witnesses, particularly expert witnesses, often attend the hearing in advance of giving evidence; they may also remain at the hearing after they have finished giving evidence. Whether or not their fees for attendance throughout these periods are recoverable depends on whether and to what extent their attendance was reasonable. In the case of experts, the relevant factors will include, *inter alia*:

(1) whether expert witnesses should be present during the presentation of the other party's evidence in order to understand and advise on the evidence being adduced; and

(2) whether the expert witnesses are required to assist the advocate in framing questions for cross-examination and/or preparation of submissions.

Similar considerations will apply to witnesses of fact; they will, however, normally have a lesser role in framing questions and assisting the advocate.

The fees for attendance by witnesses for those periods which are in excess of what is reasonable are not allowable.[82] The question of reasonableness is to be judged at the time when the decision to have them at the hearing was made and not in hindsight.[83]

5.9.5 Unused evidence

Evidence is often prepared for the hearing but not used. The costs of such evidence may be allowed if it was reasonably prepared in all the circumstances.[84] Thus, the costs of statements taken but not used at trial may be recovered if they were reasonable taken in all the circumstances.[85]

---

80. *Atwell* v. *Ministry of Public Buildings and Works* [1969] 1 W.L.R. 1074.

81. *London, Chatham and Dover Railway* v. *South Eastern Railway Company* (1889) 60 L.T. 753, *per* Kekewich J. at 755. The party paying on taxation in a large railway case argued that there was no need for the successful party to engage a famous civil engineer from London where a local Folkestone surveyor could have given the same evidence. The judge found that in all the circumstances the successful party had been quite correct in engaging the London engineer.

82. *Wright* v. *Bennett* [1948] 1 All E.R. 410.

83. *Bartlett* v. *Higgins* [1901] 2 K.B. 230, where the costs of an examination of evidence was allowed, although it turned out to be unnecessary as the case unfolded.

84. *London, Chatham and Dover Railway* v. *South Eastern Railway Company* (1889) 60 L.T. 753.

85. *Bartlett* v. *Higgins* [1901] 2 K.B. 230.

5.9 Determining the recoverable costs of the arbitration

Illustrations

London, Chatham and Dover Railway v. South Eastern Railway Company (1889) 60 L.T. 753 "The evidence which is used in court is not necessarily the evidence which is to be charged for. I think it would be very much to the disadvantage of the public if any such rule ... were laid down, because the result would be that, when one put to counsel whether they need call any other witnesses on a certain point, or put in a certain document, counsel, either actually or practically, would be obliged to say, 'I must do it, or else my client will not get it allowed on taxation'. That is a principle which, as far as I am concerned, I will do my best to keep under, and not allow to prevail. ... It does not follow because [counsel] only call 10% of the witnesses in their brief, or put in only 10% of the documents which those witnesses were prepared to prove, that therefore any one of them is to be omitted on taxation", *per* Kekewich J. at 755–6.

Wright v. Bennett [1948] 1 All E.R. 410 An expert witness for the defendant was kept in court for 13 days during the plaintiff's case. When the plaintiff had finished, it was decided that there was no need for the expert's evidence and he was released. The successful defendant claimed on taxation for the expert's time in court. The master allowed the full 13 days. On appeal to the Court of Appeal Somervell L.J. with whom the court agreed accepted that there was a recognised principle that "in the case of witnesses who are improperly and unnecessarily kept in court any costs or fees claimed in respect of the period during which they are unnecessarily kept in court should not be recoverable" (at 413). However, he was unable to infer that the master had not taken this principle into account; the costs for the full 13 days was allowed.

Atwell v. Ministry of Public Building and Works [1969] 1 W.L.R. 1074 A personal injury plaintiff sought an order that the parties be limited to one expert witness each. During argument, Fisher J. realised that the plaintiff's purpose in seeking the order was to ensure that if he were successful he would get the costs of his expert on taxation. An order limiting the number of experts was treated by taxing officers "as a conclusive indication that the calling of that number of witnesses was reasonable". But Fisher J. did not accept that an order limiting the number of experts could have any such effect. He said at 1076: "It seems to me that the court has no power in advance to give its blessing (or the opposite) to the calling of witnesses and that it is a *non sequitur* to infer from an order in the negative form saying 'you may not call more than one witness' the affirmative proposition 'it is reasonable that you call one witness', or to infer from the refusal of such an order the proposition 'it is unreasonable to call any witness'."

Mitchell v. Mulholland (1973) 117 Sol. Jo. 307 The plaintiff was severely injured in an accident. The defendant admitted liability; quantum remained at issue. The plaintiff called three expert witnesses (an economist, an actuary and an accountant) in order to prove the effect of time on any award made. The trial judge, however, placed little (if any) weight on this evidence and used instead the method of multipliers and multiplicands used habitually by the courts. The plaintiff later sought an order for the costs of these expert witnesses. Edmund Davies L.J. in the Court of Appeal said: "The evidence of the economist had been neither necessary nor proper, so specious had been his testimony, and all the costs of his evidence should be disallowed. There had been some residual, though limited, value in calling the actuary and the chartered accountant, and it had not been wholly unreasonable to call them. But as they had based their evidence largely on that of the economist it had reached more expansive dimensions than it would otherwise have done. The plaintiff should recover only one third of the cost of calling them."

5.10 CLIENT'S INTERNAL COSTS

5.10.1 General staff time

The commercial managers and professional staff of a party involved in an arbitration often dedicate substantial time to the case, including the generation of figures and attendance at the hearing. These costs, except for reasonable out-of-pocket expenses necessarily incurred in the arbitration, are generally irrecoverable on the general principle that the lay client's time in instructing those who conduct the proceedings is not allowable. This principle is not applied as strictly in commercial cases as it is to other types of proceedings.[86] An arbitrator will thus have some discretion to allow an element of costs in respect of such work if he is satisfied that the work done internally obviated the need for others to do it and hence led to an overall saving of costs. The arbitrator may determine that internal costs are to be included as part of the "... other costs of the parties".[87]

The rate which can be claimed by internal staff should not exceed the direct cost to the client, namely the salary rate plus expenses directly incurred; no allowance for general overheads should be allowed.[88]

While commercial managers may wish to attend the hearing out of interest or to report back, they will ordinarily do so at their own or their employer's expense, unless it can be shown that they attended for some purpose properly connected with the conduct of the arbitration.

5.10.2 In-house experts

In commercial proceedings it is often convenient for in-house experts to be instructed to undertake tests, perform experiments, make calculations and even to present expert evidence. The actual and direct costs of in-house experts may be allowed; but no sum for general overheads is normally allowable.[89]

5.10.3 In-house lawyers

A successful party who employs in-house lawyers is entitled to recover his costs on the normal basis as if those lawyers were in independent private practice.[90] It is assumed that a party makes no savings by employing in-house lawyers and that the process of determining the recoverable costs should not be further complicated by requiring a successful party to show a detailed breakdown of its internal costs in order to prove what sum will indemnify him in costs.

86. *Re Nossens's Letter Patent* [1969] 1 W.L.R. 638.
87. Section 59(1)(c) of the Arbitration Act 1996.
88. *Re Nossens's Letter Patent* [1969] 1 W.L.R. 638.
89. *Re Nossens's Letter Patent* [1969] 1 W.L.R. 638.
90. *Re Eastwood, deceased* [1975] 1 Ch. 112.

5.10 Determining the recoverable costs of the arbitration

Illustration

Re Nossens's Letter Patent [1969] 1 W.L.R. 638 The applicant claimed that the United Kingdom Atomic Energy Authority had infringed his patent. The UKAEA undertook experiments to refute the claim using in-house experts and later sought to recover the costs of these experts on taxation. Lloyd-Jacob J. said at 643–4: "The established practice of the courts has been to disallow any sums claimed in respect of the time spent by the litigant personally in the course of instructing his solicitors. In the case of litigation by a corporation, this has not been strictly applied, for it has been recognised that, if expert assistance is properly required, it may well occur that the corporation's own specialist employees may be the most suitable or convenient experts to employ. If the corporation litigant does decide to provide expert assistance from its own staff, as happened in this case, the taxing master has to determine the appropriate charge to allow. For an outside expert, the normal assessment would be based on current professional standards, and this in suitable cases would include a proper proportion of the overhead costs of running his office or laboratory, that is, of the costs necessarily incurred by him in his capacity as a consultant, as well as a profit element upon such expenditure. The taxing master, in the exercise of his discretion, took the view that it would be an unreasonable burden to place upon the chargeable party the inclusion of any items in respect of the respondent's own overhead expenses or any profit element referable thereto. ... In this he was plainly right, covering as he did the actual and direct costs of the work undertaken in the sense of indemnifying the respondents for the salaries, materials and out-of-pocket expenses of those engaged in the conduct of the experiments. No part of the respondents' expenditure on overheads was occasioned by this litigation and it would be unreasonable to transfer the burden to the [paying party] of meeting some part of it by reason only of the respondents' decision to prefer the services of their own staff to those of independent experts."

5.11 COSTS OF A NOTE

It is reasonable for each party to take a note of the proceedings. If a note-taker is specifically retained, his costs may be disallowed if the party already has sufficient representation (e.g. a junior led by Queen's Counsel) to enable a proper note to be taken.[91]

5.12 GENERAL EXPENSES INCURRED IN THE ARBITRATION

A party entitled to costs may claim reasonable disbursements, including the costs of travel, accommodation, etc. The class of travel, accommodation, etc. must be reasonable in all the circumstances.

---

91. The function of a qualified note-taker is not merely to produce a transcript; thus the fact that a transcript is to be produced does not necessarily preclude the fees of a legally qualified note-taker being allowed. In *Wright* v. *Bennett* [1948] 1 All E.R. 410 a second junior counsel had received a noting brief; subsequently, an agreement was made between the parties that a shorthand note should be taken. The refresher fees of counsel with the noting brief were allowed since "the noting brief was not a mere alternative to a shorthand note".

5.13 VALUE ADDED TAX

A VAT-registered arbitrator will charge VAT on his account. However, VAT charged by the successful party's lawyers and other advisers may not automatically be payable by the losing party, since these taxes may be set off against other transactions. Furthermore, the arbitrator does not have jurisdiction to make binding determinations about the level of VAT chargeable—only the Customs and Excise may do that, subject to appeals to the court. Note also that, where a litigant, including a solicitor, acts for himself, he is not to be treated as having supplied a service and hence no VAT is chargeable.[92]

5.14 SET-OFF OF COSTS

When each party is entitled to some of his costs, the amount allowed to each will be determined and the balance will be awarded to the relevant party.[93] Where there have been interlocutory proceedings or amendments and a party has been awarded costs in any event but goes on to be unsuccessful, set-off is the sensible solution. Costs of applications to the court cannot conveniently be set-off in this way since such costs will automatically be dealt with by the court.

92. See generally: Practice Direction (No. 2 of 1994) [1994] 2 All E.R. 61.
93. For example, *Welch* v. *Royal Exchange Assurance* [1939] 3 All E.R. 305, where on a taxation in court, the costs of the arbitration were set off against the costs of an application to the court.

CHAPTER 6

SECURITY FOR THE COSTS OF THE ARBITRATION

6.1 SECURITY FOR COSTS: THE RATIONALE

When a respondent succeeds in his defence, he will normally be awarded his reasonable costs. Where, however, the claimant has no funds to pay those costs, such an award will be of no value to the respondent; the respondent will be left to pay his own costs. In some situations, an arbitrator may also be at risk of not being paid.

In order to avoid these risks, a procedure has developed whereby the claimant may be ordered to provide security for some or all of the respondent's (and, where appropriate, the arbitrator's) projected costs as a condition of pursuing the arbitration.

6.2 HISTORICAL INTRODUCTION

Procedures for ordering security for costs in court actions have been well-established for many years. Prior to the 1996 legislation, the court had power to made orders for security for costs in arbitration proceedings[1] on the same basis as if the arbitration were a matter being heard in court.[2] Arbitrators could only order security for costs where the parties had expressly clothed them with authority[3]; and even here this did not deprive the court of its authority.[4]

The consideration of an application for security for costs has traditionally been dealt with in two stages. First the court considered whether it had jurisdiction; an order for security was only permissible against certain classes of plaintiff[5] and the court had to ascertain whether or not the particular plaintiff fell within the appropriate classes. If the court was satisfied that the plaintiff

---

1. Section 12(6) of the Arbitration Act 1950.
2. *Hudson Strumpffabrik G.m.b.H.* v. *Bentley Engineering Co. Ltd.* [1962] 2 Q.B. 587; *Aeronave S.P.A.* v. *Westland Charterers Ltd.* [1971] 1 W.L.R. 1445.
3. *Unione Stearinerie Lanza* v. *Wiener* [1917] 2 K.B. 558; *Mavani* v. *Ralli Brothers Ltd.* [1973] 1 All E.R. 555 at 559; *Fal Bunkering of Sharjah* v. *Grecale Inc. of Panama* [1990] 1 Lloyd's Rep. 369 at 371.
4. *Mavani* v. *Ralli Brothers Ltd.* [1973] 1 All E.R. 555 at 560.
5. Rules of the Supreme Court Order 23, rule 1.

did so, it had to exercise its discretion as to whether an order for security was appropriate in all the circumstances.

The Arbitration Act 1996 makes significant changes. The arbitrator now has power to order security against the claimant[6] unless the parties expressly deprive him of that power,[7] and the court has no such power.[8]

6.3 THE AUTHORITY TO ORDER SECURITY FOR COSTS

The arbitrator's statutory authority to make an order for security for costs derives from section 38(3) of the Arbitration Act 1996 which provides in the tersest form: "The tribunal may order a claimant to provide security for the costs of the arbitration." A "claimant" includes a counterclaimant.[9] This authority may be enlarged, constrained or restricted by the agreement of the parties.[10] The Act also stipulates that the power to order security for costs may not be exercised on the ground that the claimant is resident outside the United Kingdom, or is a body whose central management and control is exercised outside the United Kingdom.[11] While these are the only formal constraints on the exercise of the power to order security for costs, it is submitted that the arbitrator must exercise the power judicially with proper discretion. This means, in effect, that the arbitrator must consider the relevant matters put to him and must take into account no irrelevant matters in coming to his decision; furthermore he must not misdirect himself as to the exercise of his power.

Although there is no formal requirement for an application by a party, it is suggested that an arbitrator should not secure a party's costs without an application by that party. An unsolicited order may give the impression of a lack of impartiality; furthermore the arbitrator is in no position personally to investigate the circumstances (e.g. published accounts) of the claimant in order to determine whether such an order is appropriate.

---

6. Section 38(3) of the Arbitration Act 1996. This power is subject only to the agreement of the parties.

7. Section 38(2) of the Arbitration Act 1996.

8. Section 44 of the Arbitration Act 1996 lists the court's powers exercisable in support of arbitral proceedings. Section 44(5) provides: "In any case the court shall act only if or to the extent that the arbitral tribunal . . . has no power or is unable for the time being to act effectively."

9. Section 82(1) of the Arbitration Act 1996: "In this part—. . . 'claimant', unless the context otherwise requires, includes a counterclaimant, and related expressions shall be construed accordingly . . .".

10. Section 38(2) of the Arbitration Act 1996.

11. Section 38(3)(a) and (b) of the Arbitration Act 1996. These provisions were introduced to overrule the majority decision of the House of Lords in *Coppée Lavalin* v. *Ken-Ren* [1994] 2 W.L.R. 631. No discrimination would, in any event, now be possible on account of residence in the European Union: *Fitzgerald* v. *Williams* [1996] 2 W.L.R. 447.

6.4 THE ARBITRATOR MUST SATISFY HIMSELF THAT THE APPLICATION IS A PROPER ONE

Technically, there is no question as to whether the arbitrator has jurisdiction to entertain an application for security of costs: provided the application is made in respect of a claimant or a party in the position of claimant, the arbitrator may deal with it.[12]

Nevertheless, it is submitted that an arbitrator should first satisfy himself that the application is a proper one. It must be demonstrated on a balance of probabilities by credible evidence, that the claimant will be unable to pay the costs of a successful respondent at the time they would become payable.[13] However, it is normally appropriate that there is some other factor associated with the claimant's status which makes the application proper.[14] Such factors may include: (a) where the claimant is a nominal claimant[15]; here the real claimant shelters behind the limited means of a nominal intermediary; or (b) where the claimant is a limited company,[16] so that the shareholders of the company stand to gain personally from a successful claim, but may set up the limited liability as a defence to payment of the bill of costs in the event that the company cannot pay it.

6.5 THE ARBITRATOR'S DISCRETION

Where the arbitrator is satisfied that the application is a proper one, he may exercise his discretion to consider whether in all the circumstances an order for security for costs is appropriate. The arbitrator is not constrained in the factors which he may take into account when exercising his discretion.[17] He should, however, have regard to those factors which have been identified by the courts.

The principal matters to which the arbitrator should have regard are those

12. Unless the sole ground advanced in support of the application is the residence/location of the claimant: section 38(3)(a) and (b) of the Arbitration Act 1996.

13. The fact that a claimant could not pay the costs today is insufficient. The normal method of proof is the analysis of company accounts or other financial statements.

14. But one factor which must not be taken into account is the residence or location of the claimant: provisos (a) and (b) to section 38(3) of the Arbitration Act 1996.

15. A claimant who has assigned the benefit of the arbitral proceedings may be a nominal claimant: *Semler* v. *Murphy* [1968] Ch. 183. But see *Ramsey* v. *Hartley* [1977] 1 W.L.R. 686 at 696, where a claimant who is pursuing the arbitration partly for his own benefit and partly for the benefit of his trustee in bankruptcy may not be a nominal claimant, especially if the respondent contributed to the claimant's bankruptcy. In *Envis* v. *Thakkar*, *The Times*, 2 May 1995 it was held that to be a nominal plaintiff there must be some element of deliberate duplicity or window dressing to the detriment of the defendant.

16. Limited companies have long been subject to special rules relating to security for costs: see section 726(1) of the Companies Act 1985. In court proceedings, this principle is now applicable to all companies within the European Union: *Chequepoint S.A.R.L.* v. *McClelland* [1996] 3 W.L.R. 341.

17. *Sir Lindsay Parkinson Ltd.* v. *Triplan Ltd.* [1973] 1 Q.B. 609, *per* Lawton L.J. at 629.

set out by Lord Denning in *Sir Lindsay Parkinson* v. *Triplan*.[18] These factors have been the subject of later judicial comment and must be understood in the light of these subsequent clarifications. The courts have often treated the operation of the discretion using the metaphor of a balance in which the considerations pro and con an order for security are weighed. The principal factors to be weighed are:

(1) The bona fides of the claim

This is a question of fact. If it appears to the court that the claim is a serious one based on allegations which, if proved, will produce a successful result for the plaintiff, the claim is bona fide. If, however, it is scandalous or oppressive or is based on allegations which are unlikely to found a proper cause of action it is not.

(2) The prospects of success

If the merits or shortcomings of the claim are readily apparent, the arbitrator may take them into account. But the arbitrator must be careful not to prejudice himself, by coming to a partial conclusion without hearing the evidence. And, in any event, he must not undertake a specific investigation into the prospects of success, partly because it would involve the time and expense of hearing the evidence.[19]

(3) Admissions or offers

If the respondent makes admissions in his defence, the arbitrator is entitled to take this into account as going to the good faith of the claimant's claim and the likelihood of his success.

If the alleged admission takes the form of an open offer, the arbitrator may have regard to it upon an application for security for costs. Where it is wholly privileged it is inadmissible unless the party or parties who own the privilege have waived it; accordingly, where due to an inadvertence, the arbitrator knows of the offer he may not take it into account.[20] Difficult problems arise, however, where the offer is a sealed offer or Calderbank letter. Formerly, the court could look at a sealed offer upon an application for security for costs.[21] This did not prejudice the eventual outcome as the arbitrator did not know of the offer. However, now that the arbitrator is the only tribunal able to make an order for security for costs, different considerations apply.

18. [1973] 1 Q.B. 609. While this particular case concerned an application to the court and was subject to the provisions of the Companies Acts, it is submitted that the principles which emerge are of general application.

19. *Porzelack K.G.* v. *Porzelack U.K. Ltd.* [1987] 1 W.L.R. 420, *per* Sir Nicolas Browne-Wilkinson V.-C. at 423.

20. *Simaan General Contracting Co.* v. *Pilkington Glass Ltd.* [1987] 1 W.L.R. 516.

21. *Simaan General Contracting Co.* v. *Pilkington Glass Ltd.* [1987] 1 W.L.R. 516 *obiter per* Judge Newey Q.C. at 520.

On the one hand, parties should be able to make a sealed offer without the tribunal getting to see it before the decision on the substantive issues; and, on the other hand, it seems unfair that a respondent who has made a substantial offer to settle the proceedings should nevertheless seek to stifle the claim.

It is submitted that the claimant in such a case should be able to disclose the offer to the arbitrator,[22] provided that he first gives the respondent sufficient notice to apply for an injunction to restrain disclosure. If the offer is a substantial one, the arbitrator may take the view that the respondent's application lacks good faith; and even where the claimant must pay the respondent's costs, it is likely that he will have a fund from which to pay them. Where the offer is minimal, the arbitrator may properly take the view that the respondent has little faith in the claim, which may, in fact, strengthen the respondent's application.

(4) Any oppressive features of the application for security

The arbitrator should be alive to the fact that applications for security for costs may stifle a claim by a small claimant.[23] Where an application is oppressive in that it will, or is likely to, stifle a claim, the arbitrator should take this into account.

Where a claimant company is impecunious but can clearly rely on support from associated companies, this may be taken into account. In such a case, the claimant is in the best position to know the financial state of the entire group and it may be reasonable to require the claimant show that he cannot obtain the funding from elsewhere.[24]

An arbitrator should be particularly cautious when ordering security against an impecunious individual; formerly the courts did not have jurisdiction to make an order against a natural person,[25] and it is submitted that the underlying reasons for this[26] remain a proper consideration for the arbitrator.

---

22. The DAC Report (see Appendix C) recognises this. It is submitted that the key factors are: (1) that the application is made by the offeror who has control over the relative timing of offers and applications for security; and (2) an applicant with this control cannot expect to seek an order for security which may result in the permanent dismissal of the claimant's case while sheltering behind the offer.

23. On the other hand, it has also been recognised that where the costs are unsecured, the claimant may be put into an advantageous position and may use the potentially irrecoverable costs of the proceedings to force a larger settlement than is his due. See *Pearson* v. *Naydler* [1977] 1 W.L.R. 899 *per* Sir Robert Megarry V.-C. at 907.

24. *Keary Developments* v. *Tarmac Construction Ltd.* [1995] 3 All E.R. 534; *Petromin S.A.* v. *Secnav Marine Ltd.* [1995] 1 Lloyd's Rep. 603.

25. Unless they were resident abroad; this consideration can no longer be taken into account in arbitration: section 38(3) of the Arbitration Act 1996.

26. That is the need to ensure that private individuals have proper access to justice.

6.5 Security for the costs of the arbitration

(5) *The effect of the respondent's behaviour on the claimant's want of means*

Where the claimant's current poor financial state has been, or is likely to be have been, brought about as a result of non-payment in respect of matters for which the claim is made, the court will weigh this in the balance.

(6) *The timing of the application*

If the application was brought late, when arrangements for hearings or other procedures had already been made, the court or arbitrator may take this into account.[27]

Illustrations

Sir Lindsay Parkinson & Co. Ltd. v. Triplan Ltd. [1973] 1 Q.B. 609 T was a small construction company engaged by SLP to undertake certain works of construction. A dispute arose and T commenced arbitration proceedings against SLP. There was no counterclaim. SLP made an open offer to T which T rejected. SLP made a late application to the court for security for its costs, which was heard just one working day before the hearing was due to commence. The master ordered that security be provided. T could not raise the security and appealed. The judge discharged the order for security and SLP appealed. The Court of Appeal held that the court had a discretion whether or not to order security for costs. Lord Denning set out, at 626, some of the factors which may be taken into account: "[Counsel] helpfully suggests some of the matters which the court might take into account, such as whether the company's claim is bona fide and not a sham and whether the company has a reasonably good prospect of success. Again it will consider whether there is an admission by the defendants on the pleadings or elsewhere that money is due. If there was a payment into court of a substantial sum of money (not merely a payment into court to get rid of a nuisance claim), that, too, would count. The court might also consider whether the application for security was being used oppressively—so as to try to stifle a genuine claim. It would also consider whether the company's want of means has been brought about by any conduct by the defendants, such as delay in payment or delay in doing their part of the work". Lawton L.J. added that the "discretion ought not to be hampered by any special rules or regulations, nor ought it to be put into a straitjacket by considerations of burden of proof. It is a discretion which the court will exercise having regard to all the circumstances of the case". SLP's appeal was dismissed as the claim was bona fide, had reasonable prospects of success, was supported by an open offer and the application was late.

Pearson v. Naydler [1977] 3 All E.R. 531 "It seems plain enough that the inability of the plaintiff company to pay the defendant's costs is a matter which not only opens up the jurisdiction but also provides a substantial factor in the decision whether to exercise it. It is inherent in the whole concept of the section that the court is to have the power to do what the company is likely to find difficulty in doing, namely, to order the company to provide security for the costs which *ex hypothesi* it is likely to be unable to pay. At the same time, the court must not allow the section to be used as an instrument of oppression, as by shutting out a small company from making a genuine claim against a large company", *per* Sir Robert Megarry V.-C. at 536–7.

---

27. The application in *Sir Lindsay Parkinson Ltd. v. Triplan Ltd.* [1973] 1 Q.B. 609 was brought very late. Where, however, the lateness is attributable to the claimant's conduct this will not count against the applicant: *Keary Developments v. Tarmac Construction Ltd.* [1995] 3 All E.R. 534.

Porzelack K.G. v. Porzelack U.K. Ltd. [1987] 1 W.L.R. 420 "Undoubtedly, if it can clearly be demonstrated that the plaintiff is likely to succeed, in the sense that there is a very high probability of success, then that is a matter which can properly be weighed in the balance. Similarly, if it can be shown that there is a very high probability that the defendant will succeed, that is a matter which can be weighed. But for myself I deplore the attempt to go into the merits of the case, unless it can clearly be demonstrated one way or another that there is a high degree of probability of success or failure", *per* Sir Nicolas Browne-Wilkinson V.-C. at 423.

Simaan General Contracting Co. v. Pilkington Glass Ltd. [1987] 1 W.L.R. 516 SGC brought an action against PG, alleging that PG had supplied defective glass to them. PG made a "without prejudice" offer of replacement glass but did not reserve a right to produce the letter on the question of costs. PG applied for security for costs since SGC were ordinarily resident abroad in Abu Dhabi. Held, the letter was wholly without prejudice and was inadmissible. SGC were ordered to provide security. But, *obiter*, a Calderbank letter would have been admissible.

Europa Holdings Ltd. v. Circle Industries (U.K.) plc (1992) 64 Build. L.R. 21 Upon CI's application for security to be ordered against EH, the Court of Appeal stressed that the test of jurisdiction was not whether EH could provide security at the present time, but whether it would be able to do so at the time when costs were to be paid, that is at the conclusion of the arbitration (*per* Dillon L.J. at 28). On the question whether or not security should be ordered, Dillon L.J. said at 30: "It is not . . . in the least desirable that all small well-managed companies should be forced to abandon their claims for payment by building owners or main contractors or general sub-contractors because they cannot give security for the costs of expensive and protracted litigation. I say that apart from the risk . . . that where small concerns contract with bigger concerns, in hard times the bigger concerns are tempted to do what they can to avoid paying smaller sub-contractors so as to preserve cash-flow, and . . . if the small sub-contractor starts proceedings for payment by trying to stifle the claim by an application for security. Obviously the fact that the plaintiff will be unable to pay the defendant's costs if successful in his defence is a major factor. . . . But it is also a factor which carries with it the seeds of oppression."

Keary Developments v. Tarmac Construction Ltd [1995] 3 All E.R. 534 This case contains an extensive recent review of the extent of the court's discretion to order security for costs under section 726(1) of the Companies Act 1985. While the power under which an arbitrator operates is different, it is submitted that the relevant factors are broadly similar. Peter Gibson L.J. said at 539 to 542:

"The relevant principles are, in my judgment, the following.
   1. As was established by this court in *Sir Lindsay Parkinson & Co. Ltd.* v. *Triplan Ltd.* [1973] 2 All E.R. 273, [1973] Q.B. 609, the court has a complete discretion whether to order security, and accordingly it will act in the light of all the relevant circumstances.
   2. The possibility or probability that the plaintiff company will be deterred from pursuing its claim by an order for security is not without more a sufficient reason for not ordering security (see *Okotcha* v. *Voest Alpine Intertrading GmbH* [1993] B.C.L.C. 474 at 479 *per* Bingham L.J., with whom Steyn L.J. agreed). By making the exercise of discretion under s 726(1) conditional on it being shown that the company is one likely to be unable to pay costs awarded against it, Parliament must have envisaged that the order might be made in respect of a plaintiff company that would find difficulty in providing security (see *Pearson* v. *Naydler* [1977] 3 All E.R. 531 at 536–7, [1977] 1 W.L.R. 899 at 906 *per* Megarry V.-C.).
   3. The court must carry out a balancing exercise. On the one hand it must weigh the

6.5 Security for the costs of the arbitration

injustice to the plaintiff if prevented from pursuing a proper claim by an order for security. Against that, it must weigh the injustice to the defendant if no security is ordered and at the trial the plaintiff's claim fails and the defendant finds himself unable to recover from the plaintiff the costs which have been incurred by him in his defence of the claim. The court will properly be concerned not to allow the power to order security to be used as an instrument of oppression, such as by stifling a genuine claim by an indigent company against a more prosperous company, particularly when the failure to meet that claim might in itself have been a material cause of the plaintiff's impecuniosity (see *Farrer* v. *Lacy, Hartland & Co.* (1885) 28 Ch.D. 482 at 485 *per* Bowen L.J.). But it will also be concerned not to be so reluctant to order security that it becomes a weapon whereby the impecunious company can use its inability to pay costs as a means of putting unfair pressure on the more prosperous company (see *Pearson* v. *Naydler* [1977] 3 All E.R. 531 at 537, [1977] 1 W.L.R. 899 at 906).

4. In considering all the circumstances, the court will have regard to the plaintiff company's prospects of success. But it should not go into the merits in detail unless it can clearly be demonstrated that there is a high degree of probability of success or failure (see *Porzelack K.G.* v. *Porzelack (U.K.) Ltd.* [1987] 1 All E.R. 1074 at 1077, [1987] 1 W.L.R. 420 at 423 *per* Browne-Wilkinson V.-C.). In this context it is relevant to take account of the conduct of the litigation thus far, including any open offer or payment into court, indicative as it may be of the plaintiff's prospects of success. But the court will also be aware of the possibility that an offer or payment may be made in acknowledgment not so much of the prospects of success but of the nuisance value of a claim.

5. The court in considering the amount of security that might be ordered will bear in mind that it can order any amount up to the full amount claimed by way of security, provided that it is more than a simply nominal amount; it is not bound to make an order of a substantial amount (see *Roburn Construction Ltd.* v. *William Irwin (South) & Co. Ltd.* [1991] B.C.C. 726).

6. Before the court refuses to order security on the ground that it would unfairly stifle a valid claim, the court must be satisfied that, in all the circumstances, it is probable that the claim would be stifled. There may be cases where this can properly be inferred without direct evidence (see *Trident International Freight Services Ltd.* v. *Manchester Ship Canal Co.* [1990] B.C.L.C. 263). In the *Trident* case there was evidence to show that the company was no longer trading, and that it had previously received support from another company which was a creditor of the plaintiff company and therefore had an interest in the plaintiff's claim continuing; but the judge in that case did not think, on the evidence, that the company could be relied upon to provide further assistance to the plaintiff, and that was a finding which, this court held, could not be challenged on appeal.

However, the court should consider not only whether the plaintiff company can provide security out of its own resources to continue the litigation, but also whether it can raise the amount needed from its directors, shareholders or other backers or interested persons. As this is likely to be peculiarly within the knowledge of the plaintiff company, it is for the plaintiff to satisfy the court that it would be prevented by an order for security from continuing the litigation (see *Flender Werft A.G.* v. *Aegean Maritime Ltd.* [1990] 2 Lloyd's Rep 27). . . .

7. The lateness of the application for security is a circumstance which can properly be taken into account (see *The Supreme Court Practice 1993* vol. 1, para. 23/1–3/28). But what weight, if any, this factor should have and in which direction it should weigh must depend upon matters such as whether blame for the lateness of the application is to be placed at the door of the defendant or at that of the plaintiff. It is proper to take into account the fact that costs have already been incurred by the plaintiff without there being an order for security. Nevertheless it is appropriate for the court to have regard to what costs may yet be incurred.

6.6 SECURITY FOR COSTS WHERE THE ARBITRATION IS PURELY ON DOCUMENTS

When the arbitration is conducted on documents only there is a presumption that no security should be ordered.

Illustration
Mavani v. Ralli Brothers Ltd. [1973] 1 All E.R. 555 "Generally speaking I do not think that the courts should order security for costs more or less automatically in an arbitration proceeding purely on documents on the ground that one of the parties is resident outside the jurisdiction, as it generally does in an action. I also do not believe that this is the practice of the courts ... The purpose and value of such arbitrations is that they should be conducted and decided with the minimum of complexity, delay and expense. This purpose would be substantially weakened if the practice in such arbitrations were to order the claimant more or less automatically to give security for costs", *per* Kerr J. at 562.

6.7 SECURITY FOR COSTS WHEN THERE IS A COUNTERCLAIM

6.7.1 Ordering security against a counterclaimant

An order for security for costs may be made against any claimant or counterclaimant.[28] "Where the counterclaim is put forward in respect of a matter wholly distinct from the claim ... the case may be treated as if [the counterclaimant] were a plaintiff, and only a plaintiff, and an order for security for costs may be made accordingly, in the absence of anything to the contrary".[29] If the respondent raises a counterclaim which is purely defensive no order for security may be made against the respondent.

If the counterclaim contains both a defence to the claim and an independent counterclaim,[30] the arbitrator must exercise his discretion and consider what "under all the circumstances will be fair and just as between the parties".[31] There are no rules of principle that: (a) because the counterclaim contains a defensive element no security can be ordered against the respondent,[32] or (b) because the counterclaim overtops the claim that it should be ordered.[33]

---

28. Sections 38(3) and 82(1) of the Arbitration Act 1996.
29. *Neck* v. *Taylor* [1893] 1 Q.B. 560 at 562 *per* Lord Esher M.R. The last phrase of this quotation indicates clearly that the matter remains one of discretion.
30. A counterclaim by set-off will normally be considered defensive if the set-off arises out of the same contract as the claim. This will be so even where there is no right to a defence of abatement: see *Cathery* v. *Lithodmos* 41 Build. L.R. 78.
31. *Neck* v. *Taylor* [1893] 1 Q.B. 560 at 562 *per* Lord Esher M.R.
32. *New Fenix Compagnie Anonyme* v. *General Accident* [1911] 2 K.B. 619 *per* Fletcher Moulton L.J. at 628.
33. *Cathery* v. *Lithodmos Ltd.* (1987) 41 Build. L.R. 76 *per* Dillon L.J. at 80.

6.7 Security for the costs of the arbitration

6.7.2 The effect of a counterclaim on the security to be provided by the claimant

If the respondent's counterclaim is distinct from the claim and the facts which support it are different, it may be disregarded when considering the question whether or not security should be provided by the claimant, unless the arbitrator feels that it is a factor which may properly be taken into account.

If the counterclaim is of significant magnitude and the facts which found the claim are substantially the same as those which found the counterclaim, an order for security against the claimant is inappropriate if the respondent is intent on pursuing the counterclaim. Such an order may force a stay[34] and enable the respondent to pursue his counterclaim while the claimant will be forced to raise identical issues in his defence as if there were no stay; if the claimant is successful, the stay will be lifted and all that will be achieved is that the respondent has gained the tactical advantage of forcing the claimant to pursue his claim "with one hand tied behind his back".[35] In cases where the facts of the claim and counterclaim are similar but not identical and there are additional factors involved (e.g. the party resisting the application is a nominal claimant) it may be appropriate to order both parties to supply security if the applicant volunteers to do so.[36]

Illustrations
Note in several of these examples, the reason why the plaintiff or counterclaimant was liable to provide security for costs is that they are not resident/based in the U.K. This is no longer a permissible reason for an arbitrator to order security.

Neck v. Taylor [1893] 1 Q.B. 560 T was resident abroad, but while in England she stayed at N's boarding house. T provided jewellery, apparently under duress from N, as security for rent. When T left the country, N sued for unpaid rent. T denied that any rent was unpaid and further pleaded by way of counterclaim that N had kept the jewellery and sought its return. N sought security for costs on the counterclaim since T was resident abroad. Held, by the Court of Appeal, that the claim and counterclaim arose out of the same transaction and whatever the form of the pleading, the substance of the counterclaim was defensive in nature. The court had a discretion whether or not to order security to be given. "[I]t does not seem to me just or fair that the defendant should have to give security for costs as the price of being allowed to plead such defence" *per* Lindley L.J. at 563. No security was ordered.

New Fenix Compagnie Anonyme D'Assurances de Madrid v. General Accident, Fire and Life Assurance Corporation Ltd. [1911] 2 K.B. 619 GA and NF were insurance companies, which transacted insurances on behalf of one another. They were required by their contract to make periodic accounts. GA issued proceedings in which

---

34. Technically an arbitrator could dismiss the claimant's case: section 41(6) of the Arbitration Act 1996. The reasons given for not imposing a stay are *a fortiori* applicable reasons for not ordering a dismissal of the claim, since here the dismissal cannot be undone, leading to a manifest injustice.

35. *B.J. Crabtree (Insulation) Ltd.* v. *G.P.T. Communication Systems Ltd.* (1990) 59 Build. L. Rep. 43, *per* Bingham L.J. at 52.

36. *The Silver Fir* [1980] 1 Lloyd's Rep. 371; *Flender Werft* v. *Aegean Maritime* [1990] 2 Lloyd's Rep. 27 at 31; *Petromin S.A.* v. *Secnav Marine Ltd.* [1995] 1 Lloyd's Rep. 603.

they alleged that payments due from NF were unpaid. By cross-action NF sued for the reopening of all previous records and a full account. GA sought security for costs since NF were based in Spain. The Court of Appeal decided that NF's cross-claim went beyond any defensive counterclaim which it might have and considered that it raised by implication the allegation of fraud. The Court of Appeal emphasised that the matter was governed by discretion; the fact that the cross-action went beyond what was purely defensive did not mean that security should necessarily be ordered. Taking into account all the circumstances of the case, the Court of Appeal ordered that security be provided.

T. Sloyan & Sons (Builders) Ltd v. Brothers of Christian Instruction [1974] 3 All E.R. 715 A building contractor, TSS, agreed to build a school for the respondent, BCI. BCI refused to pay all the agreed money alleging defects. TSS claimed and BCI put in a much larger counterclaim. BCI sought security for costs. £8,000 was ordered. TSS appealed on the amount only. Lane J. said at 721: "In my judgment, BCI's cross-claim set out in their defence and counterclaim can properly be treated as a defence or set-off (it does not matter for present purposes which it is called) to TSS's claim, insofar as the former does not exceed the latter. But insofar as BCI's claim exceeds TSS's claim it must be treated as a counterclaim to which the builders are in the position of defendants and in respect of which they cannot as such be ordered to give security. Such a mathematical calculation and ruling should have the merit, as counsel for TSS pointed out, of discouraging massive counterclaims brought *in terrorem*. He followed that by questioning whether the fact that TSS's claim is only one-sixth of BCI's claim would not justify securing one-sixth of their costs, but it does not seem to me that this would be a proper way of fixing the security to be ordered." The judge then ordered substantial security for the proceedings of £5,000, which took into account the discount for the size of the counterclaim.

Cathery v. Lithodmos Ltd. (1987) 41 Build. L.R. 76 C was a consulting engineer engaged by L to design flats in Bath. C claimed £27,000 as unpaid fees. L counterclaimed £109,000 for professional negligence arising out of the same contract. L was "massively insolvent" and C applied for security for costs in respect of the counterclaim. The judge dismissed the application. C appealed. The counterclaim was pleaded as a true set-off rather than an abatement because of the decision in *Hutchinson* v. *Harris* (1978) 10 Build. L.R. 19 (C.A.) which required it to be dealt with thus. But L had not taken up the position of plaintiff and hence the judge was entitled to treat the counterclaim as defensive. The judge had not fallen into the error of refusing security simply because the counterclaim was to an extent defensive and had exercised a proper discretion. The appeal was dismissed.

B.J. Crabtree (Insulations) Ltd. v. G.P.T. Communication Systems Ltd. (1990) 59 Build. L.R 43 BJC, a small company, claimed £78,000 against GPT for work performed under a building contract and GPT counterclaimed for £105,000. GPT sought an order for security for costs. BJC's directors proffered undertakings that they would not draw their remuneration entitlement from BJC's accounts. The judge, however, ordered security in the sum of £30,000. The Court of Appeal decided that the issues in the claim and counterclaim were essentially the same. A stay would not affect GPT's counterclaim, which would go ahead regardless. Hence "the costs that these defendants are incurring to defend themselves might equally, and perhaps preferably, be regarded as costs necessary to prosecute their counterclaim" *per* Bingham L.J. at 53. The purpose of making an order for security for costs was to protect a defendant who was forced to defend himself, not to provide a tactical advantage to a defendant who is intent on pursuing identical issues by counterclaim. The Court of

Appeal set aside the judge's order with the undertakings of BJC's directors to remain in force.

Flender Werft A.G. v. Aegean Maritime Ltd. [1990] 2 Lloyd's Rep. *27* AM, a shipping line incorporated in the Isle of Man, engaged FW, a German shipbuilder, to construct and provide two luxury liners. AM alleged that there were defects and commenced arbitration proceedings against FW. FW counterclaimed alleging that AM had failed to make payments and had committed various other breaches. The pleadings ran to over 100 pages and the arbitration promised to be expensive. FW sought an order for security for costs against AM. FW offered to provide voluntary security of the appropriate amount if AM were required to do likewise. AM contended that the claim and counterclaim raised identical issues. Held, the fact that the claim and counterclaim were based on similar facts was a significant factor. But it was not a case where the party which appeared as claimant was "more or less accidental". Furthermore since FW has agreed to provide voluntary security, and this being a case where neither party should be at risk in costs, each party was ordered to pay £150,000 as security for the costs of the other.

6.8 THE TIMING OF AN APPLICATION FOR SECURITY FOR COSTS

An application for security for costs may be made at any stage in the proceedings,[37] although it will rarely be made during the hearing unless there has been a change in circumstances of which the applicant has only recently become aware. A delay in making such an application may be a material factor on which to base the exercise of the discretion[38] unless the delay is attributable to the conduct of the claimant.[39] In any event where the application is brought late so that the costs still to be incurred are small relative to the size of the bona fide claim that may stifled, this may be taken into account in deciding that security should not be ordered.[40]

6.9 SECURITY FOR COSTS PROVISIONS IN THE ARBITRATION AGREEMENT OR RULES

The powers of the arbitrator in respect of security for costs are subject to any agreement made by the parties. Where the arbitration is governed by agreed rules of procedure, these may supplant the statutory provisions wholly or in part. Where the agreed rules stipulate preconditions for jurisdiction or grounds for the ordering of security for costs these must be complied with. Any such rules must be properly agreed by the parties; it is insufficient that the arbitrators involved frequently or invariably operate under such terms.[41]

37. *Re Smith* (1896) L.T. 46.
38. *Sir Lindsay Parkinson Ltd. v. Triplan Ltd.* [1973] 1 Q.B. 609.
39. *Keary Developments v. Tarmac Construction Ltd.* [1995] 3 All E.R. 534.
40. *Danemark v. B.A.A.*, 9 October 1996, Phillips L.J. (C.A.).
41. *Fal Bunkering of Sharjah v. Grecale Inc. of Panama* [1990] 1 Lloyd's Rep. 369.

Since the agreed rules of procedure are contractual in nature, the parties may clothe the arbitrator with any degree of power in relation to the ordering of security for costs.

6.10 THE AMOUNT OF SECURITY

The old cases suggest that when security is ordered, the amount should be a substantial amount representing a realistic valuation of the respondent's likely costs,[42] less a discount for the possibility that the case may settle early. Traditionally, two-thirds of a realistic bill of costs is allowed.[43] It is now clear that the court "can order any amount up to the full amount claimed by way of security, provided that it is more than a simply nominal amount".[44] It is not necessary either to order no security for costs or the full two-thirds; it is proper to order an intermediate amount which is fair in all the circumstances. In any event, the case law is based on the Companies Acts which stipulate that the security to be given must be "sufficient security". Section 38(3) of the Arbitration Act 1996 contains no such stipulation. Accordingly, it seems that the arbitrator may order that the claimant should provide such proportion of the respondents costs as appears to him fair and just in balancing the interests of the parties. It is submitted, however, that it will rarely be proper to order a nominal amount of security.

The proper amount of security may be determined by a balance between the realistic value of the respondent's costs and any potential for stifling the claim. The applicant will normally submit a draft bill of costs setting out the expected time and charging rate for those engaged or to be engaged on the case. The arbitrator will have to perform a rough-and-ready computation to determine to what extent the personnel, rates and hours claimed are reasonable, giving the benefit of any doubt to the claimant. Any direction limiting the recoverable costs of the arbitration must be taken into account.[45] The arbitrator may consider that an order for security for the entire course of the arbitration is appropriate; alternatively he may decide to order security for a shorter period and allow the respondent to make a supplementary application at a later date, if appropriate. When the arbitrator has come to a view on what the respondent's likely costs may be, he must decide what proportion, if any, of those costs is fair in all the circumstances and make an order accordingly.

Where the respondent advances a large counterclaim which overtops the claim, the claimant should not in principle be required to put up the costs of

---

42. *Dominion Brewery Ltd.* v. *Foster* (1897) L.R. 507 *per* Lord Lindley M.R.

43. *T. Sloyan & Sons (Builders) Ltd.* v. *Brothers of Christian Instruction* [1974] 3 All E.R. 715.

44. *Keary Developments* v. *Tarmac Construction Ltd.* [1995] 3 All E.R. 534 at 540, *per* Peter Gibson L.J. citing *Roburn Construction Ltd.* v. *William Irwin (South) & Co. Ltd.* [1991] B.C.C. 726.

45. Section 65 of the Arbitration Act 1996. See Chapter 8.

the entire proceedings even though each item in the counterclaim may be technically available as a set-off.[46]

6.11 SECURITY FOR THE ARBITRATOR'S FEES AND EXPENSES

6.11.1 Application by the respondent for the arbitrator's fees and expenses

If the claimant is unable to pay the costs of the arbitration, the respondent will not only have to meet his own legal bill but also the fees and expenses of the arbitrator.[47] Accordingly, where a respondent applies for an order for security for costs, it is submitted that he may properly include an application for security for these fees and expenses.

An arbitrator must, of course, avoid any suspicion that he has allowed the respondent's application in order to secure his own fees and expenses; however, it is not the arbitrator, but the respondent, who benefits principally from the order because both parties are jointly and severally liable for his fees. Nevertheless, an arbitrator must be careful not to stifle a claim.

6.11.2 An order for security in the absence of an application by the respondent

An arbitrator is empowered to order a claimant[48] to provide security for his own fees and expenses[49] without receiving an application.[50] This may seem particularly attractive to an arbitrator who has engaged experts, advisers and/or assessors. However, an arbitrator is in no position to undertake investigations to determine the financial status of the claimant. He would also have to put the matter to the claimant for the claimant to make submissions, which may be unseemly.

It is submitted that, in practice, an arbitrator should recognise that both parties are liable to pay his fees; he should, therefore, be very reluctant to order his own fees to be secured unless the respondent perceives the risk and has already made a successful application which demonstrates it.

Where, however, there are agreed or adopted rules of arbitration which allow the arbitrator to secure his own fees upon demand, he may do so.

---

46. *T. Sloyan & Sons (Builders) Ltd.* v. *Brothers of Christian Instruction* [1974] 3 All E.R. 715.
47. Section 28(1) of the Arbitration Act 1996.
48. Or counterclaimant: section 82(1) of the Arbitration Act 1996.
49. Section 59 of the Arbitration Act 1996.
50. Section 38(3) of the Arbitration Act 1996 does not require an application from a party.

6.12 THE ORDERING OF SECURITY BY AN ARBITRATOR: PRACTICE AND PROCEDURE

An arbitrator may direct that an application for security for costs be considered using any procedure which to him seems appropriate provided that he abides by his general duty to act fairly and impartially and to allow both parties an opportunity of putting their cases and dealing with that of the other. In practice, the following procedures and considerations will be appropriate.

6.12.1 Request for voluntary security

The application should be made after the claimant has been given an opportunity to provide voluntary security. The applicant should show that he has asked for reasonable security with supporting reasons and that he has given the claimant a reasonable time to provide it.

6.12.2 Service

The application must be properly served on the claimant, giving him a proper opportunity to respond.

6.12.3 Submissions

The parties must be given a proper opportunity to address the arbitrator. While applications for security for costs may be dealt with solely by written submissions, it is usually appropriate to hold a short oral hearing. Wherever the respondent makes out a prima facie case for the ordering of security, the likelihood that the claimant will be unable to pay the security arises, almost by definition. Since an order for security may result in dismissal of the claimant's case, the parties should normally be allowed an opportunity to make oral submissions, unless the arbitrator considers the application to be hopeless. The points which the parties should address include:

(1) whether the application for security for costs is a proper application. It must be demonstrated at least that there is a serious risk that the claimant will be unable to pay the costs of a successful respondent;
(2) whether the arbitrator should exercise his discretion to order security. This will generally involve submissions as to whether the general criteria set out by the courts have been established;[51]
(3) whether the period for which security is requested is reasonable. The applicant will often request security for the entire proceedings up to the time of the final award; the arbitrator must consider whether

51. See §6.5 above.

security for a shorter period is more appropriate with liberty to apply for additional security at a later stage;[52]

(4) whether the amount of security requested is reasonable. This will normally involve the applicant in submitting a draft bill of costs setting out the expected time and charging rate for those engaged or to be engaged on the case. The arbitrator will have to perform a rough-and-ready determination of the extent to which personnel, time and rates claimed are reasonable, giving the benefit of the doubt to the claimant.[53] The arbitrator need not order that the amount of security to be provided shall be the full amount; traditionally two-thirds of the respondent's expected costs have been ordered.[54] However, the arbitrator may order any proportion as suits the justice of the case.[55] Where the arbitrator has made a direction limiting the recoverable costs, this will, of course, limit the amount of security which can be ordered;

(5) whether the form in which the security is requested is appropriate. The options include: cash on deposit in a bank account under the arbitrator's control; cash on deposit with an independent stakeholder (e.g. an arbitral institution); bank bond or guarantee; where the claimant is part of a group of companies, a parent company guarantee; a charge over property. Arbitrators frequently give the parties a fixed time to agree upon a stakeholder or other form of security. In default of agreement, the arbitrator will give directions as to the provision of security;

(6) how long the claimant is to have for compliance and what is to happen if he does not comply. A period of time for the provision of the security should be stipulated; the order usually provides that a failure to provide the security within the stated time will result in a stay of the proceedings. A stay has the effect that no further costs may be incurred in the substantive proceedings until the stay is lifted. Should the claimant fail to provide the security, then, whether or not a stay is ordered, the arbitrator may issue a peremptory order[56]; where the

---

52. The general practice is that a party who has successfully obtained an order for security may make a new application for increased security if the circumstances change, or if the previous order was made in respect of an application which requested security for part only of the arbitral proceedings. An unsuccessful applicant may be heard again if there is a radical change in the circumstances or if the party resisting the application wrongly suppressed the facts about his means or status.

53. The details of the costs are likely to be included within a sworn statement or affidavit. The arbitrator should, therefore, be cautious about dismissing out of hand any costs which are included. He should receive submissions from the party resisting the application. He should form his own judgment as to whether the items included in the bill are both necessary for the proper pursuit of the applicant's case and are reasonable in respect of the claimed times and charging rates.

54. *T. Sloyan & Sons (Builders) Ltd.* v. *Brothers of Christian Instruction* [1974] 3 All E.R. 715.

55. *Keary Developments* v. *Tarmac Construction Ltd.* [1995] 3 All E.R. 534; *Roburn Construction Ltd.* v. *William Irwin (South) & Co. Ltd.* [1991] B.C.C. 726.

56. That is an order in the form: "Unless the claimant complies with my order of [date of the original order] by [final date for compliance] I shall . . .".

claimant fails to comply with the peremptory order the arbitrator may by award dismiss the claim.[57]

6.12.4 The order

Where the arbitrator considers that security should be given, he should draw up a formal order, stating clearly:

(1) the amount of security to be provided;
(2) the form in which the security is to be provided;
(3) the time by which the security is to be provided;
(4) the effects of non-compliance.

6.12.5 Costs of the application

The arbitrator should consider what costs order, if any, should be made.

(1) If an application is unsuccessful, the party resisting the application will ordinarily be entitled to his costs of resisting it, unless the arbitrator feels that some other costs order is appropriate. For example, the arbitrator may have felt that there was a strong prima facie case for ordering security but that such an order may have stifled the claim; it may appear to him unfair in these circumstances to penalise the unsuccessful applicant in any event and he may decide that the costs of the application should be costs in the arbitration.

(2) If the application is successful, the arbitrator may decide that a prior request for voluntary security was very obviously reasonable, that the application was bound to succeed, and that therefore the applicant should have his costs. But this will be unusual and the normal order will be costs in the arbitration; whatever the merits of the application at the time, if it later transpires that the party resisting the application always had a good claim he should not be required to pay to provide security for prosecuting it.

In some instances, where parties prepare excessive documentation in support of their application or response, it may be appropriate to order that the excess costs are to be borne by the party incurring them in any event. If appropriate, the arbitrator should also deal specifically with any special costs associated

57. Section 41(5), (6) of the Arbitration Act 1996 provide: "(5) If without showing sufficient cause a party fails to comply with any order or directions of the tribunal, the tribunal may make a peremptory order to the same effect, prescribing such time for compliance with it as the tribunal considers appropriate. (6) If a claimant fails to comply with a peremptory order of the tribunal to provide security for costs, the tribunal may make an award dismissing his claim."

with the provision of security, such as the costs of providing a bond.[58]

6.13 CHALLENGING THE ORDER

There is no mechanism under the Arbitration Act 1996 for a party to challenge an order for security for costs unless the order indicates sufficient lack of impartiality to have the arbitrator removed. Where a party against whom such an order is made is unable to raise the security and an award is made dismissing the claim,[59] the claimant may attempt to challenge the award on the grounds that there has been a serious irregularity.[60] Provided the arbitrator allowed the claimant a proper opportunity to put his case, it is thought that the application will succeed only where the order for security was clearly wrong.

58. The costs of providing security will ordinarily be costs in the arbitration. A claimant with a good case should not have to pay for the provision of security. On the other hand, the fact that a bond is provided is usually to the benefit of the party providing the security rather than the applicant, since otherwise an immediate cash payment would be required. In this, however, as with all questions of costs, the arbitrator should exercise his own independent judgment when making his order as to costs.

59. Section 41(5), (6) of the Arbitration Act 1996.

60. Section 68(2)(a) of the Arbitration Act 1996.

CHAPTER 7

OFFERS OF SETTLEMENT: COSTS PROTECTION

7.1 OFFERS AND COSTS PROTECTION

The costs involved in commercial arbitrations can be substantial. In order to provide a degree of costs protection, a party at risk may make an offer of settlement. The law encourages the settlement of disputes[1] and generally requires a party to compromise proceedings upon being made a reasonable offer. In practice a reasonable offer is one which is equivalent to or greater than the legal entitlement of the offeree. Thus, where the offeree rejects the offer and continues with the arbitration, he will prima facie be liable for the costs incurred subsequent to the offer if he fails to recover more than the value of the offer. This basic principle is always subject to the overriding discretion of the arbitrator and to a number of refinements which will be considered in this chapter.

Illustration
Tramountana Armadora S.A. v. Atlantic Shipping Co. S.A. [1978] Lloyd's Rep.
391 "How should an arbitrator deal with costs where there has been a 'sealed offer'? I think that he should ask himself the question: 'Has the claimant achieved more by rejecting the offer and going on with the arbitration than he would have achieved if he had accepted the offer?' This is a simple question to answer. ... If the claimant in the end has achieved no more than he would have achieved by accepting the offer, the continuance of the arbitration after that date has been a waste of time and money. Prima facie, the claimant should recover his costs up to the date of the offer and should be ordered to pay the respondent's costs after that date. If he has achieved more by going on, the respondent should pay the costs throughout. Let me stress, however, that while this is the general rule, there is an overriding discretion", *per* Donaldson J. at 397–8.

---

1. In order to encourage settlement, the law provides that any negotiations which are reasonably directed towards settlement are "privileged". This means that they must not be revealed to the tribunal who has jurisdiction without the consent of all those who are entitled to the privilege. The question of privilege is of the utmost importance in relation to offers of settlement generally and is dealt with at §7.11.

7.2 PAYMENTS INTO COURT

The rules of court allow a defendant to make a payment into court which may be accepted by the plaintiff.[2] Payment is made into an official administered account. Notice is given to the plaintiff who has 21 days in which to accept the payment-in.[3] If he accepts it, he also recovers his reasonable costs. If the payment-in is not accepted, the action continues. When the court has made its decision on the substantive issues, submissions are made on costs, at which point in time the parties may refer to the payment-in. If the plaintiff "beats the payment-in" he is prima facie entitled to his costs as well as the money paid in and the excess to make up the judgment sum. If he fails to beat the payment-in, the defendant is prima facie entitled to recover the excess of the money paid in as well as his costs from the time at which the offer should have been accepted.

A defendant is not obliged to make a payment-in in respect of the totality of the plaintiff's claims but may do so in respect of specific causes of action. Furthermore, a plaintiff against whom a counterclaim is made may make a payment-in in respect of the counterclaim or any specific causes of action therein.

A payment-in may not be accepted after 21 days have elapsed without leave of the court. There is no "right" to accept payment after 21 days[4] and leave will not normally be given if the risks of the claim have changed adversely to the plaintiff.[5] If leave is given for the plaintiff to accept the money out of time, the plaintiff will be liable for the costs subsequent to the payment-in.[6]

In some circumstances, the defendant may, with the leave of the court, take the money out of court. This will only be allowed where the circumstances change significantly to the benefit of the defendant.[7]

7.3 OFFERS IN ARBITRATION PROCEEDINGS COMPARED WITH PAYMENTS INTO COURT

The provisions of the rules of court assume the existence of an administered account into which the sum offered can be paid without this fact being revealed to the tribunal. These facilities are not generally available in arbitration[8] and

2. Order 22 of the Rules of the Supreme Court. The rules are currently under review following the Woolf Report (*Access to Justice*, Lord Woolf, H.M.S.O., 1996), and it is thought that the opportunities for making offers will increase. There are proposals that the plaintiff may be entitled and encouraged to make offers as to the level of settlement which he is prepared to accept.
3. Where it is made less than 21 days before the trial, it may not be accepted after the start of the trial; where the offer is made during the trial, the 21-day period is reduced to two days.
4. *Cumper* v. *Pothecary* [1941] 2 K.B. 58.
5. *Proetta* v. *Times Newspapers* [1991] 1 W.L.R. 337.
6. *Griggs* v. *Petts* [1939] 4 All E.R. 39.
7. *Garner* v. *Cleggs* [1983] 1 W.L.R. 862.
8. Some arbitration institutions may provide in their rules that payments are to be made into an account administered by that institution. The majority of arbitrations are, however, *ad hoc* arbitrations and such facilities are unavailable.

less formal systems have been developed which the law considers to provide similar or equivalent costs protection as a payment into court.

An offer made in arbitration proceedings differs from a payment into court not only in respect of the procedures involved, but also in its legal nature. Offers made in arbitration proceedings are contractual in nature[9]; hence they may be accepted only in the manner expressly or impliedly provided for in the offer and may be withdrawn. A payment into court is not contractual but procedural and its mode of acceptance is regulated entirely by the rules of court.[10] The fact that a payment into court and an offer in arbitration proceedings are based on different legal principles means that the analogy between the two often breaks down. Arguments as to the effect of an offer in arbitration proceedings based on the practice of the courts are, therefore, frequently misleading.

7.4 CLASSIFICATION OF OFFERS IN ARBITRATION PROCEEDINGS

Three species of offer may be distinguished.

7.4.1 An offer which is wholly without prejudice

This is an offer which is made by the offeror to the offeree in terms which indicate that the offer is not to be revealed to the tribunal at any stage.[11] This species of offer cannot affect the costs position.[12]

7.4.2 An open offer

By letter the offeror invites the offeree to settle the claim for a stated sum £x (plus costs). The letter is expressed to be open or is published in circumstances where it is clear that no privilege is claimed upon it. Any party may refer to it at any stage. Where, however, an open offer is treated by both parties as a secret document and its existence is not revealed to the arbitrator, it may with time acquire a degree of privilege; a party who is minded to use it for his own purposes at a later stage in the arbitration should advise the other party of his intentions so that representations may be prepared or, if appropriate, an injunction to restrain its publication may be sought.

9. *Huron Liberian Co.* v. *Rheinoel G.m.b.H.* [1985] 2 Lloyd's Rep. 58.
10. *Cumper* v. *Pothecary* [1941] 2 K.B. 58 where Goddard L.J. said at 67 "[T]here is nothing contractual about payment into court. It is wholly a procedural matter and has no true analogy to a settlement arranged by the parties out of court, which, of course, does constitute a contract."
11. See *Simaan General Contracting Co.* v. *Pilkington Glass Ltd.* [1987] 1 W.L.R. 517 for an example of such an offer.
12. *Stotesbury* v. *Turner* [1943] 1 K.B. 370.

7.4 Offers of settlement: costs protection

7.4.3 A sealed offer or Calderbank letter

By letter, the offeror invites the offeree to accept a sealed or "without prejudice" offer of £x (plus costs) in settlement on the express or implied understanding that such offer may be revealed to the tribunal at the time when the question of costs is to be decided, but not before.

The term "sealed offer" relates to the practice of sealing a copy of the offer in an envelope which is delivered to the arbitrator (or a stakeholder), to be opened only after the substantive issues have been decided.[13] "The expression 'sealed offer' is something of a misnomer, since it is not sealed at the time when it is made"[14]; the offeree obviously sees the offer. A sealed offer is intended to reproduce, so far as it can be done, the procedure available in litigation.

It is now clear that a sealed offer need not be delivered to the arbitrator. A simple letter of offer to the offeree expressed to be "without prejudice save as to costs"[15] will produce an identical effect.[16] Such letters may still be described as sealed offers; they are also commonly referred to as Calderbank letters.[17]

Both open and sealed offers have an identical effect on costs, putting the offeree at risk for costs if he fails to recover more than the sum offered.

Illustrations

Stotesbury v. Turner [1943] 1 K.B. 370 The claimant had carried out work for the respondent for which he claimed £1,135. The respondent contended that only £120 was due. During the preliminary meeting, an informal conversation took place in the presence of the arbitrator in which the respondent said that efforts to reach a settlement had been made, without prejudice, and that he would be making an offer of £550; this offer was later rejected by the claimant in a letter expressed to be without prejudice. The letter was included in the bundle of documents for the hearing: the respondent's counsel objected to its being before the arbitrator. The arbitrator, however, said it was useless to object as he already knew of the offer. The arbitrator went on to award the claimant £350. In dealing with costs he said that he had taken the offer into account and that the claimant would be liable for the respondent's costs of the arbitration and the costs of the award. The claimant applied to have the award as to costs set aside. Atkinson J. said: "It seems to me that the arbitrator was wrong in giving any effect to the friendly talk which had taken place without prejudice and to the refusal of the offer which had been made. In my opinion, he had no material on which he could exercise his discretion in the way he did." The award as to costs was set aside and, by consent, both parties agreed to pay their own costs of the arbitration and half the arbitrator's fees.

13. See *King* v. *Thomas McKenna Ltd.* [1991] 2 Q.B. 480 at 492–3.

14. *Huron Liberian Co.* v. *Rheinoel G.m.b.H.* [1985] 2 Lloyd's Rep. 58 *per* Staughton J. at 60.

15. If it is simply headed "without prejudice" and contains a statement that the offer it contains will be brought to the tribunal's attention on the question of costs this may have the same effect (this was the situation in *Cutts* v. *Head* [1984] 1 Ch. 290). The formula "without prejudice save as to costs" is, however, safer and in all respects preferable.

16. *Cutts* v. *Head* [1984] 1 Ch. 290.

17. After *Calderbank* v. *Calderbank* [1976] Fam. 93 in which the practice was first suggested to provide costs protection in cases involving the distribution of property upon the dissolution of a marriage.

Tramountana Armadora S.A. v. Atlantic Shipping Co. S.A. [1978] 1 Lloyd's Rep. 391 "Offers of settlement in arbitral proceedings can be of three kinds, namely, 'without prejudice', 'sealed' and 'open'. [1] A 'without prejudice' offer can never be referred to by either party at any stage of the proceedings, because it is in the public interest that there should be a procedure whereby the parties can discuss their differences freely and frankly and make offers of settlement without fear of being embarrassed by these exchanges if, unhappily, they do not lead to a settlement. [2] A 'sealed offer' is the arbitral equivalent of making a payment into court in settlement of the litigation or of particular causes of action in that litigation ... it would be wholly improper for the arbitrator to look at [the sealed offer] before he has reached a final decision on the matters in dispute other than as to costs, or to revise that decision in the light of the terms of the sealed offer when he sees them. [3] An 'open offer', properly so called, is one to which either party can refer at any stage of the proceedings. In an appropriate case, it may influence the arbitrator both in his decision on the matters in dispute and on the order as to costs", *per* Donaldson J. at 396–7.

Cutts v. Head [1984] 1 Ch. 290 C claimed injunctions and damages against H in relation to C's enjoyment of fishing rights. H counterclaimed for certain rights and for damages for trespass and nuisance. C wrote to H before the trial offering a settlement, the terms of which included undertakings which could not adequately be represented by a payment into court. The letter was headed "without prejudice", but in the body of the text C reserved the right to bring the letter to the court's attention on the question of costs. At trial H obtained a judgment which was of little value to him and which was certainly less beneficial to him than the terms of the offer. When submissions were being made on costs, the judge refused to consider the letter on the ground that it was expressed to be without prejudice. He ordered H to pay one half of C's costs. C appealed on the question of costs. The Court of Appeal held that the policy underlying without prejudice offers was that they assisted in reaching compromise. The ability to bring a letter such as C's to the attention of the court did not undermine that policy. Indeed it was fully consonant with it. The order for costs was varied; C was to have half his costs until the date when the offer should have been accepted and all his costs thereafter.

7.5 THE OFFER AS A PRECISE BENCHMARK

When an offer has been made, the strict position at law is that it shall be considered by the arbitrator when making his decision as to costs. The strict position should be emphasised because the arbitrator must exercise his discretion as to costs in the light of all the circumstances and cannot be fettered by rules.

Where an effective offer is made, the practice is that, save for exceptional circumstances, the level of the offer represents a precise benchmark against which the ultimate sum recovered by the offeree is to be measured.[18] In general, if the offeree fares one penny better than the offer he is prima facie entitled to his costs. Otherwise the offeror is prima facie entitled to his costs after the date of the offer.

18. *Archital Luxfer Ltd.* v. *Henry Boot Construction Ltd.* [1981] 1 Lloyd's Rep. 642, *per* Gibson J. at 653.

If there are additional factors such as the unreasonable conduct of the parties or any of them this may be taken into account.[19] But absent such factors, the established practice seems to require the precise comparison of the offer with the eventual recovery.

In the absence of an offer, the claimant must be "substantially successful" in all the circumstances in order to recover his costs.[20] However, once his opponent makes an offer, the effect is that the opponent puts the claimant on notice that the definition of "success" is to be treated in a precise mathematical way. One of the consequences of this is that an offeror who makes an inadequate offer may put himself at more risk than if no offer had been made.[21] The wisdom of such a mechanical approach has been questioned judicially[22]; however, the Court of Appeal has not approved suggestions that some latitude be given using the concept of a *de minimis* difference between the offer and the eventual award.[23] It is submitted that the principle of the precise benchmark is entirely sound and proper, provided the arbitrator does not consider that his discretion is fettered by it. It cannot be said that an offeree who rejects the offer and subsequently recovers an award which is marginally in excess of the offer was any more unreasonable than the offeror who made the marginally inadequate offer. In reality, it is the offeror who controls the level of the offer, and it is he who should bear the responsibility for an inadequate offer.

Illustrations
Cheeseman v. Bowaters United Kingdom Paper Mills Ltd. [1971] 1 W.L.R. 1773
The plaintiff sued the defendant for personal injury. The defendant made payment into court of £750. On its pleaded case, the plaintiff recovered £749.78. The Court of

19. *Tramountana Armadora S.A.* v. *Atlantic Shipping Co. S.A.* [1978] 1 Lloyd's Rep. 391: "If, for example, the way in which the claimant conducted the arbitration in the period before the sealed offer was made is open to criticism, this may be a ground for depriving him of all or part of his costs or even, in a very extreme case, of requiring him to pay all or part of the costs of the respondent. Conversely, if after the sealed offer has been made and rejected, the conduct of the respondent is open to criticism, this may be a ground for depriving the respondent of all or part of the costs incurred by him in this period and might even, in a very extreme case, justify an order that he pay all or part of the claimant's costs" *per* Donaldson J. at 398.
20. See §3.2 generally and the cases discussed there, including *Perry* v. *Stopher* [1959] 1 All E.R. 713; *Harris* v. *Petherick* (1879) 4 Q.B.D. 611; *Anglo-Cyprian Trade Agencies Ltd.* v. *Paphos Wine Industries Ltd.* [1951] 1 All E.R. 873; *Alltrans Express Ltd.* v. *C.V.A. Holdings Ltd.* [1984] 1 W.L.R. 394; *Lipkin Gorman* v. *Karpnale Ltd.* [1989] 1 W.L.R. 1340; *Beoco Ltd.* v. *Alfa Laval Co. Ltd.* [1984] 3 W.L.R. 1179.
21. Where the claimant recovers a small amount relative to his claim, it is not unknown for the claimant to be required to pay the costs of the arbitration (see e.g. *Perry* v. *Stopher* [1959] 1 All E.R. 713). In *The Emvar* [1984] 2 Lloyd's Rep. 581 the owner made a large claim but recovered only £600 and was required to pay all the costs. If an offer of £500 had been made, the arbitrator is likely to have made the opposite order as to costs. The seeming paradox that the respondent could put himself at an advantage by failing to make an offer was raised in argument by counsel for the aggrieved owner in *The Emvar*, but to no avail. The moral seems clear: if an offer is to made, it ought to be realistic enough to create a real risk for the other party.
22. *Archital Luxfer Ltd.* v. *Henry Boot Construction Ltd.* [1981] 1 Lloyd's Rep. 642, *per* Gibson J. at 652.
23. *The Maria* [1993] 2 Lloyd's Rep. 168, *per* Sir Thomas Bingham at 175 and Evans L.J. at 181.

Appeal held that the defendants were entitled to their costs subsequent to the payment-in.

Archital Luxfer Ltd. v. Henry Boot Construction Ltd. [1981] 1 Lloyd's Rep. 642
"It is not clear to me that a fair and civilised body of law necessarily requires inclusion of a principle that, if an offer of payment into court is too small by any amount or fraction of the sum recovered, it must be wholly disregarded, but such a principle is clearly included in the law and practice which I must apply", *per* Gibson J. at 652–3.

7.6 TIME FACTORS ASSOCIATED WITH OFFERS OF SETTLEMENT

7.6.1 The duration of an offer

An offer in arbitration proceedings is contractual in nature and therefore remains open for acceptance until it is withdrawn or lapses. An offer which is not expressed to be open for any specified period of time will normally contain an implied term that it is to remain open for acceptance only until the date of the hearing; otherwise, the offeree might accept it immediately before the award is made.

7.6.2 Offers of settlement made before the arbitration commences

Arbitration proceedings generally begin when one party serves upon the other a notice to concur in the appointment of an arbitrator.[24] Costs may run from a period in advance of this notice.[25] Accordingly, it is thought that the arbitrator may properly take into account an offer made prior to the commencement of the arbitration.

7.6.3 Offers made shortly before or at the hearing

In litigation proceedings, a payment into court made before the trial must be accepted before the trial commences. Where a payment-in is made within 21 days of trial, the judge may consider it when deciding on costs, though he will take account of the shortened time available for acceptance.[26] An offer made within 21 days of the arbitration hearing may be taken into account by the arbitrator in the same way as a late payment into court.[27]

Payments into court made during the trial must be accepted within two days, but in any event before the judge begins to deliver his judgment. Costs do not automatically follow the acceptance of such a payment-in; here the judge has a wider discretion. In the absence of any inconsistent express

24. Section 14 of the Arbitration Act 1996.
25. See *Re Gibson's Settlement Trusts* [1981] Ch. 179 for an analogous litigation situation.
26. *King* v. *Weston-Howell* [1988] 2 All E.R. 375.
27. *The Angeliki* [1982] 2 Lloyd's Rep. 594.

provisions, it is thought that similar terms will be implied into an offer made during an arbitration hearing. Such an offer of settlement should, however, it is submitted, contain an offer in respect of costs and any acceptance will create a binding agreement. If such an offer is not accepted, the arbitrator will, it is submitted, have a discretion to take a broad view as to whether or not the offer should reasonably have been accepted at that stage.

7.6.4 Acceptance of an offer after more than 21 days

Where a plaintiff in litigation proceedings accepts a payment into court within 21 days, he is entitled to his costs up until the date of acceptance in addition to the amount of the payment-in. A later acceptance is possible with leave of the court; but if leave is given, the plaintiff is required to pay costs from the date at which the 21 days elapsed.[28] The 21-day period is a compromise between the need for the plaintiff to have an adequate time for consideration and the interests of the defendant in protecting his costs.

It is submitted that here the analogy with a payment into court applies in relation to offers in arbitration proceedings. If such an offer contains no express terms as to the cost effects of acceptance after a specified period, there will, it is submitted, be an implied term that it can only be accepted by the offeree on the basis that he pays the offeror's costs subsequent to the expiry of a reasonable period. This period will, it is submitted, be 21 days by analogy. There seems, however, to be no authority on this point and it is recommended, therefore, that an offer should include an express term that its acceptance after 21 days (or some other longer period) will be subject to the offeree's payment of the offeror's costs following the expiry of that period.

7.6.5 Limited duration offers and their effect on costs

An offer in arbitration proceedings is contractual. It may be expressed to be open for a limited time. If it is not accepted within that time, it lapses and may not be accepted thereafter without the consent of the offeror. Likewise, it may be withdrawn by the offeror at any time and may, if expressly rejected by the offeree, cease to be available for acceptance.

A respondent obtains the maximum protection in costs by making an offer which continues to be available for acceptance until the start of the hearing, with the proviso that if it is accepted by the claimant after 21 days, the claimant will be liable for the costs after the 21 days have expired.[29]

Respondents, however, frequently make offers open for acceptance for a limited period, usually 21 days. The effect of this is not entirely clear. While such an approach raises a number of parallels with the scheme for payment

---

28. *Griggs* v. *Petts* [1939] 4 All E.R. 39.

29. See for example the sealed offer in *Archital Luxfer Ltd.* v. *Henry Boot Construction Ltd.* [1981] 1 Lloyd's Rep. 642; the period for acceptance here was one month.

into court,[30] it does not allow the claimant to apply to accept out of time. Initial surprise has been expressed by some judges that short-lived offers are proposed as having an effect upon costs[31] and in at least three reported cases, decisions of tribunals that short-lived offers had no effect on costs have not been overturned on appeal.[32] In terms of principle, it has been suggested that a significant reason why the payment into court puts the claimant at risk is that the claimant continues with the action despite the fact that he could accept the payment-in; therefore an offer which is subsequently withdrawn bites on costs during the period when it was available for acceptance but not subsequently.[33] Nevertheless, a review of the cases suggests that there are no hard and fast rules and the matter is one for the consideration of the arbitrator in the light of all the circumstances.[34] The arbitrator may properly consider such an offer.[35] He is not required to treat it as equivalent to an offer which is available up until the date of the hearing and may even misdirect himself if he acts on the principle that a short-lived offer is equivalent to an offer which remains open.[36]

Where an offer has lapsed or been withdrawn, the offeree may later make a request to accept it out of time on the basis that he will pay the offeror's costs between the date of the offer and the date of the late request. It may be that the costs protection available to the offeror has already expired.[37] But if it is alive and the offeror refuses to allow this acceptance out of time, this will be an additional reason to take the view that the costs protection no longer exists.[38]

Illustrations
The Angeliki [1982] 2 Lloyd's Rep. 594 In a shipping arbitration, the date of the hearing was fixed for 26 January 1982. On 22 January 1982 the charterers made an offer. It was not accepted. The hearing commenced as arranged and on the following day, 27 January 1982, the arbitration was settled on the terms set out in the offer which

---

30. Most importantly, a payment into court cannot be automatically accepted after 21 days and the placing of this time limit in arbitration offers is presumably intended to create this effect.

31. In *Huron Liberian Co. v. Rheinoel G.m.b.H.* [1985] 2 Lloyd's Rep. 58, Staughton J. said at 61: "one has an initial reaction of surprise, and even disapproval, at the suggestion that a sealed offer may not still be open for acceptance until the hearing of the arbitration."

32. *The Toni* [1974] 1 Lloyd's Rep. 489; *Garner v. Cleggs* [1983] 1 W.L.R. 862; *Mark Amy Ltd. v. Olcott Investments Ltd.*, Royal Court of Jersey (Samedi Division), 4 November 1996.

33. *Garner v. Cleggs* [1983] 1 W.L.R. 862 *per* Robert Goff L.J. at 872.

34. *The Toni* [1974] 1 Lloyd's Rep. 489 *per* Cairns L.J. at 498: "I consider that no rigid rule can be laid down as to how a judge's discretion as to costs should be exercised when an offer to accept a certain proportion of responsibility has been made and later withdrawn . . ."

35. See generally *Huron Liberian Co. v. Rheinoel G.m.b.H.* [1985] 2 Lloyd's Rep. 58: "In my view, an arbitrator would be justified in exercising his discretion as to costs in favour of the respondent in an arbitration . . . where the amount recovered is less than the sealed offer, even if the offer was rejected, or expressly withdrawn, or a counter-offer was made. Whether he does so exercise his discretion is, of course, another matter", *per* Staughton J. at 61.

36. *Garner v. Cleggs* [1983] 1 W.L.R. 862.

37. Following from *Garner v. Cleggs* [1983] 1 W.L.R. 862.

38. *Huron Liberian Co. v. Rheinoel G.m.b.H.* [1985] 2 Lloyd's Rep. 58: ". . . the claimant in an arbitration should be entitled to tell the arbitrator that the offer was withdrawn; or that, although he at first rejected it or made a counter-offer, he later tried to accept it and was told that it was no longer open", *per* Staughton J. at 61.

had been made five days earlier. The question of costs was left to the arbitrators, who ignored the offer when deciding liability for costs. The charterers applied to have the award as to costs remitted. Lloyd J. said at 597: "[T]here is [in court proceedings] no rule that a defendant is automatically entitled to his costs after a payment-in if it is made less than 21 days before the trial. If, to take an extreme case, the payment-in is made on the day before the trial and the trial goes ahead, and if the plaintiff eventually recovers less than the amount of the payment-in, there is no automatic rule that, in those circumstances, the defendant should recover his costs of the trial. The matter is quite clearly one which is wholly and completely within the discretion of the court; there is no rule of thumb ... So, here, it seems to me, that the question of costs, in relation to the sealed offer, was entirely within the discretion of the arbitrators. If they took the view that this sealed offer made, as it was, on January 22, was made too late for the claimants to be able to consider it, take advice on it and decide what to do, if that was the view they took, then it was certainly within their discretion to say that it should not affect the result of the costs. . . ."

The Toni [1974] 1 Lloyd's Rep. 489 There was a collision between two ships, the Toni and the Cardo, off the coast of Africa. The parties were the owners of the ships and the dispute concerned responsibility for the collision. On 14 February 1972 the owners of the Cardo offered to settle the matter on the basis that each ship was equally to blame and that costs were to be in proportion. The owners of the Toni did not respond. The offer was then withdrawn on 29 March 1972. The trial commenced on 30 October 1972. Brandon J. decided that both ships were equally at fault. He ordered that each of the ship owners should pay half the claim and half the costs of the other party. He disregarded the offer which had been made and then withdrawn. The owners of the Cardo appealed as to costs, on the grounds that their earlier offer was as good as the final result to the owners of the Toni. They claimed, therefore, that the judge should have taken the offer into account and that the judge had wrongly exercised his discretion in making his order as to costs. Edmund Davies L.J. referred to an earlier case in which an offer had been made which affected costs and said at 494–5: "But there the offer, once made, was never withdrawn before trial, and that, in my judgment, is a most material distinction. With respect, the learned judge was right in contrasting the present situation with cases of payment into court under Order 22 ... where the position is preserved until the trial. Here the [owners of the Cardo] had terminated it months before the trial. In these circumstances, Brandon J. considered that, in exercising his discretion as to costs, he should disregard the fact that the offer had ever been made. I consider that he was entitled to do so. . . ." Megaw L.J. said at 496–7: "It is no doubt convenient, in Admiralty actions as in arbitrations, that a party should be able to encourage the other party to settle by making an open offer. It is no doubt right that, normally, where such an offer has been made and maintained, but not accepted by the other party, and the party who has made the offer obtains a result in the litigation no less favourable to him than the terms of the offer, the judge should have a discretion to make a special order as to costs in his favour. The normal exercise of the discretion would be to give the offeror his costs from the date of the offer. But it seems to me that, normally at least, the discretion would not be properly exercised in favour of the offeror unless he had maintained the offer up to the commencement of the trial of the action. I do not see why it should be thought that the offeror should acquire some kind of moral or discretionary right to the whole of the costs thereafter incurred merely because he has, for a period of time ending before the start of the hearing, held out an offer, which has not been accepted during that period. If he is to get the benefit of a subsequent order as to costs, it ought normally to be on the basis that his offer has been a continuing offer up to the start of the trial. It may be that there are exceptional cases. But I do not think that the mere fact of no response being made for six weeks is such as to bring this case within the range of such possible exceptional cases ... that would mean that a party who had once made an open offer, and thereafter wrongly thought it was over-generous, could protect himself against the consequences of his supposed over-generosity by withdrawing the offer, and yet would still be entitled to get the benefit of it. . . ."

Garner v. Cleggs [1983] 1 W.L.R. 862 The plaintiff sued the solicitor defendants for their alleged mishandling of a conveyance which resulted in the plaintiff buying a property which did not comply with his requirements. The defendants made a payment into court of £26,000 in August 1981. However, in October 1981 the defendants received information from the vendor of the property that the plaintiff had known the type of property he was purchasing all along. The defendants sought leave to withdraw the payment-in. The court gave leave and the money was withdrawn in February 1982. The trial commenced three weeks later in March 1982. At trial the informant vendor's evidence was not accepted and the plaintiff succeeded on a number of heads of claim. He recovered a sum of £24,000, which was less than the previously withdrawn offer. On the question of costs the county court judge refused to take the withdrawn payment into court into account. The defendants appealed. Lawton L.J. said at 870: "So I have come to the conclusion that if the judge meant, as I think he must be taken as meaning, that he had to disregard altogether the fact that the payment into court had been made he was wrong. What he should have done was to have regard to the fact that from the beginning of September 1981 [i.e. 21 days after the notice of payment-in, following when the plaintiff would be at risk for costs] until 13 October 1981 [the date at which the defendants would have been able to block the plaintiff's acceptance out of time because of the change in risk caused by the vendor's report], the plaintiff was taking a gamble, and during that period there may have been some costs incurred which he might have been ordered by the judge to pay, but only for that period, because after that period the plaintiff was not in a position to take a gamble at all . . ." Goff L.J. said at 872: "Subject to the two risks I have mentioned [(1) that the plaintiff will have to pay the costs after 21 days if he accepts more than 21 days after the payment-in; (2) that there may be a material change of circumstances which may prevent him from taking the money out], he can delay his decision whether or not to take the money out of court, in the knowledge that the money will still be available to him for that purpose until the time of the commencement of the trial. That being so, if, before the commencement of trial, the defendant does in fact withdraw (with leave) his notice of payment into court, it appears to me that it would be wrong in principle to order that the plaintiff should bear all the costs of the action from the date of the payment-in if the plaintiff, in the outcome, wins but recovers less than the sum previously paid in . . . However the payment into court will, in such circumstances, ordinarily be relevant in respect of costs incurred during the period between the date of payment-in and the date when the defendant's notice of payment-in is withdrawn by leave of the court. . . ."

Mark Amy Ltd. v. Olcott Investments Ltd., Royal Court of Jersey (Samedi Division), 4 November 1996 (unreported) The arbitrator in a building case made his award as to substantive issues. On the basic claim he awarded £42,000 plus £12,000 interest. On the question of costs, he was invited to consider an offer of £100,000 made by the respondent, which had been available for acceptance for 21 days. The same offer had been repeated some time later, again for a period of 21 days. However, the claimant referred the arbitrator to *The Toni* (see above) in support of the contention that the offer did not affect the position as to costs. The arbitrator concluded: "Having considered the views of the judges in all the cases to which I have been referred . . . I prefer the view expressed in *The Toni* and conclude that an offer which has lapsed prior to the start of the hearing provides no protection to the offeror with regard to costs." The judgment of the court was: ". . . the question of open offers, sealed offers and without prejudice offers were all argued in detailed pleadings before the arbitrator. He must have had the clearest indication of how to deal with this question of the purported offers; he found *The Toni* persuasive and was able, in his discretion, to ignore the offers . . . we cannot see any way that the arbitrator misdirected himself in law."

7.7 THE SCOPE AND FINANCIAL TERMS OF THE OFFER

The offer should state clearly which causes of action are to be covered by the offer. For instance, if a counterclaiming respondent makes an offer, he should make it plain whether an acceptance of the offer will dispose of the counterclaim as well as the claim.

There should be separate provisions relating to[39]:

   (1) the principal sum offered plus interest up until the date of acceptance; and
   (2) the claimant's recoverable costs and the arbitrator's fees and expenses until the date of acceptance.

7.7.1 The principal sum and interest

It is convenient to give the principal sum and interest offered as a combined lump sum. A simple offer to settle for £x will normally be construed to include both the principal sum and interest to that date.

If a principal sum is offered with interest to be assessed, assessment of the interest may prove difficult without knowing the breakdown of the offer and hence may render the offer uncertain. This may prejudice the offeree and provide grounds for asserting that the offer was reasonably rejected not-withstanding the fact that the principal sum offered exceeded that eventually awarded. If, on the other hand, separate named sums are offered for the principal and interest, the offeree may later claim that it was a reasonable to reject the offer if *either* the principal sum *or* the interest recovered exceeded that in the offer. Since arbitrations are frequently held many years after the dispute arises, and the interest may form a significant element of the final recovery, this is not a fanciful speculation. All in all, combining the principal and interest seems to produce the greatest protection for the offeror.

7.7.2 Costs

When a respondent makes an offer of settlement in which he is the net payer, it is important to offer to pay the claimant's reasonable costs to the date when

---

39. See *Tramountana Armadora S.A.* v. *Atlantic Shipping Co. S.A.* [1978] 1 Lloyd's Rep. 391.

the offer is to be accepted in addition to the sum offered by way of settlement.[40] It has in fact been judicially suggested that "If a party wishes to make a 'sealed offer' and to have it considered in the context of an order for costs, he must offer to settle the action for £x plus costs".[41] This has been explained to mean that "It will always be prudent to offer to pay taxed costs, because of the risk of error [i.e. in determining the value of the costs to the date of the offer], but the sufficiency of an offer is concerned with its demonstrable substance and not with its form".[42] If the offer is a fixed sum which includes costs, the arbitrator must determine whether, having taken the likely costs element out of that sum, what remains is demonstrably greater than the sum eventually recovered. If not, the offer has no effect on costs. If an offer by a respondent indicates that both sides should pay their own costs, this creates even greater uncertainty and less protection for the respondent; but if, having accounted for the likely costs to that date, the offer was clearly in excess of what was recovered, it will provide costs protection. Where an offer is made which does not provide for costs in addition to the sum offered, the offeror carries the burden of showing that the offer is effective.

When an offer is made in terms that the offeror is the net payee, for instance when there are competing claims and counterclaims, slightly different considerations apply. Here, the terms of settlement offered may suggest either (a) that the offeror's costs are to be paid (if the claims are to be set-off one against the other) or perhaps (b) that both parties are to pay an element of the costs (if the offer acknowledges a partial success by both parties). It is suggested that in such cases, the offer should always deal with costs on a generous basis[43] with an option exercisable by the offeree to have the costs determined by the arbitrator in the event that the offeree considers that the offer on costs tendered is inappropriate.[44] This has the advantage of putting the offer as to costs on its proper basis in law; thus if the offer is rejected, the arbitrator may consider the offer on costs to have been "whatever costs were properly due to the offeree" which has the effect of eliminating costs from the equation.

40. Note, however, that section 51(5) of the Arbitration Act 1996 provides: "[Upon reaching a settlement of the disputes] Unless the parties have also settled the matter of the payment of the costs of the arbitration, the provisions of this Part relating to costs (sections 59 to 65) continue to apply." It may seem in the light of this provision that an offeror may make an offer which affects costs without referring to costs. An offer which does not deal with costs may be accepted by the offeree; section 51(5) then comes into play. But it is submitted that the offeree may ignore an offer which does not deal with costs without putting himself at risk for costs. Otherwise he is being asked to accept an uncertain outcome as consideration for settling the proceedings.

41. *Tramountana Armadora S.A. v. Atlantic Shipping Co. S.A.* [1978] 1 Lloyd's Rep. 391 *per* Donaldson J. at 398.

42. *Archital Luxfer Ltd. v. Henry Boot Construction Ltd.* [1981] 1 Lloyd's Rep. 642 *per* Gibson J. at 654.

43. For example that each party is to bear his own costs.

44. Following the suggestion in *Archital Luxfer Ltd. v. Henry Boot Construction Ltd.* [1981] 1 Lloyd's Rep. 642 *per* Gibson J. at 655. See also section 51(5) of the Arbitration Act 1996.

7.7 Offers of settlement: costs protection

7.7.3 Ambiguous, incomplete or conditional offers

In principle, an offer should:

(1) be clear as to its monetary value;
(2) be immediately acceptable without further clarification;
(3) cover all ancillary matters such as the costs of the parties and the arbitrator's fees and expenses;
(4) set up no prejudicial conditions, such as requiring the offeree to accept fault or liability for any specific matters.

It is not uncommon, however, for a respondent to write an ambiguous offer of settlement, the monetary value of which is unclear. Likewise respondents frequently omit to mention how matters such as costs, interest, etc. are to be dealt with. On occasions, the offer may also make the acceptance conditional, as where the claimant is required to accept the validity of the counterclaim as part of the settlement. Each of these has a potential for depriving the offer of its effect. Upon receipt of such an offer the claimant has the following options:

(1) The claimant may write to the respondent pointing out that the offer is defective. This clearly puts the respondents on notice and creates the maximum protection for the claimant, particularly if the items of defect are listed.
(2) The claimant may ignore the offer hoping to persuade the arbitrator that its internal ambiguity, incompleteness and/or conditionality deprive it of effect. The claimant will argue that an offer is a device for transferring the risk of costs from the respondent to the claimant and that the claimant's representatives can be under no duty to undermine the claimant's interests by pointing out that the offer is defective.

It is submitted that there are no hard-and-fast rules. An arbitrator is entitled to examine the offer and all the circumstances and to make his decision accordingly. He should, however, bear in mind that an offer of settlement is designed to protect the offeror in costs and that the offeror must take care to ensure that the offer is proper. Where, however, what has been offered is clearly greater than the eventual recovery when a liberal assessment is taken into account, then the offer may be treated as effective.[45]

Illustrations
Tramountana Armadora S.A. v. Atlantic Shipping Co. S.A. [1978] 1 Lloyd's Rep. 391 Shipowners claimed $20,000. The charterers counterclaimed for $8,000. The shipowner recovered $7,000 and the charterers $4,000, giving the shipowners a net recovery of $3,000. The hearing took place in two phases a year apart. Following the first phase, the charterer made a sealed offer of $6,000, which required both parties to pay their own costs. Held, the failure to offer costs invalidated the offer since their value to some point in the middle of the arbitration was likely to be significant in

---

45. *Tramountana Armadora S.A. v. Atlantic Shipping Co. S.A.* [1978] 1 Lloyd's Rep. 391.

relation to the offer and was a "completely unknown factor which the arbitrator is not in a position to assess", *per* Donaldson J. at 398.

Archital Luxfer Ltd. v. Henry Boot Construction Ltd. [1981] 1 Lloyd's Rep. 642
HB claimed £93,000 against AL and AL claimed £29,000 against HB. AL made an offer that HB be allowed £12,000 on its claim and that AL be allowed £17,000 on its counterclaim, with a net payment to AL of £5,000. The offer stated that "there shall be no order as to costs". The offer was rejected. HB recovered £5,000 and AL recovered £15,000, i.e. a net payment of £10,000 to AL. The arbitrator decided that this was not an effective offer because it was not in the form "£X plus costs". Held, by Gibson J., the offer was valid. Since it was clear that HB had achieved a good deal less than if they had accepted the offer, AL were prima facie entitled to their costs subsequent to the date of the offer.

The Maria [1993] 2 Lloyd's Rep. 168 The owner chartered The Maria on a time charter. The charterer withheld $70,000 of the hire claimed because, he said, the ship's master had wrongly refused to enter the port of discharge. The owner referred the matter to arbitration. The charterer made a sealed offer of $15,000 plus costs to date. The owner rejected the offer and the arbitration proceeded. The arbitrators awarded $16,500 to the owner. As requested by the parties they held over their decision on costs until they had sight of the sealed offer. After submissions, the arbitrators awarded the charterers their costs, despite the fact that, on the face of it, the offer was less than the eventual recovery. Their reasons were as follows. Because of the manner in which the owner had conducted the arbitration (for example he had wrongly accused the charterer of attempting to bribe the arbitrators) the arbitrators had in mind to order the successful owner to pay their own costs if successful. They took the view that $15,000 plus costs was a better offer than $16,500 without costs. Thus, they reasoned, the offer was of greater value than the eventual recovery and so they ordered the owner to pay the charterer's costs. The owner appealed. Held by the judge at first instance that the arbitrators were only entitled to take into account the principal (and interest) when comparing an offer with the sum ultimately recovered and that the order would be varied so that both parties would bear their own costs (which was the costs order which the arbitrators had said they would make if the owners had been successful). The Court of Appeal (Sir Thomas Bingham M.R. dissenting) upheld the judge's varied order on the principle that costs follow the event, but do not determine it.

7.8 OFFERS WHERE THERE IS A COUNTERCLAIM

Where a claim and a counterclaim are both being advanced, the arbitrator may make a single combined order as to costs or he may, if the claim and counter-claim arise from distinct facts, make two separate orders.[46]

Where there is both a claim and a counterclaim, it is most common for the respondent to make an aggregate offer to settle the entire proceedings. However, some counterclaiming respondents may prefer to make an offer which is specifically directed to the claim alone; and, the claimant may in some cases consider it appropriate to make an offer in respect of the respondent's counterclaim. If the arbitrator considers it appropriate to make separate costs

---

46. See generally §3.2 for the principles applicable to the question whether a combined order or separate orders are appropriate.

orders in respect of the claim and counterclaim, any offers directed specifically to the claim and/or counterclaim may simply be compared with the success achieved to determine which party should bear the costs of each, subject as always to the arbitrator's overriding discretion. If, however, the arbitrator decides that a single costs order is appropriate,[47] he must then consider what effect, if any, an offer directed solely to the claim or counterclaim is to have. Suppose, for instance, that the respondent makes an offer to compromise the entire proceedings for £x and the claimant offers to compromise the counterclaim for £y. If the claimant's net recovery exceeds £x, the claimant would normally, in the absence of his own offer, be awarded his costs both on the claim and counterclaim. The arbitrator may thus properly consider it inequitable to deduct costs from the claimant even if the respondent's success in respect of his counterclaim exceeded £y. In such circumstances, however, it is suggested that the arbitrator should always invite the parties to address him on the question of the appropriate costs order and proceed to make the order which to him seems appropriate to the justice of the case.

7.9 COUNTEROFFERS: REVERSE CALDERBANK LETTERS

Offers in arbitration proceedings are contractual in nature[48] and are not dictated by procedural rules; there seems no reason in principle why a counteroffer should be ineffective.[49] It is submitted that an arbitrator may take into account any counteroffer, providing it can be evaluated and it can be said that the offeree has not achieved more by rejecting the offer and going on with the arbitration than he would have achieved if he had accepted the offer.

The claimant may write to the respondent "without prejudice save as to costs" stating the amount and terms on which he would be prepared to settle the arbitration. This is appropriate where the respondent has either not made an offer or the offer which has been made is not sufficiently attractive to the claimant (or indeed where a previous offer has lapsed). This "reverse Calderbank letter" indicates that if the offer is not accepted by the respondent and the claimant recovers more than the value of the offer, he reserves the right to disclose the letter to the arbitrator in support of the submission that, for the period following the time when the offer should have been accepted, he should recover his costs on a more generous basis than the standard basis.[50] It is submitted that the arbitrator is entitled to allow costs on a more generous basis, providing he acts judicially.

47. See e.g. *Hanak* v. *Green* [1958] 2 Q.B. 9.
48. See *Huron Liberian Co.* v. *Rheinoel G.m.b.H.* [1985] 2 Lloyd's Rep. 58.
49. Indeed counteroffers in litigation proceedings have been treated as unremarkable in a number of cases, e.g. *Harrison* v. *Thompson* [1989] 1 W.L.R. 1325; *Gojkovic* v. *Gojkovic* (No. 2) [1992] 1 All E.R. 267.
50. Section 63(5) of the Arbitration Act 1996.

7.10 AMENDMENTS MADE TO CASE SUBSEQUENT TO AN OFFER

An offer of settlement necessarily addresses the issues in dispute at the time it is made. Where either party subsequently modifies his case by amendment,[51] adding new or enhanced claims or defences, the force of the offer may change.

The classical situation is where the respondent makes an offer relatively early in the proceedings and the claimant makes a late amendment close to or at the hearing.[52] Here, the broad principle is that the arbitrator should "consider what would have been the result but for the amendment".[53] This is straight-forward where a claimant amends to introduce a new or enhanced claim or the respondent amends to introduce a new or enhanced counterclaim.[54]

Where a new defence is introduced, however, the position is somewhat different. While the purpose of pleadings is to identify the issues, the funda-mental burden of proof lies with the claimant; it is he who must prove his claim. It is not for the defendant to defeat it.[55] In its extreme form, this suggests that an amendment to the defence should, therefore, have no effect on the validity or scope of the offer. This is, however, to overstate the position. "[T]he general rule [i.e. the test 'what would have been the result but for the amendment'] should apply where the defendant amends to plead a new defence of which the burden rests on him, for example, a plea of limitation or of some relevant contractual exception. In such a case, if the effect of the amendment is to reduce what would otherwise have been awarded below the sum paid in, it would usually be just to give the plaintiff his costs".[56]

Different considerations may apply where amendments are made by the claimant at an earlier stage in the proceedings so that the respondent has ample time to respond. It is submitted that just as an offeree has a reasonable time to consider an offer, the offeror has a reasonable time to consider an amendment[57]; if he feels that his existing offer is inadequate in the light of the

51. Or by particularisation if the strict rules which apply to pleadings in court are not being used in the arbitration.

52. Cases where late amendments were made include: *Anglo-Cyprian Trade Agencies Ltd.* v. *Paphos Wine Industries Ltd.* [1951] 1 All E.R. 873; *Cheeseman* v. *Bowaters United Kingdom Paper Mills Ltd.* [1971] 1 W.L.R.1773; *Lipkin Gorman* v. *Karpnale Ltd.* [1989] 1 W.L.R. 1340; *Blexen Ltd.* v. *G Percy Trentham Ltd.* (1990) 54 Build. L.R. 37 *per* Lloyd L.J. at 47; *Beoco Ltd.* v. *Alfa Laval Co. Ltd.* [1994] 3 W.L.R. 1179.

53. *Blexen Ltd.* v. *G Percy Trentham Ltd.* (1990) 54 Build. L.R. 37 *per* Lloyd L.J. at 47.

54. As in *Cheeseman* v. *Bowaters United Kingdom Paper Mills Ltd.* [1971] 1 W.L.R. 1773.

55. *Beoco Ltd.* v. *Alfa Laval Co. Ltd.* [1994] 3 W.L.R. 1179: "it is for the plaintiff to establish causation in respect of the damage claimed. While the defendant must plead [a defence which is specific—in this case a novus actus interveniens] on which he is going to rely, if the plaintiff's case failed because he fails to establish causation, in the ordinary case the defendant will recover all the costs of the action and not merely those after the service of the defence raising the specific matters", *per* Stuart-Smith L.J. at 1193.

56. *Blexen Ltd.* v. *G Percy Trentham Ltd.* (1990) 54 Build. L.R. 37 *per* Lloyd L.J. at 47.

57. In *Beoco Ltd.* v. *Alfa Laval Co. Ltd.* [1994] 3 W.L.R. 1179, the plaintiff made a late amendment which enabled him to avoid failure on his claim; in dealing with costs, the judge considered that upon the amendment being made, the defendant should have protected himself by sending a Calderbank letter. The Court of Appeal clearly disagreed. Stuart-Smith L.J. at 1193

amendment, he must revise it to retain costs protection.[58] When dealing with costs, the arbitrator is then required to consider the costs incurred during three distinct periods. First, he should deal with costs for the period before any offer is made. Second, he should consider whether or not the original offer was successful on the claims advanced at that time. Third, he should consider whether or not the later offer exceeds the sum recovered by the offeree and on that basis, award costs from the date of the later offer to the conclusion of the proceedings.

Illustrations

Cheeseman v. Bowaters United Kingdom Paper Mills Ltd. [1971] 1 W.L.R. 1773
The plaintiff sued the defendant for personal injury. The defendant made payment into court of £750. The plaintiff recovered £749 on the case as originally pleaded. But during the course of the trial the plaintiff's case was amended with the result that more than £750 was recovered. The Court of Appeal held that the defendants were entitled to their costs subsequent to the payment-in.

Blexen Ltd. v. G Percy Trentham Ltd. (1990) 54 Build. L.R. 37 B was engaged as a subcontractor by GPT. B claimed £220,000 against GPT. GPT made a sealed offer of £77,000 plus costs, which B rejected. The proceedings continued. Immediately before the hearing, GPT amended its defence, claiming that certain elements in the claim should be valued in accordance with specific clauses in the agreement. That defence was successful and reduced the amount recovered by B by £34,000. The arbitrator awarded B £50,000. It was argued by B that, without the amendment, B would have recovered £84,000, which was in excess of the sealed offer and hence were entitled to their costs. The arbitrator awarded B its costs to the date of the sealed offer, and GPT its costs thereafter on the grounds that B would have continued with the arbitration anyway. The Court of Appeal decided that "it is normally preferable for the judge or an arbitrator to consider what would have been the result but for the amendment, rather than the ... elusive question whether the plaintiff would or would not have accepted the offer, had he known of future amendments" (*per* Lloyd L.J. at 47). However, the matter was both considered by the arbitrator and within his discretion and his award was allowed to stand.

Beoco Ltd. v. Alfa Laval Co. Ltd. [1994] 3 W.L.R. 1179 "As a general rule, where a plaintiff makes a late amendment ... which substantially alters the case the defendant has to meet and without which the action will fail, the defendant is entitled to the costs of the action down to the date of the amendment", *per* Stuart-Smith L.J. at 1193.

felt that the judge's reasoning "ignores the reality of the situation or the difficulty in which the defendant was placed. ... There was no proper pleading of the alternative case, there had been no discovery, and the defendant's experts had no opportunity to investigate or make any estimate of the proper value of the claim."

58. It is submitted that this new offer need not include an offer to pay costs up to the date of acceptance of the new offer. Here it is thought that the respondent can make a money offer with costs to be determined. The claimant may be left in doubt as to what the value of this offer is to him, but he created this doubt by failing to plead properly in the first place.

7.11 OFFERS AND PRIVILEGE

The law considers bona fide negotiations with a view to settlement to be "privileged" and the fact and content of such negotiations cannot be revealed to any tribunal which has jurisdiction over the issues in dispute.[59] This privilege is often expressly claimed, usually by the formula "without prejudice",[60] but it arises automatically during bona fide negotiations whether claimed or not.[61] Likewise, the fact that privilege is claimed does not create it if it would not otherwise exist.[62]

A privileged document, including an offer, may be revealed to the tribunal if all those who are entitled to the privilege waive it. Any party who makes an offer or indicates that he might do so, is entitled to the relevant privilege and other parties may not reveal the fact or content of the offer to the tribunal.[63] While the privilege belongs principally to the offeror, the offeree's response (or lack of response) is also entitled to a degree of privilege,[64] since this may put the offeree's reasonableness during negotiations in issue.

Offers which are wholly without prejudice cannot be revealed to the arbitrator at any stage unless both the offeror and offeree consent. Sealed offers and Calderbank letters clearly attract privilege and may not be revealed to the arbitrator against the privilege of any party until all issues of liability and quantum have been determined. An open offer is not privileged unless both parties treat it as a secret document thereby endowing it over time with a degree of privilege.

59. *Rush & Tomkins Ltd.* v. *Greater London Council* [1989] A.C. 1280.

60. *Walker* v. *Wilsher* (1889) 23 Q.B.D. 335; *Stotesbury* v. *Turner* [1943] K.B. 370; *Tomlin* v. *Standard Telephones and Cables Ltd.* [1969] 1 W.L.R. 1378.

61. *Stotesbury* v. *Turner* [1943] K.B. 370.

62. *Dixon Stores Group Ltd.* v. *Thames Television plc per* Drake J. at 351: "The mere fact of heading a letter 'without prejudice' is not in the least decisive as to whether or not the letter is in fact privileged. The privilege exists in order to encourage bona fide attempts to negotiate a settlement of an action and if the letter is not written to initiate or continue such a bona fide attempt to effect a settlement it will not be protected by privilege. But, conversely, if it is written in the course of such a bona fide attempt, it will be covered by privilege, and the absence of any heading or reference in the letter to show it is without prejudice will not be fatal."

63. See *Ian Keith Brown* v. *C.B.S. (Contractors) Ltd.* [1987] 1 Lloyd's Rep. 279 where an unsuccessful application was made to remove an arbitrator on the grounds that the lack of agreement reached during a privileged meeting had been revealed to him.

64. See the general remarks on privileged communications in *Cutts* v. *Head* [1984] 1 Ch. 290.

CHAPTER 8

LIMITATION OF RECOVERABLE COSTS

8.1 SECTION 65: THE POWER TO LIMIT COSTS

Section 65 of the Arbitration Act 1996 provides:

65 Power to limit the recoverable costs

(1) Unless otherwise agreed by the parties, the tribunal may direct that the recoverable costs of the arbitration, or of any part of the arbitral proceedings, shall be limited to a specified amount.

(2) Any direction may be made or varied at any stage, but this must be done sufficiently in advance of the incurring of costs to which it relates, or the taking of any steps in the proceeding which may be affected by it, for the limit to be taken into account.

This is a new power which enables the arbitrator to limit the recoverable costs of the arbitration. It allows the arbitrator to (a) control costs before they are incurred, (b) ensure that costs are proportionate to the importance and complexity of the case and/or the sums in issue, and (c) make costs more predictable.

The power in section 65 is designed to support the exercise of the arbitrator's general duty to adopt fair and cost-effective procedures.[1] Accordingly, the arbitrator must not direct a costs limit which denies either party a reasonable opportunity of putting his case or dealing with that of his opponent or which prevents a fair resolution of the disputes. The exercise of the power under section 65 requires a balance to be struck between the parties' opportunity to advance their cases and the avoidance of unnecessary delay and expense, judged against the key factor, namely the fair resolution of the disputes.

---

1. Section 33 of the Arbitration Act 1996.

8.2 THE ELEMENTS OF SECTION 65

8.2.1 "Unless otherwise agreed by the parties"

Section 65 of the Arbitration Act 1996 is a non-mandatory provision. It may be excluded by an express agreement in writing[2] that the arbitrator does not have the power set out in section 65.

Where, however, the parties simply agree their own limit on recoverable costs, it is submitted that this does not exclude the power entirely. The words "Unless otherwise agreed . . . the tribunal may direct . . ." seem to indicate that, in order to deprive the arbitrator of his power under the section, the agreement in question must deal specifically with the power to direct a limit rather than to the amount of the limit. Nevertheless, where the parties agree their own limit this will, it is submitted, deprive the arbitrator of the power to direct a higher limit on costs and will be a major factor in the exercise of his discretion if an application is made to direct a lower limit.

Where an arbitrator is proposing to direct a limit on recoverable costs and he receives representations from both parties that no limit is to be directed, the arbitrator is, it is submitted, obliged to accede to those representations provided they are agreed in writing and the arbitrator is satisfied that they are properly authorised by the clients.

Where a limit has already been directed, the parties may by subsequent agreement in writing agree that a specified higher limit is applicable.[3]

8.2.2 The power is a discretionary one

The arbitrator's power to limit the recoverable costs is a discretionary one. This discretion must be exercised judicially. The arbitrator must not misdirect himself, for example by considering irrelevant matters. The arbitrator must have primary regard to his general duty to "act fairly and impartially . . . giving each party a reasonable opportunity of putting his case and dealing with that of his opponent, and . . . [to] adopt procedures suitable to the circumstances of the particular case, avoiding unnecessary delay or expense, so as to provide a fair means for the resolution of the matters falling to be determined".[4]

8.2.3 The direction relates to the recoverable costs

The arbitrator cannot restrict the costs expended by any party. A party may engage such representatives[5] and advisers as he considers appropriate. He may undertake such investigations as he wishes. A direction under section 65 merely

2. Section 5(1) of the Arbitration Act 1996.
3. Section 63(1) of the Arbitration Act 1996.
4. Section 33 of the Arbitration Act 1996.
5. Subject to any agreement as to representation: section 36 of the Arbitration Act 1996.

limits the liability of the other party for those costs if that other party is unsuccessful.

8.2.4 "any part of the arbitral proceedings"

The arbitrator may direct different limits in relation to different parts of the arbitration. Thus he may specify a limit for the legal costs of the parties without limiting his own fees and expenses.[6] He may direct different limits for different parts of the proceedings. For example, he may establish detailed budgetary control by directing costs' limits to each element of the arbitration such as "analysis of case", "statements of case", "witness statements", etc. so that the parties know the way in which their potential liability may change as the arbitration proceeds.

Upon an analysis of costs to be incurred, it may appear that the costs to be expended by one party are reasonably likely to be greater than those of the other party. It is submitted, however, that, save in exceptional circumstances, it would be wrong for a different limit to be specified for each party.

8.2.5 "a specified amount"

The direction must limit the recoverable costs to a "specified amount". It is submitted that the "specified amount" must be determinable at the date of the direction. It may be proper for the arbitrator to direct that the recoverable costs for the hearing are to be limited to a specified amount per day or per week. However, the arbitrator cannot direct a "contingency limit", for example, that the limit is to be proportional to the amount recovered under the award.

8.2.6 Direction may be made at any stage

It is convenient for any direction to be made shortly after the arbitrator's appointment provided that the arbitrator is able, at that stage, to appreciate the scope and scale of the issues involved. The direction must be made "sufficiently in advance of the incurring of costs to which it relates, or the taking of any steps in the proceedings which may be affected by it, for the limit to be taken into account".[7] There is no power to limit costs retrospectively; where costs have been expended by the time that a limit is directed, those costs will be recoverable unless those costs were incurred unreasonably or prematurely in accordance with the normal rules.[8]

Where it is proposed that a direction be made, the arbitrator must have

6. It may be difficult to compute how much time the arbitrator will need to spend on the case; there should be no suspicion that the arbitrator has accelerated the case in order not to be out of pocket.

7. Section 56(2) of the Arbitration Act 1996.

8. See Chapter 5 and, in particular, *Harrison* v. *Leutner* (1881) 16 Ch.D. 559; *Thomas* v. *Palin* (1882) 21 Ch.D. 360.

regard to any costs which are by then reasonably and irretrievably committed. For example, a brief fee in instalments may have been agreed with counsel. This agreement may not be readily renegotiated; and the engagement of new counsel will not only be disruptive, but may possibly be more expensive in the long run. Similar problems may arise in connection with experts, other personnel and accommodation for the hearing.

8.2.7 Varying the direction

After a direction is made, it may appear that an adjustment to the specified limit is warranted. Such an adjustment should not be made lightly. The parties, or any of them may have relied upon the first limit when appointing representation, conducting settlement negotiations, etc. and may have taken a different approach had they known that the limit would be revised.

An application to vary the limit may be appropriate where, for instance, new evidence comes to light or events arise which could not reasonably have been expected at the time of the original offer.

8.3 THE EXERCISE OF THE POWER TO LIMIT COSTS

When exercising his discretion under section 65 of the Arbitration Act 1996, the arbitrator must act judicially. He must take into account those factors which are relevant and must not base his decision on factors which are irrelevant. He must have full regard to his general duty to act fairly and to give the parties a reasonable opportunity to put their arguments in the proceedings.[9] It is submitted that the following matters are relevant:

(1) *The complexity of the issues and the risk of injustice being done if the costs actually spent are restricted to the proposed limit*

An arbitrator cannot restrict the costs which a party actually spends; he can only limit the costs recoverable by a successful party. Nevertheless, in setting a limit on costs, he should consider whether or not a party who keeps his spending within the limit will be unreasonably handicapped. The function of an award of costs is to ensure that a party who has had to go to arbitration to assert or defend his rights is compensated.[10] That party should not be reimbursed in full where he spends more on costs than it was reasonable for him to spend; but neither should he be penalised for spending a proper amount. Accordingly, the limit should reflect what is a proper amount in all the circumstances.

This consideration will involve an analysis of the nature of the

9. Section 33 of the Arbitration Act 1996.
10. *London Scottish Benefit Society* v. *Chorley* (1884) 13 Q.B.D. 873 *per* Bowen L.J. at 876.

claims and defences being advanced, including whether or not complex analyses are required and whether or not the legal issues warrant senior representation. In order for the arbitrator to understand the complexities of the case, he should invite the parties to indicate what the issues are, by what means they propose to prove them and at what cost. The arbitrator should consider whether alternative procedures may enable the same results to be achieved at less cost.

(2) The sums in dispute

In setting a costs limit, the arbitrator will seek to ensure that the recoverable costs are to some degree proportionate to the sums in issue.[11] But every case will be different. Some cases in which the amount in dispute is £x may turn upon the construction of a single contract term; other cases with the same amount in dispute may require the analysis of thousands of documents.

It is not always easy to determine the real amount in dispute at the outset of the case; it may be unfair to the respondent to have an inflated costs limit imposed as a result of the claimant making an exaggerated claim. The arbitrator must be careful, of course, not to prejudice himself by taking an early view as to the proper value of the claim. He may, nevertheless, give the parties notice and then state in any direction that the costs limit is based, in part, on the amount claimed; and if it is shown that the claims were grossly exaggerated he reserves the right to take that into account when the question of costs comes to be decided. The arbitrator may not retrospectively revise his direction as to the limit of recoverable costs[12]; but he may award a successful claimant a proportion only of his costs on the grounds that the value of the claim was grossly exaggerated.[13]

(3) The importance of the case to each of the parties[14]

Where, for instance, the dispute concerns allegations of serious culp-

11. See the 1995 Freshfields Lecture (*Arbitration Journal*, August 1996 supplement). Arthur Marriott suggests an example which reflects this principle of computation. "Thus, for example, in a construction case if there was a claim for damages amounting to say £1m, the arbitrator and the parties would together work out, and in the absence of agreement, the arbitrator would decide, by what procedures and how long it would take to resolve the dispute, having regard to the amount at stake. ... A timetable would be worked out and costed. If for the sake of argument it was considered reasonable for the parties to spend a total of £100,000, the expenditure of each party, again to make the example simple, would be estimated at £50,000 and that would be the limit of recoverable costs."

12. Section 65(2) of the Arbitration Act 1996.

13. *The Rozel* [1994] 2 Lloyd's Rep. 161. Phillips J. said at 170 that where the claims are grossly exaggerated the arbitrator may deprive the successful party of "some of his costs". See also *Perry* v. *Stopher* [1959] 1 All E.R. 713 and *Dineen* v. *Walpole* [1969] 1 Lloyd's Rep. 261.

14. See for example the considerations used by the courts to determine whether it was appropriate to engage senior counsel: *Simpsons Motor Sales (London) Ltd.* v. *Hendon Borough Council* [1965] 1 W.L.R. 112.

able negligence this may warrant more rigorous investigation than where the issue concerns a minor dispute over the meaning of words in a commercial agreement.

(4) The cost-benefits of discovery, expert evidence and extensive analyses

In many fields of commercial arbitration it is traditional for full discovery to be ordered, with extensive expert evidence involving testing, calculation, analyses, etc. In many situations the expense of such measures is justifiable. In other cases, however, the benefits may be marginal compared to the cost. It is for the arbitrator to consider whether and to what extent the expenditure of such costs is warranted in the case before him.

8.4 OPERATION OF THE SECTION 65 POWER IN PRACTICE

8.4.1 The application

While the power will be exercised most frequently following an application by a party, there is nothing to prevent an arbitrator from exercising the power to limit recoverable costs upon his own initiative.

An application may be in any convenient format. It may be useful for the applicant to set out a proposed programme for the proceedings, with timings and costings so that the arbitrator can see how any costs limit contended for has been arrived at.

8.4.2 Submissions

Where the arbitrator considers that he may limit the recoverable costs, he should give the parties a reasonable opportunity to make representations as to:

(1) whether or not the power should be exercised;
(2) the principal factors which should be taken into account when arriving at a limit for recoverable costs; and
(3) the amount of the appropriate limit.

8.4.3 The interaction between the recoverable costs limit and other powers

The arbitrator has a number of powers which may interact with the power to limit the recoverable costs. For example, the appointment of an expert by the arbitrator will affect the costs which the parties may reasonably expend on their own experts; consequently, where there is a possibility that an expert may be appointed by the arbitrator it may be convenient to deal with that issue before dealing with the costs limit.

Where no limit on costs has been directed and an application is made by a respondent[15] for security for costs against a claimant, the claimant may submit in his response that, if any security be ordered, it should be limited to a "specified amount" to be determined in accordance with section 65. The arbitrator now has two distinct applications which should not be coupled. The arbitrator should first consider whether a costs limit is appropriate and, if so, he should make his direction. He should then go on to consider whether the conditions for ordering security have been met. The maximum sum which the claimant must provide by way of security is the maximum amount of costs which is likely to be due to the respondent if he is successful, namely any specified limit.[16] Note, however, that the specified costs limit is an upper limit rather than necessarily the amount that will be recoverable; it is proper for the arbitrator to order that some proportion of that limit is the correct amount of security to be ordered.

If the arbitrator orders security for costs, he may make his order on terms that he will entertain a further application in the event that the specified costs limit is subsequently varied.

8.4.4 The terms of the direction

The direction should be formally drawn up. It should state or identify:

(1) *The date when the direction comes into effect*

This will normally be the date of the direction itself, but provision should be made for costs reasonably committed before this date which cannot be renegotiated or cancelled. Costs incurred before the date on which the direction comes into effect will not be subject to the direction. However, the direction may make specific provision for any costs which were prematurely incurred in this earlier period and which should properly have fallen within the post-direction period.

(2) *The elements of work to which the limit or limits relate*

The direction should clearly define which elements of the costs are being referred to. For instance the direction: "the recoverable costs of the arbitration will be limited to £x" is highly ambiguous; it may have been the arbitrator's intention to limit the costs recoverable by a successful party from an unsuccessful party to £x. However, the definition of "costs of the arbitration"[17] suggests that the limit of £x relates to the total costs of both parties and the arbitrator's fees and expenses. Thus where the arbitrator's fees and expenses are £a, this

15. Section 38(3) of the Arbitration Act 1996.
16. Where the arbitrator considers that the security to be ordered should include for his own fees and expenses, this must be added to the limit: see §6.11.
17. Section 59 of the Arbitration Act 1996.

means that the successful party can only recover $£\frac{1}{2}(x-a)$ from the other party.

Identifying the work to which the limit relates may, where appropriate, be achieved by reference to the categories set out in section 59 of the Arbitration Act 1996. Where there are different limits for different components of the arbitration, these may be listed in a schedule.

(3)   *The effect of a settlement part way through the proceedings*

It is submitted that the effect of a direction which sets an overall limit on the recoverable costs is not only to place an upper limit on the costs; it also requires that the reasonable recoverable costs in respect of any item will be consistent with the overall costs not exceeding the limit. Where, therefore, there is a settlement part way through the proceedings, the recoverable costs will be limited to a proportionate amount of the specified limit. Where the direction is expressly given in these terms, this creates additional certainty and assists the parties in evaluating costs when considering terms of settlement.

(4)   *Under what circumstance the limit may be revised*

The arbitrator should be prepared to hear a renewed application at any time. Nevertheless it is frequently of value to the parties to be advised as to when an application will be most properly made. It is submitted that an indication such as "in the event that circumstances arise which could not reasonably have been foreseen at the time of this direction ..." is appropriate.

8.5 DETERMINING THE RECOVERABLE COSTS WHERE THERE IS A DIRECTION

Where an arbitrator sets a limit on costs, the successful party is not automatically entitled to the costs limit. The arbitrator (or court) must determine the reasonable costs and only when they exceed the specified amount does the limit become relevant. Where a successful party has clearly spent reasonable sums in presenting his case which exceed the specified limit, the losing party may concede that the value of the limit is payable without a formal determination, thus avoiding the costs of determining the reasonable amount.

8.6 CHALLENGING THE DIRECTION

There is no mechanism under the Arbitration Act 1996 for a party to challenge a direction under section 65. Where both parties find a direction unacceptable, they may make an agreement which supersedes it.[18] Where the arbitrator appreciates that the matter involves difficult questions he may give permission for an application for the determination of a preliminary point of law.[19] But where the complaining party cannot get the agreement of the other or the permission of the arbitrator he seems to have no option but to make his protest[20] and await the award so that he may challenge it.[21] It may be that, in the most extreme cases, where the arbitrator has "failed properly to conduct the proceedings . . . and . . . substantial injustice will be caused", the court may entertain an application to remove the arbitrator.[22]

18. Section 63(1) of the Arbitration Act 1996.

19. Section 45 of the Arbitration Act 1996. The question may be framed in the following terms: "Will the arbitrator misdirect himself in law if, purporting to act pursuant to section 65 of the Act, he directs a limit on costs which . . . [set out specific grounds of complaint, e.g. 'takes into account . . .' or 'is so restrictive that . . .']." Note that the applicant must show that there is likely to be a substantial saving in costs—section 45(2)(b)(i); he will have to show that an award will in all likelihood be successfully challenged if the current direction stands.

20. Section 73 of the Arbitration Act 1996.

21. Section 68 of the Arbitration Act 1996. See §9.4. It is thought that such an application will only succeed in the clearest cases of injustice.

22. Section 24 of the Arbitration Act 1996.

CHAPTER 9

APPLICATIONS TO THE COURT IN RESPECT OF COSTS

9.1 APPLICATIONS TO THE COURT IN RESPECT OF COSTS

A variety of applications may be made to the court in respect of costs, including[1]:

(1) an application under section 28(2) of the Arbitration Act 1996 to have the amount of the arbitrator's fees and expenses considered and adjusted;

(2) an application under section 56(2) of the Arbitration Act 1996 for a review of the fees and expenses claimed by the arbitrator;

(3) an application under section 63(4) of the Arbitration Act 1996 for the determination of the recoverable costs of the arbitration;

(4) an application under section 64(2) of the Arbitration Act 1996 for the determination of any question as to the reasonable fees and expenses of the arbitrator;

(5) an application under section 68 of the Arbitration Act 1996 on the grounds that there has been a serious irregularity;

(6) an appeal under section 69 of the Arbitration Act 1996 on the grounds of a serious error of law in the award as to costs; or an ancillary application under section 70(4) of the Arbitration Act 1996 for an order that the arbitrator supplies proper reasons for his award as to costs.

---

1. This list is not exhaustive. An arbitrator who resigns his appointment may apply for an order as to his liability, fees and expenses: section 25(3) of the Arbitration Act 1996. An application may be made under section 45 for the determination of a preliminary point of law as to the proper use of powers under the Arbitration Act 1996. An application which is not specifically provided for by the Arbitration Act 1996 is unlikely to succeed, even though the prohibition in section 1(c) of the Act is not absolute. In particular, any application for an injunction or declaration which seeks to interfere with an arbitrator's procedural order or direction will rarely, if ever, succeed: see *K/S A/S Bill Biakh* v. *Hyundai Corporation* [1988] 1 Lloyd's Rep. 187 *per* Steyn J. at 189 and *Three Valleys Water Committee* v. *Binnie & Partners* (1990) 52 Build. L. R. 47 *per* Steyn J. at 54.

9.2 APPLICATIONS IN RESPECT OF THE ARBITRATOR'S FEES AND EXPENSES

9.2.1 An application under section 28(2) of the Arbitration Act 1996 to have the amount of the arbitrator's fees and expenses adjusted

Section 28(2) of the Arbitration Act 1996 enables a party to apply to the court to have the amount of the arbitrator's fees and expenses considered and adjusted. This power of review does not affect any agreement as to costs properly made between the arbitrator and the parties.[2]

No time limits are expressly stipulated; the application may, for instance, be made as soon as an appointed arbitrator sends an indication of his proposed charges. An application will not be prevented by the fact that payment has already been made to the arbitrator[3] (e.g. where stage payments are requested and paid). Where money is paid over to the arbitrator, however, there may be circumstances in which it is unreasonable to order repayment and so an early application may be appropriate.[4]

9.2.2 Application under section 56(2) of the Arbitration Act 1996 for a review of the fees claimed by the arbitrator

The arbitrator may refuse to deliver up any award except upon full payment of his fees and expenses,[5] including the fees and expenses of experts, legal advisers and assessors appointed by him[6] and those of former arbitrators.

Where a party considers that the fees and expenses demanded are excessive, he may pay into court the amount demanded, or such lesser amount as the court may specify.[7] The court will order that the award be delivered.[8] Out of the money paid in, the arbitrator will be paid the "fees and expenses properly payable".[9] This means "the amount the applicant is liable to pay under section 28 or any agreement relating to the payment of the arbitrators."[10] The balance between the money paid into court and the fees and expenses properly payable will be repaid to the applicant.[11]

2. Section 28(5) of the Arbitration Act 1996.
3. Section 28(3) of the Arbitration Act 1996.
4. Note, however, that there may be reasons why a party may be uneasy about making an application part way through an arbitration. Order 73, rule 10(2) of the Rules of the Supreme Court provides that the arbitrator is to be made a respondent to the application. Furthermore, the application is required to identify the respondent against whom an order for costs is made—rule 4(2)(c)—and this is likely to be the arbitrator.
5. Section 56(1) of the Arbitration Act 1996. This right has been recognised in the decided cases since the nineteenth century and it was implied by the pre-1996 legislation: see section 19 of the Arbitration Act 1950.
6. Section 37(2) of the Arbitration Act 1996.
7. Section 56(2)(a) of the Arbitration Act 1996.
8. Section 56(2)(a) of the Arbitration Act 1996.
9. Section 56(2)(b) of the Arbitration Act 1996.
10. Section 56(3) of the Arbitration Act 1996.
11. Section 56(2)(c) of the Arbitration Act 1996.

An application for the court to consider and adjust the amount of fees and expenses under section 28 of the Arbitration Act 1996 is not excluded where payment has been made to obtain the award.[12]

9.3 APPLICATIONS FOR THE COURT TO DETERMINE THE RECOVERABLE COSTS OF THE ARBITRATION

Section 63(4) of the Arbitration Act 1996 provides that: "If the tribunal does not determine the recoverable costs of the arbitration" any party may apply to the court to have them determined. Where there is any question as to the arbitrator's reasonable fees and expenses recoverable under an award, a party may apply to the court under section 64(2) of the Act for the matter to be determined. There may be an overlap between an application under section 63(4) and one under section 64(2); in either case, the court may determine the recoverable costs itself or order that they be determined by such means and upon such terms as the court may specify. Ordinarily the court would pass the matter over to a taxing officer of the court for determination.

9.4 CHALLENGES ON THE GROUNDS OF SERIOUS IRREGULARITY IN RESPECT OF COSTS

9.4.1 The nature of an application under section 68 of the Arbitration Act 1996

Where a party alleges that there has been a serious irregularity, the appropriate application is under section 68 of the Arbitration Act 1996. The irregularity may be in relation to (a) the tribunal, (b) the proceedings, or (c) the award. The challenge is made in relation to the award; a significant period of time may, therefore, elapse between the alleged irregularity and the application.

Irregularities relating to the tribunal, such as bias, fraud, etc. are not dealt with here. Irregularities relating to the proceedings and the award which fall within the compass of section 68 are dealt with below.

9.4.2 Prerequisites

The prerequisites to a successful challenge under section 68 of the Arbitration Act 1996 are:

(1) The challenge must be made to an award. Where, for instance, an irregular order or direction is made, no challenge is possible until an award is made which is affected by the irregularity.

(2) The irregularity must be properly classifiable under one or more of

12. Section 56(8) of the Arbitration Act 1996.

the grounds set out in section 68(2). These are widely drawn. Where the court perceives an injustice, it is likely that an appropriate ground will be found.

(3) The irregularity complained of "has caused or will cause substantial injustice to the applicant".[13]

(4) The applicant must not have lost his right to object.[14] Where there has been a failure to comply with the Act or the proceedings have been improperly conducted, or there has been any irregularity, the applicant must raise his objection "forthwith" unless he could not reasonably have known of the irregularity and raises his objection as soon as he knows of it.[15]

(5) The applicable time limits have not expired.[16] The time limits require that a challenge is made within 28 days of the date of the award.[17]

9.4.3 Serious irregularity affecting the proceedings

Such irregularities include:

(1) Where a party has not been give a reasonable opportunity to make representations in respect of costs,[18] for example where the arbitrator fails to allow one or both parties a sufficient opportunity to make representations as to: (a) a direction limiting costs; (b) an order for security; or (c) generally on the question of costs prior to the making of an award as to liability or determining the recoverable costs.

(2) Where there has been a procedural mishap.[19] For example, where an advocate inadvertently fails to request that a decision on costs be reserved for further submissions and the arbitrator proceeds to award costs without being aware of an offer, the court may remit the award for his reconsideration[20]; or where the award on costs is made because of a mistake or a possible misapprehension[21] on the arbitrator's part.

(3) Where an unfair limit on recoverable costs is directed. Where, for example, the arbitrator directs a limit on recoverable costs under section 65 of the Arbitration Act 1996 which is so restrictive that a party was unable properly to advance its case or to meet that of the other, this may be a matter which amounts to a serious irregularity.[22]

13. Section 68(2) of the Arbitration Act 1996: opening sentence.
14. Section 73 of the Arbitration Act 1996.
15. Section 73(1) of the Arbitration Act 1996.
16. Section 70(2), (3) of the Arbitration Act 1996.
17. Section 70(3) of the Arbitration Act 1996.
18. Section 68(2)(a) of the Arbitration Act 1996.
19. This may well amount to an irregularity under grounds set out in sections 68(2)(a) and (i) of the Arbitration Act 1996.
20. *King* v. *Thomas McKenna Ltd.* [1991] 2 Q.B. 480.
21. *The Angeliki* [1982] 2 Lloyd's Rep. 594.
22. Section 68(2)(a) of the Arbitration Act 1996.

It is thought that the application will succeed only in the clearest cases.

(4) Where an unfair order for security for costs is made. Where a party against whom such an order is made manages to raise the security, it is unlikely that the application will succeed. Where, however, the party is unable to do so, and the arbitrator makes an award dismissing a claim[23] following the inability of a claimant to provide security for costs, the claimant may protest that there has been a serious irregularity. It is thought that the application will succeed only where the order for security was clearly wrong.

9.4.4 Serious irregularity affecting the award

Such irregularities include:

(1) Where no award is made in respect of costs or some element of them.[24] Note that section 57(3)(b) of the Arbitration Act 1996 empowers the arbitrator to "make an additional award in respect of any claim (including a claim for interest or costs) which was presented to the tribunal but was not dealt with in the award". The time limits in section 70(3) of the Arbitration Act 1996 are extended where such an application is made.

(2) Where the award as to costs is uncertain or ambiguous.[25]

(3) Where the award deals with elements of costs which are not within the arbitrator's jurisdiction.[26] An example arises where two arbitrations are heard concurrently without being formally consolidated and a party in one arbitration is ordered to pay the costs of a party in respect of the other arbitration.[27]

(4) Where the award as to costs is defective as to form.[28] This may create substantial injustice where the defect renders the award unenforceable in the place where it is to be enforced.

9.4.5 Where the award is successfully challenged

Where an application under section 68 is successful, the court may remit the award to the arbitrator, set it aside or declare it to be of no effect.[29] Ordinarily the award will be remitted unless this is inappropriate.

---

23. Section 41(6) of the Arbitration Act 1996.
24. Section 68(2)(d) of the Arbitration Act 1996: "failure by the tribunal to deal with all the issues that were put to it". An arbitrator is obliged to make an award as to costs (see §3.1) unless there is an enforceable agreement (see §1.5) that there will be no order as to costs.
25. Section 68(2)(f) of the Arbitration Act 1996.
26. Section 68(2)(b) of the Arbitration Act 1996.
27. *The Catherine L* [1982] 1 Lloyd's Rep. 484.
28. Section 68(2)(h) of the Arbitration Act 1996.
29. Section 68(3) of the Arbitration Act 1996.

9.5 AN APPEAL ON A POINT OF LAW

If either party considers the award as to costs to be wrong in principle, an appeal under section 69 of the Arbitration Act 1996 will be the appropriate and, usually, the only permissible application.[30] If the award as to costs does not clearly follow the general principle that costs follow the event and no reasons are given, an application under section 70(4) of the 1996 Act for reasons should be made.[31]

If both parties consent to an appeal, it will be heard by the court [32] provided all arbitral processes of appeal have been exhausted and the application is brought within 28 days of the date of the award.[33] Where only one party wishes to appeal, leave to appeal is required.[34] The courts have adopted a policy of giving leave only in serious cases of injustice based on an error of law or when there is a major point of principle which is of importance to the development of the commercial law[35]; this policy is now succinctly set out in section 69(3) of the Arbitration Act 1996. While reference to the pre-1996 cases may be of assistance in exceptional circumstances, it is submitted that the principles in section 69(3) of the Arbitration Act 1996 provide an exhaustive code.[36]

The situations where leave may be given are restrictive.[37] It will often be difficult to establish either that the decision is obviously wrong or that the point at issue is of general public importance.[38] In practice leave will be given:

(1) where the award is so perverse that no proper discretion can have

---

30. The distinction drawn in the Arbitration Act 1996 between an appeal on a point of law and other applications relating to "irregularities" was first established by the Arbitration Act 1979, section 1 of which provided for a right of appeal on points of law. Despite this, many applications continued to be made under section 22 of the Arbitration Act 1950—which is akin to section 68 of the 1996 Act—even though the principal basis of the application was that there was an error in principle. Errors of principle are, of course, errors of law, rather than procedural irregularities. In 1990 the Court of Appeal insisted on the demarcation between errors of law and irregularities. In *Blexen Ltd.* v. *G. Percy Trentham* (1990) 54 Build. L.R. 37, Lloyd L.J. said at 43: "Whatever may have been the position as to costs in the old days, the only course open today, where an arbitrator states his reasons, is to challenge those reasons by seeking leave to appeal on a question of law. . . ." Affirmed by Lord Donaldson M.R. in *King* v. *Thomas McKenna Ltd.* [1991] 2 Q.B. 480. Applied in *President of India* v. *Jadranska Slobodna Plovidba* [1992] 2 Lloyd's Rep. 274 and *Cohen* v. *Baram* [1994] 2 Lloyd's Rep. 138.

31. Where a party make an application under section 67, 68 or 69 of the Arbitration Act 1996, the court may also order the arbitrator to state his reasons in sufficient detail for that purpose. The court may also make a further order with respect to any additional costs of the arbitration arising from the order to state reasons: section 70(5) of the Arbitration Act 1996. See *President of India* v. *Jadranska Slobodna Plovidba* [1992] 2 Lloyd's Rep. 274 *per* Hobhouse J. at 279–80 for a statement as to what reasons are sufficient.

32. Section 69(2)(a) of the Arbitration Act 1996.

33. See sections 69 and 70(2), (3) of the Arbitration Act 1996.

34. Section 69(2)(b) of the Arbitration Act 1996. The costs of obtaining leave will normally be costs in the appeal: *The Oinoussian Virtue* [1981] 1 Lloyd's Rep. 533.

35. *The Nema* [1982] A.C. 724 and *The Antaios* [1985] A.C. 191.

36. Note the use of the word "only" in the first line of the subsection.

37. Note that each of the four criteria in (a) to (d) in section 69(3) must be satisfied simultaneously.

38. See section 69(3)(c) of the Arbitration Act 1996.

been exercised and the amount of costs at stake is large relative to the amounts in dispute; or

(2) where the arbitrator sets out reasons for his award as to costs which clearly demonstrate that he has used his discretion on an incorrect basis in law[39] and the amount of costs at stake is large relative to the amounts in dispute; or

(3) where the arbitrator purports to apply a principle of law and in so doing undermines the very principle which he seeks to apply.[40]

If no appeal is made within 28 days,[41] the award as to costs becomes "final, valid and unassailable".[42] If the parties have entered into an exclusion agreement,[43] no appeal in relation to costs will be possible. If the appeal is heard, the court may confirm, vary, set aside or remit the award with its opinion.[44]

Illustration
President of India v. Jadranska Slobodna Plovidba [1992] 2 Lloyd's Rep. 274
"It will be appreciated that in order to succeed on an application for leave to appeal in respect of an award on costs a party will normally have to be prepared to satisfy the highest category of test in the *The Nema* [i.e. the case which established the principles which are largely enacted in section 69(3) of the Arbitration Act 1996] which is tantamount to persuading the court that the appeal will almost certainly be successful. The point will be 'one off'; the decision being attacked is the exercise of a discretion which is *a fortiori* a question of mixed fact and law. Further there will often be other factors present which make it inappropriate that the court should grant leave to appeal", *per* Hobhouse J. at 280–81.

9.6 BRIEF NOTES ON PROCEDURES RELATING TO THE CHALLENGE OF AN AWARD AS TO COSTS

Applications are ordinarily made to the High Court.[45] The procedural aspects of applications to the court are governed by rules of court. At the time of writing,[46] the relevant rules are those in Order 73 of the Rules of the Supreme

39. *Metro-Cammell Hong Kong Ltd.* v. *F.K.I. Engineering plc* [1996] A.D.R.L.N. May 1996.
40. *The Maria* [1993] 2 Lloyd's Rep. 168.
41. Section 70(3) of the Arbitration Act 1996. This time may be extended by the court if the court is satisfied that a substantial injustice would otherwise be done: see section 79 of the Arbitration Act 1996.
42. *Cohen* v. *Baram* [1994] 2 Lloyd's Rep. 138, per Hirst L.J. at 143.
43. Section 69(1) of the Arbitration Act 1996.
44. Section 69(7) of the Arbitration Act 1996.
45. See Order 73, rule 5 of the Rules of the Supreme Court and the High Court and County Courts (Allocation of Arbitration Proceedings) Order 1996, S.I. 1996 No. 3215. The latter provides for applications in and transfers to and from the Central London County Court Business List.
46. Proposals for reform of the civil court system following Lord Woolf's report (*Access to Justice*, H.M.S.O. 1996) will result in revised rules of court.

9.6 Applications to the court in respect of costs

Court.[47] An application for a declaration or injunction (if permitted[48]) may not fall within the definition of "arbitration application" in Order 73 and hence may be commenced by the ordinary originating processes.

Applications under sections 68 and 69 of the Arbitration Act 1996 must ordinarily be brought within 28 days of the date of the award.[49] Compliance with this time means not only must the arbitration application be issued, but that all the affidavits in support have been sworn and filed by the expiry of that time limit.[50] The date of the award is the date given in the award.[51] The fact that the parties have not collected the award does not stop time running.[52] The court may extend the time limit, but only if it satisfied that a substantial injustice would otherwise be done.[53]

---

47. The Supreme Court Rule Committee has drawn up a revised version of Order 73 to accommodate the Arbitration Act 1996: Rules of the Supreme Court (Amendment) Order 1996, S.I. 1996 No. 3219. Applications where the dates of commencement of the arbitration and the making of the application are both later than 31 January 1997 will be made under Part I of the Order.
48. Section 1(c) of the Arbitration Act 1996.
49. Section 70(3) of the Arbitration Act 1996.
50. Order 73, rule 22(1) of the Rules of the Supreme Court.
51. Section 52(5) of the Arbitration Act 1996. If no date is given, the date will be taken to be the date of the (last) signature: section 54 of the Arbitration Act 1996.
52. *The Faith* [1993] 2 Lloyd's Rep. 408 *per* Hobhouse J. at 411.
53. See sections 79 and 80(5) of the Arbitration Act 1996; and Order 73, rule 22(2), (3).

APPENDIX A

PRECEDENTS

A.1 COSTS ORDERS IN RESPECT OF PRELIMINARY MATTERS

Following any interlocutory proceeding including a preliminary meeting, application for security for costs, application for specific discovery, etc., an order may be made in terms such as those below.

IN THE MATTER OF THE ARBITRATION ACT 1996
and
IN THE MATTER OF AN ARBITRATION
between:

A.B.

Claimant

—and—

C.D.

Respondent

ORDER No. [State Number]

[State section of the Arbitration Act etc. if appropriate]

Upon the [Respondent's/Claimant's] application for [state the nature of the application]

And upon hearing [name] on behalf of the Claimant and [name] on behalf of the Respondent, it is hereby directed and ordered that:

1   [set out the substantive orders]
2   [set out the substantive orders]
3   [If appropriate] I reserve the right to supplement the above and/or to issue further orders with liberty to the parties to apply.
4   The costs of this application shall be [state the order, e.g. costs in the arbitration; or Claimant's costs in any event; or Respondent's costs in any event; or Claimant's costs in the arbitration; or Respondent's costs in the arbitration; or paid by the party which incurred them]

Signed E.F., Arbitrator; dated [date].

Notes: 1   The expression "upon hearing" is the standard formula following an oral hearing. Where the proceedings were conducted solely in writing, the expression "upon reading written submissions by . . ." etc. may be appropriate.

133

A.1 Precedents

2 The costs orders appropriate following interlocutory proceedings are set out and discussed in Chapter 4.

A.2 DIRECTION LIMITING THE RECOVERABLE COSTS

A number of possible types of direction may be given under section 65 of the Arbitration Act 1996. Below are found an indicative range.

A.2.1 Limitation of the overall costs of the arbitration

ORDER No. [State Number]

DIRECTION UNDER SECTION 65
OF THE ARBITRATION ACT 1996

Upon the [Respondent's/Claimant's/parties' joint] application for an order that the recoverable costs of the arbitration be limited pursuant to section 65 of the Arbitration Act 1996 ("The Act")

And upon hearing [name] on behalf of the Claimant and [name] on behalf of the Respondent, it is hereby directed and ordered that:

1 The legal and other costs of the parties, as defined in section 59(1)(c) of the Act, recoverable in these proceedings shall be limited to £x for each party.
2 In the event that the arbitration is concluded prior to a full reasoned substantive award, whether by settlement or otherwise, the recoverable costs under paragraph 1 herein shall be limited to such proportion of the limit there stated as is reasonable in all the circumstances.
3 The limit in paragraph 1 herein excludes the costs of or incidental to proceedings to determine the amount of recoverable costs as defined in section 59(2) of the Act.
4 If either party considers that the cost limit set out in paragraph 1 herein has become inappropriate, by reason of any factor which could not reasonably have been foreseen at the date of this application, that party may apply for an increase or decrease in the said costs limit. The costs of any such application may be the subject of an additional order.
5 The costs of this application and order are costs in the arbitration [or other order as appropriate].

Signed E.F., Arbitrator on [date].

Notes: 1 The costs which are limited are defined by reference to the definition set out in section 59(1) of the Arbitration Act 1996. This is useful shorthand and clearly indicates that the fees and expenses of the arbitrator are not included.
2 It is not entirely clear under the Act whether the arbitrator has power to make the order in paragraph 2. If not, he still has power to make an award of costs in these terms at the end of the proceedings, and it is worthwhile putting the parties on notice as to his method of determining reasonable costs.
3 The costs of determining the recoverable costs of the proceedings have been excluded. It is suggested that this allows the costs limit to operate clearly on the central core of costs, namely the parties' costs of the substantive proceedings.
4 It is made explicit that the cost limit relates to the costs of each party, not the aggregate costs. Expressions such as: "the recoverable costs defined in section 59(1)(c) shall be limited to £2,000" may be uncertain. For example where the claimant is successful, is he to recover a maximum of £1,000 (which is arguably his share of the £2,000) or £2,000, being the "recoverable" costs?

5   Paragraph 4 allows either party to seek an adjustment of the order. It is worthwhile setting out the grounds upon which a reapplication may be received. Here a "reasonable foreseeability" test is used.

A.2.2 Limitation of the overall costs of the arbitration: late application

Where an application is made at the outset of the proceeding, all the costs to be incurred may be made subject to the limitation. Where, however, the application is made during the proceedings, some costs will already have been incurred by the parties without notice of the limit. In order to cater for this, the main body of the order will need to be adapted to separate out the costs prior to and those after the order. The operative part of the order may read:

1   The legal and other costs, as defined in section 59(1)(c) of the Act, recoverable in these proceedings shall be limited as follows:

   (a)   costs incurred by the parties up to the date of this direction shall be limited to such costs as have reasonably and not prematurely been incurred;
   (b)   costs incurred from the date of this direction until the conclusion of proceedings shall be limited to £x for each party.
   (c)   for the avoidance of doubt, any costs which are not recoverable under (a) by reason of having been prematurely incurred, will be recoverable, if appropriate under (b).

2   In the event that the arbitration is concluded prior to a full reasoned substantive award, whether by settlement or otherwise, the recoverable costs under paragraph 1(b) herein shall be limited to such proportion of the limit there stated as is reasonable in all the circumstances.
3   The limit in paragraph 1(b) herein excludes the costs of or incidental to proceedings to determine the amount of recoverable costs as defined in section 59(2) of the Act.
4   If either party considers that the costs limit in paragraph 1(b) herein has become inappropriate, by reason of any factor which could not reasonably have been foreseen at the date of this application, that party may apply for an increase or decrease in the said costs limit. The costs of any such application may be the subject of an additional order.

Note: 1   Paragraph 1(a) allows only such costs as have not been prematurely incurred. However, even where an element of costs has been prematurely incurred, a time may come when such costs become recoverable. The clarification in 1(c) is designed to ensure this.

A.2.3 Limitation of specific costs of the arbitration: limitation by activity

Section 65 of the Arbitration Act 1996 enables the arbitrator to make an order with respect to any part of the proceedings. The "part" may be the costs of the parties, specifically excluding the costs of the arbitrator; it may be the costs of a specific application or activity; or it may be the costs of a particular issue or issues.

   In this section, an example is given of an order which may be made where the arbitrator decides to make separate cost limits applicable to different activities. The operative part of the direction may read:

1   The legal and other costs, as defined in section 59(1)(c) of the Act, recoverable in respect of:

   (a)   preparation of statements of case (including all associated instructions and analysis) shall be limited to £x for each party;
   (b)   discovery and inspection of documents (including all incidental costs and charges) shall be limited to £y for each party;

135

     (c)   preparation of witness statements (including all incidental costs and charges) shall be limited to £z for each party;

     (d)   [etc.]

2   If either party considers that the costs limits or any of them set out in paragraph 1 herein have become inappropriate, by reason of any factor which could not reasonably have been foreseen at the date of this application, that party may apply for an increase or decrease in the limits or any of them. The costs of any such application may be the subject of an additional order.

Where the limit relates to a specific proceeding, the order may read:

1   The legal and other costs, as defined in section 59(1)(c) of the Act, recoverable in respect of the hearing of the preliminary issue as to [identify the issue] (as directed in my Order No. X dated [date]) shall be limited to £y for each party.

2   The costs limit in paragraph 1 herein shall include for all advice, preparation and representation in connection with and/or arising out of the hearing of the said preliminary issue.

A.3 DIRECTION FOLLOWING AN APPLICATION FOR SECURITY FOR COSTS

A.3.1 Where there is no independent counterclaim

Where the Claimant advances claims and the Respondent's case is purely defensive, the order for security for costs is straightforward.

IN THE MATTER OF THE ARBITRATION ACT 1996
and
IN THE MATTER OF AN ARBITRATION
between:

A.B.
Claimant

—and

C.D.
Respondent

ORDER No. [State Number]
ORDER FOR SECURITY FOR COSTS
UNDER SECTION 38(3) OF THE ARBITRATION ACT 1996

Upon the Respondent's application for an order that the Claimant do provide security for costs of the arbitration pursuant to section 38(3) of the Arbitration Act 1996 ("the Act")

And upon hearing [name] on behalf of the Claimant and [name] on behalf of the Respondent, it is hereby directed and ordered that:

1   The Claimant shall provide security in the amount of £x for the Respondent's costs in these proceedings. This security shall be provided by way of [state the form the security should take, or state that the parties are to agree on the form with power to apply for further directions].

2   The security shall be provided within N days of the date of this order. If it is not, the proceedings will automatically be stayed.

3   At any time after the proceedings are stayed, the Respondent may apply for me to issue a peremptory order under section 41(5) of the Act, requiring compliance with paragraph 1 of this order, prescribing a time for compliance. I may, in any event, issue a peremptory order following the expiry of M months from the date of this order.

4   If the Claimant fails to comply with the peremptory order, I may, upon the application of the Respondent, and, may in any event following the expiry of L months of the date of the failure to comply, make an award dismissing the claims of the Claimant.

5   The costs of this application and order shall be costs in the arbitration. The costs of any proceedings in this arbitration (if any) consequent upon the Claimant's failure to provide security in accordance with my order in paragraph 1 herein shall be borne by the Claimant in any event.

Signed E.F., Arbitrator on [date].

Notes: 1   It is not necessary to set out the detailed consequences of failing to comply with the Order. Nevertheless, it is frequently valuable for the parties to see in advance what will happen.

2   The arbitrator must use his discretion at each stage and hence the word "may" (e.g. "I may, in any event, issue a peremptory order") is used in preference to "shall". For the same reason, no exact time for compliance is stated in relation to the peremptory order.

3   The form of the security may be stated. Alternatively, the arbitrator may direct that unless the Claimant offers security acceptable to the Respondent, the arbitrator may make further directions.

4   The order preserves the right of the arbitrator to make directions following a period of inactivity. This is helpful to the arbitrator. He has at all stages a continuing duty under section 33 of the Arbitration Act 1996. In practice, arbitrations sometimes go very quiet and this provision may help to ensure that the parties advise the arbitrator, e.g. of any settlement which has been made.

5   Where the security is to be given in the form of a bond etc., the arbitrator should make provision for those costs.

A.3.2 Where there are independent claims and counterclaims

Where both the Claimant and the Respondent advance independent claims and only one party is ordered to provide security for costs the position is more complex. Below is given a possible operative part of an order.

1   The Claimant shall provide security in the sum of £x for the Respondent's costs of defending against the Claimant's claims. The security shall be provided by way of [state the form the security should take, or state that the parties are to agree on the form with power to apply for further directions].

2   The security shall be provided within N days of the date of this order. In the event that the security is not provided within N days of the date of this order, the proceedings on the Claimant's claims will be stayed. For the avoidance of doubt, the Respondent's counterclaims will not be stayed.

3   At any time after the Claimant's claims have been stayed, the Respondent may apply to me for:

(a)   the issue of a peremptory order under section 41(5) of the Act, requiring compliance with paragraph 1 herein, prescribing a time for compliance.

(b)   further directions as to the hearing of the Respondent's counterclaims.

4   If no application is received from the Respondent as provided in paragraph 3(a) herein, I may, in any event, issue to the Claimant following the expiry of M months from the date of this order, a peremptory order requiring compliance

with paragraph 1 herein, prescribing a time for compliance.

5 If the Claimant fails to comply with the peremptory order, I may, upon the application of the Respondent, and may, in any event following the expiry of L months of the date of the failure to comply, make an award dismissing the claims of the Claimant.

Note: 1 It is worth stating expressly that the Claimant's failure to supply the security will not affect the Respondent's independent claims.

A.4 AWARD AS TO COSTS

In order for a party to recover his costs, he must produce an award as to costs which entitles him to them. A number of types of award as to costs may be drawn. In these examples, it is assumed that the following sequence of awards is produced:

(1) First Award: this is an award as to liability and quantum on substantive claims.
(2) Second Award: this is the award as to liability for costs. This award is dealt with in the present section.
(3) Third Award: this award deals with the determination of recoverable costs. This award is dealt with in section A.6.

IN THE MATTER OF THE ARBITRATION ACT 1996
and
IN THE MATTER OF AN ARBITRATION
between:

A.B.
Claimant
—and—

C.D.
Respondent

SECOND AWARD

My First Award in these proceedings was made on [date]. It dealt with the substantive claims in this arbitration.

Following the publication of my First Award, I invited the parties to make written submissions as to liability for the recoverable costs of the arbitration. Having received submissions from both parties, I called a short hearing on [date].

The Claimant was represented by [name] and [name] the Respondent was represented by [name].

This is my Second Award. It deals with liability for the recoverable costs of the arbitration (except the costs of determining the recoverable costs of the arbitration). It also deals with my fees and expenses of my First and Second Awards.

Reasons for this, my Second Award

A Under my First Award, the Claimant recovered £80,000 in respect of his claims. The Respondent recovered £32,000 in respect of his counterclaim. The net recovery by the Claimant was £48,000.

B The Claimant commenced the proceedings properly. The Respondent owed him a considerable amount of money. The Claimant is entitled to his reasonable costs for commencing and proceeding with the arbitration. However, on [date], the Respondent made a written offer in which the Claimant was offered £60,000 plus his reasonable costs to settle the proceedings at that date. The Claimant did not accept the offer. The value of the offer was more than the net sum eventually recovered by the Claimant. I adjudge that the offer was successful in protecting the Respondent's costs from the date when it should reasonably have been accepted. I adjudge that that date was [date x]; this date was 21 days after the receipt of the offer by the Claimant, by analogy with the period used in litigation proceedings.

C   Accordingly, I adjudge that prior to the date when the offer should have been accepted, namely [date x], the Claimant is entitled to his recoverable costs. And I adjudge that following that date, the Respondent is entitled to his recoverable costs.

D   The Respondent is, however, to be liable for his own costs and the costs of the Claimant in respect of his application for [state nature of application] which was dismissed with costs in my Order No. X. The application was ill-founded.

E   As to my own fees, I have decided that the Respondent shall pay one quarter of my fees and expenses which corresponds approximately to the proportion of my fees and expenses for the period prior to his making the offer. The Claimant shall pay the remainder.

F   As set out in my interim account dated [date] my fees and expenses up until the date of my First Award were £3,000 plus VAT. My fees and expenses of this, my Second Award, are £500 plus VAT as set out in the Schedule appended hereto.

ACCORDINGLY I HEREBY AWARD and DIRECT that:

1   The Respondent shall pay the Claimant's recoverable legal and other costs of the arbitration up until [date x]. Thereafter, the Claimant shall pay (a) the respondent's legal and other recoverable costs of the arbitration, except those costs specifically set out in paragraph 2 below and (b) the costs of determining the recoverable costs, which will be dealt with in a subsequent award. The net costs payable shall attract interest at a rate of 8 per cent per annum simple from the date of this award.

2   The Respondent shall pay his own costs and the recoverable legal and other costs of the Claimant in relation to his application which was dismissed with costs in my Order No. X dated [date]. That order in appended hereto and now takes effect as part of this award.

3   Unless the amounts of the above costs are agreed by the parties, I shall determine them under section 63(3) of the Arbitration Act 1996 ("the Act") on the basis given in section 63(5) of the Act.

4   I determine that the total amount of my recoverable fees and expenses is £3,500 [Three thousand five hundred pounds Sterling] plus VAT. The Claimant shall pay 75 per cent of this and the Respondent shall pay the remaining 25 per cent. If either party has already paid any sum in excess of their liability, the other shall refund him immediately.

This Award was made on [date] by me, E.F., arbitrator, in London, England. The Seat of this arbitration is England.

Notes: 1   The award must comply with the formalities prescribed in section 52 of the Arbitration Act 1996. It must set out the seat, give the date, contain reasons and be signed.

2   The reasons given in this example are rather obvious. They are included, however, so that the parties and the court can see the process by which the award is arrived at. In complex cases, reasons become more important.

3   The award is principally concerned with the liability for costs. In order to allow the parties to agree the amount of costs payable, the amount of the arbitrators's fees are stated. This is subject, of course, to an application by either party under section 64(2) of the Arbitration Act 1996.

4   The basis on which the costs will be determined (i.e. under section 63(5) of the Arbitration Act 1996) is stated so as to enable the parties to agree amongst themselves with greater certainty what the recoverable costs are to be.

A.5 DIRECTION AS TO THE DETERMINATION OF THE RECOVERABLE COSTS

IN THE MATTER OF THE ARBITRATION ACT 1996
and
IN THE MATTER OF AN ARBITRATION
between:

A.B.
Claimant
—and—

C.D.
Respondent

ORDER No. [State Number]
DIRECTIONS AS TO THE DETERMINATION OF RECOVERABLE COSTS

In my award dated [date] I awarded the [Claimant/Respondent—the receiving party] his recoverable costs to be paid by the [Respondent/Claimant—the paying party].

I further directed that, unless the parties reached agreement as to the recoverable costs, I would determine them under section 63(3) of the Arbitration Act 1996. Further to that award and having received an application from the [receiving party] asserting that the costs have not been agreed I direct and order that:

1 The [receiving party] shall supply me and the [paying party] with a schedule of the costs which he has actually incurred in connection with these proceedings for which a claim is made.
2 Where a claim is made, it is to be particularised in sufficient detail for me and the [paying party] to be able to identify how and why the item of costs was incurred.
3 The schedule is to indicate whether and, if so, the dates when any payments were made by the [receiving party] or his representatives.
4 Where, in respect of any item of costs, the [receiving party] claims less than the full amount shown in the schedule, this is to be clearly indicated.
5 Within N days of receipt of the [receiving party]'s schedule, the [paying party] will supply me with full details of its objections to any costs claimed. Within M days of receipt of such objections, the [receiving party] may reply in writing.
6 At that stage, I may direct that a telephone conference or meeting be held in order to allow the parties to make such further submissions as may be appropriate, including as to the costs of determining the recoverable costs.

E.F., Arbitrator, dated [date].

Notes: 1 This order for direction sets out one possible approach to the determination of recoverable costs. Many arbitrators would associate this order with a "commercial basis" of determining the recoverable costs.
2 The arbitrator might direct the precise format in which he wishes to receive documents. For instance: "The receiving party will supply me and the other party with a four-column schedule giving (a) date and reference for each entry, (b) a chronological schedule of the full costs liability of the receiving party supported by receipts or a sworn statement, (c) a corresponding list of amounts claimed in respect thereof, together with a brief explanation associated with each item claimed describing it in the context of the proceedings as a whole and (d) a column for the paying party to make comments and/or objections. . . ."

A.6 AWARD AS TO RECOVERABLE COSTS

IN THE MATTER OF THE ARBITRATION ACT 1996
and
IN THE MATTER OF AN ARBITRATION
between:

A.B.

Claimant

—and—

C.D.

Respondent

THIRD AWARD

My First Award in these proceedings was made on [date]. It dealt with the substantive claims in this arbitration.

My Second Award dealt with liability for the recoverable costs of the arbitration. In my Second Award I directed that if the parties were unable to agree the amount of costs recoverable under my Second Award I would determine them under section 63(3) of the Arbitration Act 1996 in accordance with the provisions of section 63(5) of that Act.

No such agreement was reached and I issued an order on [date] giving directions for the determination of the recoverable costs.

Now having received documents in support of the claims of the parties as to costs; and having received written objections to the claims as to costs; and having heard [name] for the Claimant and [name] for the Respondent on [date] I have considered carefully the amount of costs properly payable under the terms of my Second Award.

This is my Third Award. It deals with the determination of the recoverable costs of the arbitration and the costs of that determination.

Reasons for this, my Third Award

A   I have set out the claims for costs made by the Claimant and the Respondent in Schedules 1 and 2 attached hereto. I have marked on the schedules a list of deductions and disallowances with manuscript reasons.

B   The basis upon which I have acted is that set out in section 63(5) of the Arbitration Act 1996, namely that a reasonable amount has been allowed in respect of all costs reasonably incurred; and any doubt as to whether costs were reasonably incurred or were reasonable in amount were resolved in favour of the paying party.

C   As to the costs which the Claimant claims: the costs recoverable by the Claimant from the Respondent amount to £2,000.

D   As to the costs which the Respondent claims: the costs recoverable by the Respondent from the Claimant amount to £6,000.

E   The Respondent is entitled to receive a net payment from the Claimant in respect of recoverable legal and other costs of the parties of £4,000.

F   At the conclusion of the hearing I invited the parties to address me as to what order should be made as to the costs of determining the recoverable costs. The Claimant accepted that the Respondent was entitled to his costs in that respect. I received a brief description of the costs involved. I have determined that, in all the circumstances, an appropriate amount is £550 which is to be paid by the Claimant to the Respondent.

G   I have also determined my fees and expenses in connection with determining the recoverable costs as £350 plus VAT.

ACCORDINGLY I HEREBY AWARD and DETERMINE that:

1   The Claimant shall pay the Respondent £4,000 [Four thousand pounds Sterling] in respect of the recoverable legal and other costs of the parties with interest at 8 per cent per annum simple from the date of my Second Award dated [date].

2   The Claimant will pay the Respondent's costs of determining the recoverable costs of the arbitration in the sum of £550 [Five hundred and fifty pounds Sterling] with interest at 8 per cent per annum simple from the date of this, my Third award.

3   The Claimant will pay my fees and expenses in respect of determining the recoverable costs of the arbitration in the sum of £350 [Three hundred and fifty pounds Sterling] plus VAT, with interest at 8 per cent per annum simple from the date of this, my Third Award.

This Award was made on [date] by me, E.F., arbitrator, in London, England. The Seat of this arbitration is England.

Notes: 1   This award sets out the history of the awards made as a preamble. This assists a court in interpreting such an award.

            2   The determination of the recoverable costs is to be by award. Such award must comply with the formalities prescribed in section 52 of the Arbitration Act 1996. Like any other award, it must set out the seat, give the date, contain reasons and be signed.

            3   By section 63(3) of the Arbitration Act 1996, the award must specify the basis for the determination and the items of recoverable cost and the amounts referable to each. The basis is set out in paragraph B of the Award. It is thought sufficient, if the items of recoverable costs and the amounts referable to each are dealt with by way of a schedule with manuscript disallowances. This is certainly a cost effective method.

            4   At some point a final award must be issued. This is it. All costs, including the costs of determining the recoverable costs are collected in this award.

A.7 OFFERS OF SETTLEMENT

A.7.1 Calderbank letter

Calderbank letters have received substantial judicial approval: see Chapter 7. The form below sets out a typical example.

WITHOUT PREJUDICE SAVE AS TO COSTS
Dear Sirs
Arbitration between A.B. and C.D.
We are instructed by our clients, C.D. to make your clients, A.B., an offer to settle the above proceedings, in the following terms.

1   Neither the existence nor the contents of this offer shall be disclosed to the arbitrator until he has determined all issues of liability and quantum on the substantive claims and counterclaims in these proceedings.

2   Our clients offer your clients the sum of £[state the amount] (inclusive of interest) plus their reasonable costs in consideration for settling all claims and counterclaims in the above proceedings. Our clients will pay the arbitrator's fees and expenses.

3   This offer will remain open for acceptance at any time until the start of the substantive hearing with the proviso that if it is not accepted within 21 days from the date upon which it is received, your clients will pay our clients' reasonable costs and the arbitrator's fees and expenses incurred after the expiry of that period.

4   If your clients do not accept the offer and they go on to recover less than its value in the award as to substantive issues, our clients will bring this letter to the arbitrator's

attention when the question of costs is to be decided. It will be our clients' contention that, based on the authorities, they are entitled to their reasonable costs of these proceedings from the date when the 21-day period (referred to in paragraph 3) expired.

Yours etc.

Note: 1   The offer is kept open until the start of the hearing, subject to the usual terms. Following *The Toni* [1974] 1 Lloyd's Rep. 489 and *Garner* v. *Cleggs* [1983] 1 W.L.R. 862 (see Chapter 7) it is thought that time limited offers are unsafe. An arbitrator who chooses to ignore such an offer will not misdirect himself: *Mark Amy Ltd.* v. *Olcott Investments Ltd.*, Royal Court of Jersey (Samedi Division), 4 November 1996 (unreported).

A.7.2 Reverse Calderbank letter

A reverse Calderbank letter is written by a Claimant to the Respondent setting out the terms on which the proceedings may be settled. Such a device has not been judicially approved. Nevertheless it seems in keeping with the philosophy that parties should be rewarded for making reasonable offers of settlement.

WITHOUT PREJUDICE SAVE AS TO COSTS
Dear Sirs
Arbitration between A.B. and C.D.
We are instructed by our clients, A.B. to make your clients, C.D., an offer to settle the above proceedings, in the following terms.

1   Neither the existence nor the contents of this offer shall be disclosed to the arbitrator until he has determined all issues of liability and quantum on the substantive claims and counterclaims in these proceedings.
2   Our clients will accept the sum of £[state the amount] plus their reasonable costs to today's date in consideration of settling all claims and counterclaims in these proceedings. Both parties will pay the arbitrator's fees and expenses in equal shares.
3   This offer will remain open for acceptance at any time until the start of the substantive hearing with the proviso that if it is not accepted within 21 days from the date upon which it is received, your clients will pay our clients' reasonable costs and the arbitrator's fees and expenses incurred after the expiry of that period.
4   If your clients do not accept the offer and our clients go on to recover more than its value in the award as to substantive issues, our clients will bring this letter to the arbitrator's attention when the question of costs is to be decided. It will be our clients' contention that they are entitled to their reasonable costs until the date when this offer should have been accepted; and thereafter they are entitled to receive costs on a more generous basis than that set out in section 63(5) of the Arbitration Act 1996.
5   For the avoidance of doubt, this letter will not have any effect on costs in the event that our clients recover less than the value of the offer.

Yours etc.

Notes: 1   The offer as to costs is generous to the Respondent. If the Respondent were to offer £x, he would have to offer to pay the Claimant's costs up until then and for another, say, 21 days. By requiring payment of costs only until the date of the letter, the Claimant is offering a more generous settlement than is strictly necessary. Likewise, in offering to share the arbitrator's fees and expenses, the Claimant is being generous. While such generosity is not strictly necessary, it does assist the Claimant in his ultimate contention that here was an offer which was so reasonable that there could be no excuse for the offeree to continue with the proceedings; and therefore the offeree ought to pay all the additional costs incurred on an indemnity basis.
        2   The letter uses the reference to section 63(5) of the Arbitration Act 1996. This

provides for a basis of costs which is equivalent to the "standard basis" in court proceedings. This part of the letter, therefore, is not expressly asking for "indemnity costs"; but the effect is clear.

3   In the final paragraph the letter preserves the position where the Claimant recovers less than the value of the offer. It would be unfortunate if an offer such as this might deprive the Claimant of costs where otherwise he would recover them.

4   Where the Respondent has made a Calderbank offer, a reverse Calderbank is still possible. It may be worthwhile including a statement that the reverse offer is an independent offer and is not intended to reject the offer already made by the Respondent.

APPENDIX B

ARBITRATION ACT 1996

The Arbitration Act 1996 contains a group of sections (sections 59 to 65 inclusive) under the title "Costs of the arbitration". There is much material relevant to the subject of this book outside these sections. The interactions between the various sections of the statute make it impractical to separate out those provisions which deal with or bear upon the question of costs. Accordingly, the Act is reproduced in its entirety, save for Schedule 3 (Consequential amendments) and Schedule 4 (Repeals).

Note that in the order bringing the Act into force,[1] sections 85 to 87 (which would have created a special regime for domestic arbitrations) were specifically not brought into force.

ARRANGEMENT OF SECTIONS

Part I   Arbitration pursuant to an arbitration agreement

INTRODUCTORY

THE ARBITRATION AGREEMENT

STAY OF LEGAL PROCEEDINGS

COMMENCEMENT OF ARBITRAL PROCEEDINGS

1. The Arbitration Act 1996 (Commencement No. 1) Order 1996.

General principles

1. The provisions of this Part are founded on the following principles, and shall be construed accordingly—
- (a) the object of arbitration is to obtain the fair resolution of disputes by an impartial tribunal without unnecessary delay or expense;
- (b) the parties should be free to agree how their disputes are resolved, subject only to such safeguards as are necessary in the public interest;
- (c) in matters governed by this Part the court should not intervene except as provided by this Part.

Scope of application of provisions

2.—(1) The provisions of this Part apply where the seat of the arbitration is in England and Wales or Northern Ireland.

(2) The following sections apply even if the seat of the arbitration is outside England and Wales or Northern Ireland or no seat has been designated or determined—
- (a) sections 9 to 11 (stay of legal proceedings, &c.), and
- (b) section 66 (enforcement of arbitral awards).

(3) The powers conferred by the following sections apply even if the seat of the arbitration is outside England and Wales or Northern Ireland or no seat has been designated or determined—
- (a) section 43 (securing the attendance of witnesses), and
- (b) section 44 (court powers exercisable in support of arbitral proceedings);

but the court may refuse to exercise any such power if, in the opinion of the court, the fact that the seat of the arbitration is outside England and Wales or Northern Ireland, or that when designated or determined the seat is likely to be outside England and Wales or Northern Ireland, makes it inappropriate to do so.

(4) The court may exercise a power conferred by any provision of this Part not mentioned in subsection (2) or (3) for the purpose of supporting the arbitral process where—

    (a) no seat of the arbitration has been designated or determined, and

    (b) by reason of a connection with England and Wales or Northern Ireland the court is satisfied that it is appropriate to do so.

(5) Section 7 (separability of arbitration agreement) and section 8 (death of a party) apply where the law applicable to the arbitration agreement is the law of England and Wales or Northern Ireland even if the seat of the arbitration is outside England and Wales or Northern Ireland or has not been designated or determined.

The seat of the arbitration

3. In this Part "the seat of the arbitration" means the juridical seat of the arbitration designated—

    (a) by the parties to the arbitration agreement, or

    (b) by any arbitral or other institution or person vested by the parties with powers in that regard, or

    (c) by the arbitral tribunal if so authorised by the parties,

or determined, in the absence of any such designation, having regard to the parties' agreement and all the relevant circumstances.

Mandatory and non-mandatory provisions

4.—(1) The mandatory provisions of this Part are listed in Schedule 1 and have effect notwithstanding any agreement to the contrary.

(2) The other provisions of this Part (the "non-mandatory provisions") allow the parties to make their own arrangements by agreement but provide rules which apply in the absence of such agreement.

(3) The parties may make such arrangements by agreeing to the application of institutional rules or providing any other means by which a matter may be decided.

(4) It is immaterial whether or not the law applicable to the parties' agreement is the law of England and Wales or, as the case may be, Northern Ireland.

(5) The choice of a law other than the law of England and Wales or Northern Ireland as the applicable law in respect of a matter provided for by a non-mandatory provision of this Part is equivalent to an agreement making provision about that matter.

For this purpose an applicable law determined in accordance with the parties' agreement, or which is objectively determined in the absence of any express or implied choice, shall be treated as chosen by the parties.

Agreements to be in writing

5.—(1) The provisions of this Part apply only where the arbitration agreement is in writing, and any other agreement between the parties as to any matter is effective for the purposes of this Part only if in writing.

The expressions "agreement", "agree" and "agreed" shall be construed accordingly.

(2) There is an agreement in writing—

    (a) if the agreement is made in writing (whether or not it is signed by the parties),

    (b) if the agreement is made by exchange of communications in writing, or

    (c) if the agreement is evidenced in writing.

(3) Where parties agree otherwise than in writing by reference to terms which are in writing, they make an agreement in writing.

(4) An agreement is evidenced in writing if an agreement made otherwise than in

writing is recorded by one of the parties, or by a third party, with the authority of the parties to the agreement.

(5) An exchange of written submissions in arbitral or legal proceedings in which the existence of an agreement otherwise than in writing is alleged by one party against another party and not denied by the other party in his response constitutes as between those parties an agreement in writing to the effect alleged.

(6) References in this Part to anything being written or in writing include its being recorded by any means.

Definition of arbitration agreement

6.—(1) In this Part an "arbitration agreement" means an agreement to submit to arbitration present or future disputes (whether they are contractual or not).

(2) The reference in an agreement to a written form of arbitration clause or to a document containing an arbitration clause constitutes an arbitration agreement if the reference is such as to make that clause part of the agreement.

Separability of arbitration agreement

7. Unless otherwise agreed by the parties, an arbitration agreement which forms or was intended to form part of another agreement (whether or not in writing) shall not be regarded as invalid, non-existent or ineffective because that other agreement is invalid, or did not come into existence or has become ineffective, and it shall for that purpose be treated as a distinct agreement.

Whether agreement discharged by death of party

8.—(1) Unless otherwise agreed by the parties, an arbitration agreement is not discharged by the death of a party and may be enforced by or against the personal representatives of that party.

(2) Subsection (1) does not affect the operation of any enactment or rule of law by virtue of which a substantive right or obligation is extinguished by death.

Stay of legal proceedings

9.—(1) A party to an arbitration agreement against whom legal proceedings are brought (whether by way of claim or counterclaim) in respect of a matter which under the agreement is to be referred to arbitration may (upon notice to the other parties to the proceedings) apply to the court in which the proceedings have been brought to stay the proceedings so far as they concern that matter.

(2) An application may be made notwithstanding that the matter is to be referred to arbitration only after the exhaustion of other dispute resolution procedures.

(3) An application may not be made by a person before taking the appropriate procedural step (if any) to acknowledge the legal proceedings against him or after he has taken any step in those proceedings to answer the substantive claim.

(4) On an application under this section the court shall grant a stay unless satisfied that the arbitration agreement is null and void, inoperative, or incapable of being performed.

(5) If the court refuses to stay the legal proceedings, any provision that an award is a condition precedent to the bringing of legal proceedings in respect of any matter is of no effect in relation to those proceedings.

Reference of interpleader issue to arbitration

10.—(1) Where in legal proceedings relief by way of interpleader is granted and any issue between the claimants is one in respect of which there is an arbitration agreement between them, the court granting the relief shall direct that the issue be determined in accordance with the agreement unless the circumstances are such that proceedings brought by a claimant in respect of the matter would not be stayed.

(2) Where subsection (1) applies but the court does not direct that the issue be determined in accordance with the arbitration agreement, any provision that an award is a condition precedent to the bringing of legal proceedings in respect of any matter shall not affect the determination of that issue by the court.

Retention of security where Admiralty proceedings stayed

11.—(1) Where Admiralty proceedings are stayed on the ground that the dispute in question should be submitted to arbitration, the court granting the stay may, if in those proceedings property has been arrested or bail or other security has been given to prevent or obtain release from arrest—

    (a) order that the property arrested be retained as security for the satisfaction of any award given in the arbitration in respect of that dispute, or

    (b) order that the stay of those proceedings be conditional on the provision of equivalent security for the satisfaction of any such award.

(2) Subject to any provision made by rules of court and to any necessary modifications, the same law and practice shall apply in relation to property retained in pursuance of an order as would apply if it were held for the purposes of proceedings in the court making the order.

Power of court to extend time for beginning arbitral proceedings, &c

12.—(1) Where an arbitration agreement to refer future disputes to arbitration provides that a claim shall be barred, or the claimant's right extinguished, unless the claimant takes within a time fixed by the agreement some step—

    (a) to begin arbitral proceedings, or

    (b) to begin other dispute resolution procedures which must be exhausted before arbitral proceedings can be begun,

the court may by order extend the time for taking that step.

(2) Any party to the arbitration agreement may apply for such an order (upon notice to the other parties), but only after a claim has arisen and after exhausting any available arbitral process for obtaining an extension of time.

(3) The court shall make an order only if satisfied—

    (a) that the circumstances are such as were outside the reasonable contemplation of the parties when they agreed the provision in question, and that it would be just to extend the time, or

    (b) that the conduct of one party makes it unjust to hold the other party to the strict terms of the provision in question.

(4) The court may extend the time for such period and on such terms as it thinks fit, and may do so whether or not the time previously fixed (by agreement or by a previous order) has expired.

(5) An order under this section does not affect the operation of the Limitation Acts (see section 13).

(6) The leave of the court is required for any appeal from a decision of the court under this section.

Application of Limitation Acts

13.—(1) The Limitation Acts apply to arbitral proceedings as they apply to legal proceedings.

(2) The court may order that in computing the time prescribed by the Limitation Acts for the commencement of proceedings (including arbitral proceedings) in respect of a dispute which was the subject matter—

    (a) of an award which the court orders to be set aside or declares to be of no effect, or

    (b) of the affected part of an award which the court orders to be set aside in part, or declares to be in part of no effect,

the period between the commencement of the arbitration and the date of the order referred to in paragraph (a) or (b) shall be excluded.

(3) In determining for the purposes of the Limitation Acts when a cause of action accrued, any provision that an award is a condition precedent to the bringing of legal proceedings in respect of a matter to which an arbitration agreement applies shall be disregarded.

(4) In this Part "the Limitation Acts" means—

    (a) in England and Wales, the Limitation Act 1980, the Foreign Limitation Periods Act 1984 and any other enactment (whenever passed) relating to the limitation of actions;

    (b) in Northern Ireland, the Limitation (Northern Ireland) Order 1989, the Foreign Limitation Periods (Northern Ireland) Order 1985 and any other enactment (whenever passed) relating to the limitation of actions.

Commencement of arbitral proceedings

14.—(1) The parties are free to agree when arbitral proceedings are to be regarded as commenced for the purposes of this Part and for the purposes of the Limitation Acts.

(2) If there is no such agreement the following provisions apply.

(3) Where the arbitrator is named or designated in the arbitration agreement, arbitral proceedings are commenced in respect of a matter when one party serves on the other party or parties a notice in writing requiring him or them to submit that matter to the person so named or designated.

(4) Where the arbitrator or arbitrators are to be appointed by the parties, arbitral proceedings are commenced in respect of a matter when one party serves on the other party or parties notice in writing requiring him or them to appoint an arbitrator or to agree to the appointment of an arbitrator in respect of that matter.

(5) Where the arbitrator or arbitrators are to be appointed by a person other than a party to the proceedings, arbitral proceedings are commenced in respect of a matter when one party gives notice in writing to that person requesting him to make the appointment in respect of that matter.

The arbitral tribunal

15.—(1) The parties are free to agree on the number of arbitrators to form the tribunal and whether there is to be a chairman or umpire.

(2) Unless otherwise agreed by the parties, an agreement that the number of arbitrators shall be two or any other even number shall be understood as requiring the appointment of an additional arbitrator as chairman of the tribunal.

(3) If there is no agreement as to the number of arbitrators, the tribunal shall consist of a sole arbitrator.

Procedure for appointment of arbitrators

16.—(1) The parties are free to agree on the procedure for appointing the arbitrator or arbitrators, including the procedure for appointing any chairman or umpire.

(2) If or to the extent that there is no such agreement, the following provisions apply.

(3) If the tribunal is to consist of a sole arbitrator, the parties shall jointly appoint the arbitrator not later than 28 days after service of a request in writing by either party to do so.

(4) If the tribunal is to consist of two arbitrators, each party shall appoint one arbitrator not later than 14 days after service of a request in writing by either party to do so.

(5) If the tribunal is to consist of three arbitrators—

    (a) each party shall appoint one arbitrator not later than 14 days after service of a request in writing by either party to do so, and

    (b) the two so appointed shall forthwith appoint a third arbitrator as the chairman of the tribunal.

(6) If the tribunal is to consist of two arbitrators and an umpire—

    (a) each party shall appoint one arbitrator not later than 14 days after service of a request in writing by either party to do so, and

    (b) the two so appointed may appoint an umpire at any time after they themselves are appointed and shall do so before any substantive hearing or forthwith if they cannot agree on a matter relating to the arbitration.

(7) In any other case (in particular, if there are more than two parties) section 18 applies as in the case of a failure of the agreed appointment procedure.

Power in case of default to appoint sole arbitrator

17.—(1) Unless the parties otherwise agree, where each of two parties to an arbitration agreement is to appoint an arbitrator and one party ("the party in default") refuses to do so, or fails to do so within the time specified, the other party, having duly appointed his arbitrator, may give notice in writing to the party in default that he proposes to appoint his arbitrator to act as sole arbitrator.

(2) If the party in default does not within 7 clear days of that notice being given—

    (a) make the required appointment, and

    (b) notify the other party that he has done so,

the other party may appoint his arbitrator as sole arbitrator whose award shall be binding on both parties as if he had been so appointed by agreement.

(3) Where a sole arbitrator has been appointed under subsection (2), the party in default may (upon notice to the appointing party) apply to the court which may set aside the appointment.

(4) The leave of the court is required for any appeal from a decision of the court under this section.

Failure of appointment procedure

18.—(1) The parties are free to agree what is to happen in the event of a failure of the procedure for the appointment of the arbitral tribunal.

There is no failure if an appointment is duly made under section 17 (power in case of default to appoint sole arbitrator), unless that appointment is set aside.

(2) If or to the extent that there is no such agreement any party to the arbitration agreement may (upon notice to the other parties) apply to the court to exercise its powers under this section.

(3) Those powers are—

    (a) to give directions as to the making of any necessary appointments;

(b) to direct that the tribunal shall be constituted by such appointments (or any one or more of them) as have been made;

(c) to revoke any appointments already made;

(d) to make any necessary appointments itself.

(4) An appointment made by the court under this section has effect as if made with the agreement of the parties.

(5) The leave of the court is required for any appeal from a decision of the court under this section.

Court to have regard to agreed qualifications

19. In deciding whether to exercise, and in considering how to exercise, any of its powers under section 16 (procedure for appointment of arbitrators) or section 18 (failure of appointment procedure), the court shall have due regard to any agreement of the parties as to the qualifications required of the arbitrators.

Chairman

20.—(1) Where the parties have agreed that there is to be a chairman, they are free to agree what the functions of the chairman are to be in relation to the making of decisions, orders and awards.

(2) If or to the extent that there is no such agreement, the following provisions apply.

(3) Decisions, orders and awards shall be made by all or a majority of the arbitrators (including the chairman).

(4) The view of the chairman shall prevail in relation to a decision, order or award in respect of which there is neither unanimity nor a majority under subsection (3).

Umpire

21.—(1) Where the parties have agreed that there is to be an umpire, they are free to agree what the functions of the umpire are to be, and in particular—

(a) whether he is to attend the proceedings, and

(b) when he is to replace the other arbitrators as the tribunal with power to make decisions, orders and awards.

(2) If or to the extent that there is no such agreement, the following provisions apply.

(3) The umpire shall attend the proceedings and be supplied with the same documents and other materials as are supplied to the other arbitrators.

(4) Decisions, orders and awards shall be made by the other arbitrators unless and until they cannot agree on a matter relating to the arbitration.

In that event they shall forthwith give notice in writing to the parties and the umpire, whereupon the umpire shall replace them as the tribunal with power to make decisions, orders and awards as if he were sole arbitrator.

(5) If the arbitrators cannot agree but fail to give notice of that fact, or if any of them fails to join in the giving of notice, any party to the arbitral proceedings may (upon notice to the other parties and to the tribunal) apply to the court which may order that the umpire shall replace the other arbitrators as the tribunal with power to make decisions, orders and awards as if he were sole arbitrator.

(6) The leave of the court is required for any appeal from a decision of the court under this section.

Decision-making where no chairman or umpire

22.—(1) Where the parties agree that there shall be two or more arbitrators with no chairman or umpire, the parties are free to agree how the tribunal is to make decisions, orders and awards.

(2) If there is no such agreement, decisions, orders and awards shall be made by all or a majority of the arbitrators.

Revocation of arbitrator's authority

23.—(1) The parties are free to agree in what circumstances the authority of an arbitrator may be revoked.

(2) If or to the extent that there is no such agreement the following provisions apply.

(3) The authority of an arbitrator may not be revoked except—

    (a) by the parties acting jointly, or

    (b) by an arbitral or other institution or person vested by the parties with powers in that regard.

(4) Revocation of the authority of an arbitrator by the parties acting jointly must be agreed in writing unless the parties also agree (whether or not in writing) to terminate the arbitration agreement.

(5) Nothing in this section affects the power of the court—

    (a) to revoke an appointment under section 18 (powers exercisable in case of failure of appointment procedure), or

    (b) to remove an arbitrator on the grounds specified in section 24.

Power of court to remove arbitrator

24.—(1) A party to arbitral proceedings may (upon notice to the other parties, to the arbitrator concerned and to any other arbitrator) apply to the court to remove an arbitrator on any of the following grounds—

    (a) that circumstances exist that give rise to justifiable doubts as to his impartiality;

    (b) that he does not possess the qualifications required by the arbitration agreement;

    (c) that he is physically or mentally incapable of conducting the proceedings or there are justifiable doubts as to his capacity to do so;

    (d) that he has refused or failed—

        (i) properly to conduct the proceedings, or

        (ii) to use all reasonable despatch in conducting the proceedings or making an award,

and that substantial injustice has been or will be caused to the applicant.

(2) If there is an arbitral or other institution or person vested by the parties with power to remove an arbitrator, the court shall not exercise its power of removal unless satisfied that the applicant has first exhausted any available recourse to that institution or person.

(3) The arbitral tribunal may continue the arbitral proceedings and make an award while an application to the court under this section is pending.

(4) Where the court removes an arbitrator, it may make such order as it thinks fit with respect to his entitlement (if any) to fees or expenses, or the repayment of any fees or expenses already paid.

(5) The arbitrator concerned is entitled to appear and be heard by the court before it makes any order under this section.

(6) The leave of the court is required for any appeal from a decision of the court under this section.

Resignation of arbitrator

25.—(1) The parties are free to agree with an arbitrator as to the consequences of his resignation as regards—

(a) his entitlement (if any) to fees or expenses, and

(b) any liability thereby incurred by him.

(2) If or to the extent that there is no such agreement the following provisions apply.

(3) An arbitrator who resigns his appointment may (upon notice to the parties) apply to the court—

(a) to grant him relief from any liability thereby incurred by him, and

(b) to make such order as it thinks fit with respect to his entitlement (if any) to fees or expenses or the repayment of any fees or expenses already paid.

(4) If the court is satisfied that in all the circumstances it was reasonable for the arbitrator to resign, it may grant such relief as is mentioned in subsection (3)(a) on such terms as it thinks fit.

(5) The leave of the court is required for any appeal from a decision of the court under this section.

Death of arbitrator or person appointing him

26.—(1) The authority of an arbitrator is personal and ceases on his death.

(2) Unless otherwise agreed by the parties, the death of the person by whom an arbitrator was appointed does not revoke the arbitrator's authority.

Filling of vacancy, &c

27.—(1) Where an arbitrator ceases to hold office, the parties are free to agree—

(a) whether and if so how the vacancy is to be filled,

(b) whether and if so to what extent the previous proceedings should stand, and

(c) what effect (if any) his ceasing to hold office has on any appointment made by him (alone or jointly).

(2) If or to the extent that there is no such agreement, the following provisions apply.

(3) The provisions of sections 16 (procedure for appointment of arbitrators) and 18 (failure of appointment procedure) apply in relation to the filling of the vacancy as in relation to an original appointment.

(4) The tribunal (when reconstituted) shall determine whether and if so to what extent the previous proceedings should stand.

This does not affect any right of a party to challenge those proceedings on any ground which had arisen before the arbitrator ceased to hold office.

(5) His ceasing to hold office does not affect any appointment by him (alone or jointly) of another arbitrator, in particular any appointment of a chairman or umpire.

Joint and several liability of parties to arbitrators for fees and expenses

28.—(1) The parties are jointly and severally liable to pay to the arbitrators such reasonable fees and expenses (if any) as are appropriate in the circumstances.

(2) Any party may apply to the court (upon notice to the other parties and to the arbitrators) which may order that the amount of the arbitrators' fees and expenses shall be considered and adjusted by such means and upon such terms as it may direct.

(3) If the application is made after any amount has been paid to the arbitrators by way of fees or expenses, the court may order the repayment of such amount (if any) as is shown to be excessive, but shall not do so unless it is shown that it is reasonable in the circumstances to order repayment.

(4) The above provisions have effect subject to any order of the court under section 24(4) or 25(3)(b) (order as to entitlement to fees or expenses in case of removal or resignation of arbitrator).

(5) Nothing in this section affects any liability of a party to any other party to pay all or any of the costs of the arbitration (see sections 59 to 65) or any contractual right of an arbitrator to payment of his fees and expenses.

(6) In this section references to arbitrators include an arbitrator who has ceased to act and an umpire who has not replaced the other arbitrators.

Immunity of arbitrator

29.—(1) An arbitrator is not liable for anything done or omitted in the discharge or purported discharge of his functions as arbitrator unless the act or omission is shown to have been in bad faith.

(2) Subsection (1) applies to an employee or agent of an arbitrator as it applies to the arbitrator himself.

(3) This section does not affect any liability incurred by an arbitrator by reason of his resigning (but see section 25).

Competence of tribunal to rule on its own jurisdiction

30.—(1) Unless otherwise agreed by the parties, the arbitral tribunal may rule on its own substantive jurisdiction, that is, as to—
  (a) whether there is a substantive arbitration agreement,
  (b) whether the tribunal is properly constituted, and
  (c) what matters have been submitted to arbitration in accordance with the arbitration agreement.
(2) Any such ruling may be challenged by any available arbitral process of appeal or review or in accordance with the provisions of this Part.

Objection to substantive jurisdiction of the tribunal

31.—(1) An objection that the arbitral tribunal lacks substantive jurisdiction at the outset of the proceedings must be raised by a party not later than the time he takes the first step in the proceedings to contest the merits of any matter in relation to which he challenges the tribunal's jurisdiction.
A party is not precluded from raising such an objection by the fact that he has appointed or participated in the appointment of the arbitrator.

(2) Any objection during the course of the arbitral proceedings that the arbitral tribunal is exceeding its substantive jurisdiction must be made as soon as possible after the matter alleged to be beyond its jurisdiction is raised.

(3) The arbitral tribunal may admit an objection later than the time specified in subsection (1) or (2) if it considers the delay justified.

(4) Where an objection is duly taken to the tribunal's substantive jurisdiction and the tribunal has power to rule on its own jurisdiction, it may—
  (a) rule on the matter in an award as to jurisdiction;
  (b) deal with the objection in its award on the merits.
If the parties agree which of these courses the tribunal should take, the tribunal shall proceed accordingly.

(5) The tribunal may in anay case, and shall if the parties so agree, stay proceedings whilst an application is made to the court under section 32 (determination of preliminary point of jurisdiction).

Determination of preliminary point of jurisdiction

32.—(1) The court may, on the application of a party to arbitral proceedings (upon notice to the other parties), detyermine any questions as to the substantive jurisdiction of the tribunal.
A party may lose the right to object (see section 73).

(2) An application under this section shall not be considered unless—

(a) it is made with the agreement in writing of all the other parties to the proceedings, or

(b) it is made with the permission of the tribunal and the court is satisfied—

(i) that the determination of the question is likely to produce substantial savings in costs,

(ii) that the application was made without delay,

(iii) that there is good reason why the matter should be decided by the court.

(3) An application under this section, unless made with the agreement of all the other parties to the proceedings, shall state the grounds on which it is said that the matter should be decided by the court.

(4) Unless otherwise agreed by the parties, the arbitral tribunal may continue the arbitral proceedings and make an award while an application to the court under this section is pending.

(5) Unless the court gives leave, no appeal lies from a decision of the court whether the conditions specified in subsection (2) are met.

(6) The decision of the court on the question of jurisdiction shall be treated as a judgment of the court for the purposes of an appeal.
But no appeal lies without the leave of the court which shall not be given unless the court considers that the question involves a point of law which is one of general importance or is one for which for some other special reason should be considered by the Court of Appeal.

General duty of the tribunal

33.—(1) The tribunal shall—

(a) act fairly and impartially as between the parties, giving each party a reasonable opportunity of putting his case and dealing with that of his opponent, and

(b) adopt procedures suitable to the circumstances of the particular case, avoiding unnecessary delay or expense, so as to provide a fair means for the resolution of the matters falling to be determined.

(2) The tribunal shall comply with that general duty in conducting the arbitral proceedings, in its decisions on matters of procedure and evidence and in the exercise of all other powers conferred on it.

Procedural and evidential matters

34.—(1) It shall be for the tribunal to decide all procedural and evidential matters, subject to the right of the parties to agree any matter.

(2) Procedural and evidential matters include—

(a) when and where any part of the proceedings is to be held;

(b) the language or languages to be used in the proceedings and whether translations of any relevant documents are to be supplied;

(c) whether any and if so what form of written statements of claim and defence are to be used, when these should be supplied and the extent to which such statements can be later amended;

(d) whether any and if so which documents or classes of documents should be disclosed between and produced by the parties and at what stage;

(e) whether any and if so what questions should be put to and answered by the respective parties and when and in what form this should be done;

(f) whether to apply strict rules of evidence (or any other rules) as to the admissibility, relevance or weight of any material (oral, written or other) sought to be tendered on any matters of fact or opinion, and the time, manner and form in which such material should be exchanged and presented;

(g) whether and to what extent the tribunal should itself take the initiative in ascertaining the facts and the law;

(h) whether and to what extent there should be oral or written evidence or submissions.

(3) The tribunal may fix the time within which any directions given by it are to be complied with, and may if it thinks fit extend the time so fixed (whether or not it has expired).

Consolidation of proceedings and concurrent hearings

35.—(1) The parties are free to agree—

(a) that the arbitral proceedings shall be consolidated with other arbitral proceedings, or

(b) that concurrent hearings shall be held,

on such terms as may be agreed.

(2) Unless the parties agree to confer such power on the tribunal, the tribunal has no power to order consolidation of proceedings or concurrent hearings.

Legal or other representation

36. Unless otherwise agreed by the parties, a party to arbitral proceedings may be represented in the proceedings by a lawyer or other person chosen by him.

Power to appoint experts, legal advisers or assessors

37.—(1) Unless otherwise agreed by the parties—

(a) the tribunal may—

(i) appoint experts or legal advisers to report to it and the parties, or

(ii) appoint assessors to assist it on technical matters,

and may allow any such expert, legal adviser or assessor to attend the proceedings and

(b) the parties shall be given a reasonable opportunity to comment on any information, opinion or advice offered by any such person.

(2) The fees and expenses of an expert, legal adviser or assessor appointed by the tribunal for which the arbitrators are liable are expenses of the arbitrators for the purposes of this Part.

General powers exercisable by the tribunal

38.—(1) The parties are free to agree on the powers exercisable by the arbitral tribunal for the purposes of and in relation to the proceedings.

(2) Unless otherwise agreed by the parties the tribunal has the following powers.

(3) The tribunal may order a claimant to provide security for the costs of the arbitration. This power shall not be exercised on the ground that the claimant is—

(a) an individual ordinarily resident outside the United Kingdom, or

(b) a corporation or association incorporated or formed under the law of a country outside the United Kingdom, or whose central management and control is exercised outside the United Kingdom.

(4) The tribunal may give directions in relation to any property which is the subject of the proceedings or as to which any question arises in the proceedings, and which is owned by or is in the possession of a party to the proceedings—
(a) for the inspection, photographing, preservation, custody or detention of the property by the tribunal, an expert or a party, or
(b) ordering that samples be taken from, or any observation be made of or experiment conducted upon, the property.

(5) The tribunal may direct that a party or witness shall be examined on oath or affirmation, and may for that purpose administer any necessary oath or take any necessary affirmation.

(6) The tribunal may give directions to a party for the preservation for the purposes of the proceedings of any evidence in his custody or control.

Power to make provisional awards

39.—(1) The parties are free to agree that the tribunal shall have power to order on a provisional basis any relief which it would have power to grant in a final award.

(2) This includes, for instance, making—
(a) a provisional order for the payment of money or the disposition of property as between the parties, or
(b) an order to make an interim payment on account of the costs of the arbitration.

(3) Any such order shall be subject to the tribunal's final adjudication and the tribunal's final award, on the merits or as to costs, shall take account of any such order.

(4) Unless the parties agree to confer such power on the tribunal, the tribunal has no such power.
This does not affect its powers under section 47 (awards on different issues, &c).

General duty of parties

40.—(1) The parties shall do all things necessary for the proper and expeditious conduct of the arbitral proceedings.

(2) This includes—
(a) complying without delay with any determination of the tribunal as to pro-cedural or evidential matters, or with any order or directions of the tribunal, and
(b) where appropriate, taking without delay any necessary steps to obtain a decision of the court on a preliminary question of jurisdiction or law (see sections 32 and 45).

Powers of tribunal in case of party's default

41.—(1) The parties are free to agree on the powers of the tribunal in case of a party's failure to do something necessary for the proper and expeditious conduct of the arbitration.

(2) Unless otherwise agreed by the parties, the following provisions apply.

(3) If the tribunal is satisfied that there has been inordinate and inexcusable delay on the part of the claimant in pursuing his claim and that the delay—
(a) gives rise, or is likely to give rise, to a substantial risk that it is not possible to have a fair resolution of the issues in that claim, or
(b) has caused, or is likely to cause, serious prejudice to the respondent,
the tribunal may make an award dismissing the claim.

(4) If without showing sufficient cause a party—
(a) fails to attend or be represented at an oral hearing of which due notice was given, or

(b) where matters are to be dealt with in writing, fails after due notice to submit written evidence or make written submissions,

the tribunal may continue the proceedings in the absence of that party or, as the case may be, without any written evidence or submissions on his behalf, and may make an award on the basis of the evidence before it.

(5) If without showing sufficient cause a party fails to comply with any order or directions of the tribunal, the tribunal may make a peremptory order to the same effect, prescribing such time for compliance with it as the tribunal considers appropriate.

(6) If a claimant fails to comply with a peremptory order of the tribunal to provide security for costs, the tribunal may make an award dismissing his claim.

(7) If a party fails to comply with any other kind of peremptory order, then, without prejudice to section 42 (enforcement by court of tribunal's peremptory orders), the tribunal may do any of the following—

(a) direct that the party in default shall not be entitled to rely upon any allegation or material which was the subject matter of the order;

(b) draw such adverse inferences from the act of non-compliance as the circumstances justify;

(c) proceed to an award on the basis of such materials as have been properly provided to it;

(d) make such order as it thinks fit as to the payment of costs of the arbitration incurred in consequence of the non-compliance.

Enforcement of peremptory orders of tribunal

42.—(1) Unless otherwise agreed by the parties, the court may make an order requiring a party to comply with a peremptory order made by the tribunal.

(2) An application for an order under this section may be made—

(a) by the tribunal (upon notice to the parties),

(b) by a party to the arbitral proceedings with the permission of the tribunal (and upon notice to the other parties), or

(c) where the parties have agreed that the powers of the court under this section shall be available.

(3) The court shall not act unless it is satisfied that the applicant has exhausted any available arbitral process in respect of failure to comply with the tribunal's order.

(4) No order shall be made under this section unless the court is satisfied that the person to whom the tribunal's order was directed has failed to comply with it within the time prescribed in the order or, if no time was prescribed, within a reasonable time.

(5) The leave of the court is required for any appeal from a decision of the court under this section.

Securing the attendance of witnesses

43.—(1) A party to arbitral proceedings may use the same court procedures as are available in relation to legal proceedings to secure the attendance before the tribunal of a witness in order to give oral testimony or to produce documents or other material evidence.

(2) This may only be done with the permission of the tribunal or the agreement of the other parties.

(3) The court procedures may only be used if—

(a) the witness is in the United Kingdom, and

(b) the arbitral proceedings are being conducted in England and Wales or, as the case may be, Northern Ireland.

(4) A person shall not be compelled by virtue of this section to produce any document

or other material evidence which he could not be compelled to produce in legal proceedings.

Court powers exercisable in support of arbitral proceedings

44.—(1) Unless otherwise agreed by the parties, the court has for the purposes of and in relation to arbitral proceedings the same power of making orders about the matters listed below as it has for the purposes of and in relation to legal proceedings.

(2) Those matters are—

    (a) the taking of the evidence of witnesses;

    (b) the preservation of evidence;

    (c) making orders relating to property which is the subject of the proceedings or as to which any question arises in the proceedings—

        (i) for the inspection, photographing, preservation, custody or detention of the property, or

        (ii) ordering that samples be taken from, or any observation be made of or experiment conducted upon, the property;

and for that purpose authorising any person to enter any premises in the possession or control of a party to the arbitration;

    (d) the sale of any goods the subject of the proceedings;

    (e) the granting of an interim injunction or the appointment of a receiver.

(3) If the case is one of urgency, the court may, on the application of a party or proposed party to the arbitral proceedings, make such orders as it thinks necessary for the purpose of preserving evidence or assets.

(4) If the case is not one of urgency, the court shall act only on the application of a party to the arbitral proceedings (upon notice to the other parties and to the tribunal) made with the permission of the tribunal or the agreement in writing of the other parties.

(5) In any case the court shall act only if or to the extent that the arbitral tribunal, and any arbitral or other institution or person vested by the parties with power in that regard, has no power or is unable for the time being to act effectively.

(6) If the court so orders, an order made by it under this section shall cease to have effect in whole or in part on the order of the tribunal or of any such arbitral or other institution or person having power to act in relation to the subject-matter of the order.

(7) The leave of the court is required for any appeal from a decision of the court under this section.

Determination of preliminary point of law

45.—(1) Unless otherwise agreed by the parties, the court may on the application of a party to arbitral proceedings (upon notice to the other parties) determine any question of law arising in the course of the proceedings which the court is satisfied substantially affects the rights of one or more of the parties.

An agreement to dispense with reasons for the tribunal's award shall be considered an agreement to exclude the court's jurisdiction under this section.

(2) An application under this section shall not be considered unless—

    (a) it is made with the agreement of all the other parties to the proceedings, or

    (b) it is made with the permission of the tribunal and the court is satisfied—

        (i) that the determination of the question is likely to produce substantial savings in costs, and

        (ii) that the application was made without delay.

(3) The application shall identify the question of law to be determined and, unless made with the agreement of all the other parties to the proceedings, shall state the grounds on which it is said that the question should be decided by the court.

(4) Unless otherwise agreed by the parties, the arbitral tribunal may continue the arbitral proceedings and make an award while an application to the court under this section is pending.

(5) Unless the court gives leave, no appeal lies from a decision of the court whether the conditions specified in subsection (2) are met.

(6) The decision of the court on the question of law shall be treated as a judgment of the court for the purposes of an appeal.

But no appeal lies without the leave of the court which shall not be given unless the court considers that the question is one of general importance, or is one which for some other special reason should be considered by the Court of Appeal.

Rules applicable to substance of dispute

46.—(1) The arbitral tribunal shall decide the dispute—
- (a) in accordance with the law chosen by the parties as applicable to the substance of the dispute, or
- (b) if the parties so agree, in accordance with such other considerations as are agreed by them or determined by the tribunal.

(2) For this purpose the choice of the laws of a country shall be understood to refer to the substantive laws of that country and not its conflict of laws rules.

(3) If or to the extent that there is no such choice or agreement, the tribunal shall apply the law determined by the conflict of laws rules which it considers applicable.

Awards on different issues, &c

47.—(1) Unless otherwise agreed by the parties, the tribunal may make more than one award at different times on different aspects of the matters to be determined.

(2) The tribunal may, in particular, make an award relating—
- (a) to an issue affecting the whole claim, or
- (b) to a part only of the claims or cross-claims submitted to it for decision.

(3) If the tribunal does so, it shall specify in its award the issue, or the claim or part of a claim, which is the subject matter of the award.

Remedies

48.—(1) The parties are free to agree on the powers exercisable by the arbitral tribunal as regards remedies.

(2) Unless otherwise agreed by the parties, the tribunal has the following powers.

(3) The tribunal may make a declaration as to any matter to be determined in the proceedings.

(4) The tribunal may order the payment of a sum of money, in any currency.

(5) The tribunal has the same powers as the court—
- (a) to order a party to do or refrain from doing anything;
- (b) to order specific performance of a contract (other than a contract relating to land);
- (c) to order the rectification, setting aside or cancellation of a deed or other document.

Interest

49.—(1) The parties are free to agree on the powers of the tribunal as regards the award of interest.

(2) Unless otherwise agreed by the parties the following provisions apply.

(3) The tribunal may award simple or compound interest from such dates, at such

rates and with such rests as it considers meets the justice of the case—
    (a) on the whole or part of any amount awarded by the tribunal, in respect of any period up to the date of the award;
    (b) on the whole or part of any amount claimed in the arbitration and outstanding at the commencement of the arbitral proceedings but paid before the award was made, in respect of any period up to the date of payment.

(4) The tribunal may award simple or compound interest from the date of the award (or any later date) until payment, at such rates and with such rests as it considers meets the justice of the case, on the outstanding amount of any award (including any award of interest under subsection (3) and any award as to costs).

(5) References in this section to an amount awarded by the tribunal include an amount payable in consequence of a declaratory award by the tribunal.

(6) The above provisions do not affect any other power of the tribunal to award interest.

Extension of time for making award

50.—(1) Where the time for making an award is limited by or in pursuance of the arbitration agreement, then, unless otherwise agreed by the parties, the court may in accordance with the following provisions by order extend that time.

(2) An application for an order under this section may be made—
    (a) by the tribunal (upon notice to the parties), or
    (b) by any party to the proceedings (upon notice to the tribunal and the other parties),
but only after exhausting any available arbitral process for obtaining an extension of time.

(3) The court shall only make an order if satisfied that a substantial injustice would otherwise be done.

(4) The court may extend the time for such period and on such terms as it thinks fit, and may do so whether or not the time previously fixed (by or under the agreement or by a previous order) has expired.

(5) The leave of the court is required for any appeal from a decision of the court under this section.

Settlement

51.—(1) If during arbitral proceedings the parties settle the dispute, the following provisions apply unless otherwise agreed by the parties.

(2) The tribunal shall terminate the substantive proceedings and, if so requested by the parties and not objected to by the tribunal, shall record the settlement in the form of an agreed award.

(3) An agreed award shall state that it is an award of the tribunal and shall have the same status and effect as any other award on the merits of the case.

(4) The following provisions of this Part relating to awards (sections 52 to 58) apply to an agreed award.

(5) Unless the parties have also settled the matter of the payment of the costs of the arbitration, the provisions of this Part relating to costs (sections 59 to 65) continue to apply.

Form of award

52.—(1) The parties are free to agree on the form of an award.

(2) If or to the extent that there is no such agreement, the following provisions apply.

(3) The award shall be in writing signed by all the arbitrators or all those assenting to the award.

(4) The award shall contain the reasons for the award unless it is an agreed award or the parties have agreed to dispense with reasons.

(5) The award shall state the seat of the arbitration and the date when the award is made.

Place where award treated as made

53. Unless otherwise agreed by the parties, where the seat of the arbitration is in England and Wales or Northern Ireland, any award in the proceedings shall be treated as made there, regardless of where it was signed, despatched or delivered to any of the parties.

Date of award

54.—(1) Unless otherwise agreed by the parties, the tribunal may decide what is to be taken to be the date on which the award was made.

(2) In the absence of any such decision, the date of the award shall be taken to be the date on which it is signed by the arbitrator or, where more than one arbitrator signs the award, by the last of them.

Notification of award

55.—(1) The parties are free to agree on the requirements as to notification of the award to the parties.

(2) If there is no such agreement, the award shall be notified to the parties by service on them of copies of the award, which shall be done without delay after the award is made.

(3) Nothing in this section affects section 56 (power to withhold award in case of non-payment).

Power to withhold award in case of non-payment

56.—(1) The tribunal may refuse to deliver an award to the parties except upon full payment of the fees and expenses of the arbitrators.

(2) If the tribunal refuses on that ground to deliver an award, a party to the arbitral proceedings may (upon notice to the other parties and the tribunal) apply to the court, which may order that—

    (a) the tribunal shall deliver the award on the payment into court by the applicant of the fees and expenses demanded, or such lesser amount as the court may specify,

    (b) the amount of the fees and expenses properly payable shall be determined by such means and upon such terms as the court may direct, and

    (c) out of the money paid into court there shall be paid out such fees and expenses as may be found to be properly payable and the balance of the money (if any) shall be paid out to the applicant.

(3) For this purpose the amount of fees and expenses properly payable is the amount the applicant is liable to pay under section 28 or any agreement relating to the payment of the arbitrators.

(4) No application to the court may be made where there is any available arbitral process for appeal or review of the amount of the fees or expenses demanded.

(5) References in this section to arbitrators include an arbitrator who has ceased to act and an umpire who has not replaced the other arbitrators.

(6) The above provisions of this section also apply in relation to any arbitral or other institution or person vested by the parties with powers in relation to the delivery of the tribunal's award.

As they so apply, the references to the fees and expenses of the arbitrators shall be construed as including the fees and expenses of that institution or person.

(7) The leave of the court is required for any appeal from a decision of the court under this section.

(8) Nothing in this section shall be construed as excluding an application under section 28 where payment has been made to the arbitrators in order to obtain the award.

Correction of award or additional award

57.—(1) The parties are free to agree on the powers of the tribunal to correct an award or make an additional award.

(2) If or to the extent there is no such agreement, the following provisions apply.

(3) The tribunal may on its own initiative or on the application of a party—

- (a) correct an award so as to remove any clerical mistake or error arising from an accidental slip or omission or clarify or remove any ambiguity in the award, or
- (b) make an additional award in respect of any claim (including a claim for interest or costs) which was presented to the tribunal but was not dealt with in the award.

These powers shall not be exercised without first affording the other parties a reasonable opportunity to make representations to the tribunal.

(4) Any application for the exercise of those powers must be made within 28 days of the date of the award or such longer period as the parties may agree.

(5) Any correction of an award shall be made within 28 days of the date the application was received by the tribunal or, where the correction is made by the tribunal on its own initiative, within 28 days of the date of the award or, in either case, such longer period as the parties may agree.

(6) Any additional award shall be made within 56 days of the date of the original award or such longer period as the parties may agree.

(7) Any correction of an award shall form part of the award.

Effect of award

58.—(1) Unless otherwise agreed by the parties, an award made by the tribunal pursuant to an arbitration agreement is final and binding both on the parties and on any persons claiming through or under them.

(2) This does not affect the right of a person to challenge the award by any available arbitral process of appeal or review or in accordance with the provisions of this Part.

Costs of the arbitration

59.—(1) References in this Part to the costs of the arbitration are to—

- (a) the arbitrators' fees and expenses,
- (b) the fees and expenses of any arbitral institution concerned, and
- (c) the legal or other costs of the parties.

(2) Any such reference includes the costs of or incidental to any proceedings to determine the amount of the recoverable costs of the arbitration (see section 63).

Agreement to pay costs in any event

60. An agreement which has the effect that a party is to pay the whole or part of the costs of the arbitration in any event is only valid if made after the dispute in question has arisen.

Award of costs

61.—(1) The tribunal may make an award allocating the costs of the arbitration as between the parties, subject to any agreement of the parties.

(2) Unless the parties otherwise agree, the tribunal shall award costs on the general principle that costs should follow the event except where it appears to the tribunal that in the circumstances this is not appropriate in relation to the whole or part of the costs.

Effect of agreement or award about costs

62. Unless the parties otherwise agree, any obligation under an agreement between them as to how the costs of the arbitration are to be borne, or under an award allocating the costs of the arbitration, extends only to such costs as are recoverable.

The recoverable costs of the arbitration

63.—(1) The parties are free to agree what costs of the arbitration are recoverable.

(2) If or to the extent there is no such agreement, the following provisions apply.

(3) The tribunal may determine by award the recoverable costs of the arbitration on such basis as it thinks fit.
If it does so, it shall specify—

    (a) the basis on which it has acted, and

    (b) the items of recoverable costs and the amount referable to each.

(4) If the tribunal does not determine the recoverable costs of the arbitration, any party to the arbitral proceedings may apply to the court (upon notice to the other parties) which may—

    (a) determine the recoverable costs of the arbitration on such basis as it thinks fit, or

    (b) order that they shall be determined by such means and upon such terms as it may specify.

(5) Unless the tribunal or the court determines otherwise—

    (a) the recoverable costs of the arbitration shall be determined on the basis that there shall be allowed a reasonable amount in respect of all costs reasonably incurred, and

    (b) any doubt as to whether costs were reasonably incurred or were reasonable in amount shall be resolved in favour of the paying party.

(6) The above provisions have effect subject to section 64 (recoverable fees and expenses of arbitrators).

(7) Nothing in this section affects any right of the arbitrators, any expert, legal adviser or assessor appointed by the tribunal, or any arbitral institution, to payment of their fees and expenses.

Recoverable fees and expenses of arbitrators

64.—(1) Unless otherwise agreed by the parties, the recoverable costs of the arbitration shall include in respect of the fees and expenses of the arbitrators only such reasonable fees and expenses as are appropriate in the circumstances.

(2) If there is any question as to what reasonable fees and expenses are appropriate in the circumstances, and the matter is not already before the court on an application

under section 63(4), the court may on the application of any party (upon notice to the other parties)—
    (a) determine the matter, or
    (b) order that it be determined by such means and upon such terms as the court may specify.

(3) Subsection (1) has effect subject to any order of the court under section 24(4) or 25(3)(b) (order as to entitlement to fees or expenses in case of removal or resignation of arbitrator).

(4) Nothing in this section affects any right of the arbitrator to payment of his fees and expenses.

Power to limit recoverable costs

65.—(1) Unless otherwise agreed by the parties, the tribunal may direct that the recoverable costs of the arbitration, or of any part of the arbitral proceedings, shall be limited to a specified amount.

(2) Any direction may be made or varied at any stage, but this must be done sufficiently in advance of the incurring of costs to which it relates, or the taking of any steps in the proceedings which may be affected by it, for the limit to be taken into account.

Enforcement of the award

66.—(1) An award made by the tribunal pursuant to an arbitration agreement may, by leave of the court, be enforced in the same manner as a judgment or order of the court to the same effect.

(2) Where leave is so given, judgment may be entered in terms of the award.

(3) Leave to enforce an award shall not be given where, or to the extent that, the person against whom it is sought to be enforced shows that the tribunal lacked substantive jurisdiction to make the award.
The right to raise such an objection may have been lost (see section 73).

(4) Nothing in this section affects the recognition or enforcement of an award under any other enactment or rule of law, in particular under Part II of the Arbitration Act 1950 (enforcement of awards under Geneva Convention) or the provisions of Part III of this Act relating to the recognition and enforcement of awards under the New York Convention or by an action on the award.

Challenging the award: substantive jurisdiction

67.—(1) A party to arbitral proceedings may (upon notice to the other parties and to the tribunal) apply to the court—
    (a) challenging any award of the arbitral tribunal as to its substantive jurisdiction or
    (b) for an order declaring an award made by the tribunal on the merits to be of no effect, in whole or in part, because the tribunal did not have substantive jurisdiction.
A party may lose the right to object (see section 73) and the right to apply is subject to the restrictions in section 70(2) and (3).

(2) The arbitral tribunal may continue the arbitral proceedings and make a further award while an application to the court under this section is pending in relation to an award as to jurisdiction.

(3) On an application under this section challenging an award of the arbitral tribunal as to its substantive jurisdiction, the court may by order—
    (a) confirm the award,

  (b) vary the award, or

  (c) set aside the award in whole or in part.

  (4) The leave of the court is required for any appeal from a decision of the court under this section.

Challenging the award: serious irregularity

68.—(1) A party to arbitral proceedings may (upon notice to the other parties and to the tribunal) apply to the court challenging an award in the proceedings on the ground of serious irregularity affecting the tribunal, the proceedings or the award.

  A party may lose the right to object (see section 73) and the right to apply is subject to the restrictions in section 70(2) and (3).

  (2) Serious irregularity means an irregularity of one or more of the following kinds which the court considers has caused or will cause substantial injustice to the applicant—

  (a) failure by the tribunal to comply with section 33 (general duty of tribunal);

  (b) the tribunal exceeding its powers (otherwise than by exceeding its substantive jurisdiction: see section 67);

  (c) failure by the tribunal to conduct the proceedings in accordance with the procedure agreed by the parties;

  (d) failure by the tribunal to deal with all the issues that were put to it;

  (e) any arbitral or other institution or person vested by the parties with powers in relation to the proceedings or the award exceeding its powers;

  (f) uncertainty or ambiguity as to the effect of the award;

  (g) the award being obtained by fraud or the award or the way in which it was procured being contrary to public policy;

  (h) failure to comply with the requirements as to the form of the award or

  (i) any irregularity in the conduct of the proceedings or in the award which is admitted by the tribunal or by any arbitral or other institution or person vested by the parties with powers in relation to the proceedings or the award.

  (3) If there is shown to be serious irregularity affecting the tribunal, the proceedings or the award, the court may—

  (a) remit the award to the tribunal, in whole or in part, for reconsideration,

  (b) set the award aside in whole or in part, or

  (c) declare the award to be of no effect, in whole or in part.

The court shall not exercise its power to set aside or to declare an award to be of no effect, in whole or in part, unless it is satisfied that it would be inappropriate to remit the matters in question to the tribunal for reconsideration.

  (4) The leave of the court is required for any appeal from a decision of the court under this section.

Appeal on point of law

69.—(1) Unless otherwise agreed by the parties, a party to arbitral proceedings may (upon notice to the other parties and to the tribunal) appeal to the court on a question of law arising out of an award made in the proceedings.

An agreement to dispense with reasons for the tribunal's award shall be considered an agreement to exclude the court's jurisdiction under this section.

  (2) An appeal shall not be brought under this section except—

  (a) with the agreement of all the other parties to the proceedings, or

  (b) with the leave of the court.

  The right to appeal is also subject to the restrictions in section 70(2) and (3).

  (3) Leave to appeal shall be given only if the court is satisfied—

    (a) that the determination of the question will substantially affect the rights of one or more of the parties,

    (b) that the question is one which the tribunal was asked to determine,

    (c) that, on the basis of the findings of fact in the award—

        (i) the decision of the tribunal on the question is obviously wrong, or

        (ii) the question is one of general public importance and the decision of the tribunal is at least open to serious doubt, and

    (d) that, despite the agreement of the parties to resolve the matter by arbitration, it is just and proper in all the circumstances for the court to determine the question.

(4) An application for leave to appeal under this section shall identify the question of law to be determined and state the grounds on which it is alleged that leave to appeal should be granted.

(5) The court shall determine an application for leave to appeal under this section without a hearing unless it appears to the court that a hearing is required.

(6) The leave of the court is required for any appeal from a decision of the court under this section to grant or refuse leave to appeal.

(7) On an appeal under this section the court may by order—

    (a) confirm the award,

    (b) vary the award,

    (c) remit the award to the tribunal, in whole or in part, for reconsideration in the light of the court's determination, or

    (d) set aside the award in whole or in part.

The court shall not exercise its power to set aside an award, in whole or in part, unless it is satisfied that it would be inappropriate to remit the matters in question to the tribunal for reconsideration.

(8) The decision of the court on an appeal under this section shall be treated as a judgment of the court for the purposes of a further appeal.

But no such appeal lies without the leave of the court which shall not be given unless the court considers that the question is one of general importance or is one which for some other special reason should be considered by the Court of Appeal.

Challenge or appeal: supplementary provisions

70.—(1) The following provisions apply to an application or appeal under section 67, 68 or 69.

(2) An application or appeal may not be brought if the applicant or appellant has not first exhausted—

    (a) any available arbitral process of appeal or review, and

    (b) any available recourse under section 57 (correction of award or additional award).

(3) Any application or appeal must be brought within 28 days of the date of the award or, if there has been any arbitral process of appeal or review, of the date when the applicant or appellant was notified of the result of that process.

(4) If on an application or appeal it appears to the court that the award—

    (a) does not contain the tribunal's reasons, or

    (b) does not set out the tribunal's reasons in sufficient detail to enable the court properly to consider the application or appeal,

the court may order the tribunal to state the reasons for its award in sufficient detail for that purpose.

(5) Where the court makes an order under subsection (4), it may make such further order as it thinks fit with respect to any additional costs of the arbitration resulting from its order.

(6) The court may order the applicant or appellant to provide security for the costs

of the application or appeal, any may direct that the application or appeal be dismissed if the order is not complied with.

The power to order security for costs shall not be exercised on the ground that the applicant or appellant is—

(a) an individual ordinarily resident outside the United Kingdom, or

(b) a corporation or association incorporated or formed under the law of a country outside the United Kingdom, or whose central management and control is exercised outside the United Kingdom.

(7) The court may order that any money payable under the award shall be brought into court or otherwise secured pending the determination of the application or appeal, and may direct that the application or appeal be dismissed if the order is not complied with.

(8) The court may grant leave to appeal subject to conditions to the same or similar effect as an order under subsection (6) or (7).

Challenge or appeal: effect of order of court

71.—(1) The following provisions have effect where the court makes an order under section 67, 68 or 69 with respect to an award.

(2) Where the award is varied, the variation has effect as part of the tribunal's award.

(3) Where the award is remitted to the tribunal, in whole or in part, for reconsideration, the tribunal shall make a fresh award in respect of the matters remitted within three months of the date of the order for remission or such longer or shorter period as the court may direct.

(4) Where the award is set aside or declared to be of no effect, in whole or in part, the court may also order that any provision that an award is a condition precedent to the bringing of legal proceedings in respect of a matter to which the arbitration agreement applies, is of no effect as regards the subject matter of the award or, as the case may be, the relevant part of the award.

Saving for rights of person who takes no part in proceedings

72.—(1) A person alleged to be a party to arbitral proceedings but who takes no part in the proceedings may question—

(a) whether there is a valid arbitration agreement,

(b) whether the tribunal is properly constituted, or

(c) what matters have been submitted to arbitration in accordance with the arbitration agreement,

by proceedings in the court for a declaration or injunction or other appropriate relief.

(2) He also has the same right as a party to the arbitral proceedings to challenge an award—

(a) by an application under section 67 on the ground of lack of substantive jurisdiction in relation to him, or

(b) by an application under section 68 on the ground of serious irregularity (within the meaning of that section) affecting him;

and section 70(2) (duty to exhaust arbitral procedures) does not apply in this case.

Loss of right to object

73.—(1) If a party to arbitral proceedings takes part, or continues to take part, in the proceedings without making, either forthwith or within such time as is allowed by the arbitration agreement or the tribunal or by any Provision of this Part, any objections—

(a) that the tribunal lacks substantive jurisdiction,

(b) that the proceedings have been improperly conducted,

(c) that there has been a failure to comply with the arbitration agreement or with any provision of this Part, or

(d) that there has been any other irregularity affecting the tribunal or the proceedings,

he may not raise that objection later, before the tribunal or the court, unles he shows that, at the time he took part or continued to take part in the proceedings, he did not know and could not with reasonable diligence have discovered the grounds for the objection.

(2) Where the arbitral tribunal rules that it has substantive jurisdiction and a party to arbitral proceedings who could have questioned that ruling—

(a) by any available arbitral process of appeal or review, or

(b) by challenging the award,

does not do so, or does not do so within the time allowed by the arbitration agreement or any provision of this Part, he may not object later to the tribunal's substantive jurisdiction on any ground which was the subject of that ruling.

Immunity of arbitral institutions, &c

74.—(1) An arbitral or other institution or person designated or requested by the parties to appoint or nominate an arbitrator is not liable for anything done or omitted in the discharge or purported discharge of that function unless the act or omission is shown to have been in bad faith.

(2) An arbitral or other institution or person by whom an arbitrator is appointed or nominated is not liable, by reason of having appointed or nominated him, for anything done or omitted by the arbitrator (or his employees or agents) in the discharge or purported discharge of his functions as arbitrator.

(3) The above provisions apply to an employee or agent of an arbitral or other institution or person as they apply to the institution or person himself.

Charge to secure payment of solicitors' costs

75. The powers of the court to make declarations and orders under section 73 of the Solicitors Act 1974 or Article 71H of the Solicitors (Northern Ireland) Order 1976 (power to charge property recovered in the proceedings with the payment of solicitors' costs) may be exercised in relation to arbitral proceedings as if those proceedings were proceedings in the court.

Service of notice

76.—(1) The parties are free to agree on the manner of service of any notice or other document required or authorised to be given or served in pursuance of the arbitration agreement or for the purpose of the arbitral proceedings.

(2) If or to the extent that there is no such agreement the following provisions apply.

(3) A notice or other document may be served on a person by any effective means.

(4) If a notice or other document is addressed, pre-paid and delivered by post—

(a) to the addressee's last known principal residence or, if he is or has been carrying on a trade, profession or business, his last known principal business address, or

(b) where the addressee is a body corporate, to the body's registered or principal office,

it shall be treated as effectively served.

(5) This section does not apply to the service of documents for the purposes of legal proceedings, for which provision is made by rules of court.

(6) References in this Part to a notice or other document include any form of communication in writing and references to giving or serving a notice or other document shall be served accordingly.

Powers of court in relation to service of documents

77.—(1) This section applies where service of a document on a person in the manner agreed by the parties, or in accordance with the provisions of section 76 having effect in default of agreement , is not reasonably practicable.

(2) Unless otherwise agreed by the parties, the court may make such order as it thinks fit—

(a) for service in such manner as the court may direct, or

(b) dispensing with service of the document.

(3) Any party to the arbitration agreement may apply for an order, but only after exhausting any available arbitral process for resolving the matter.

(4) The leave of the court is required for any appeal from a decision of the court under this section.

Reckoning periods of time

78.—(1) The parties are free to agree on the method of reckoning periods of time for the purposes of any provision agreed by them or any provision of this Part having effect in default of such agreement.

(2) If or to the extent there is no such agreement, periods of time shall be reckoned in accordance with the following provisions.

(3) Where the act is required to be done within a specified period after or from a specified date, the period begins immediately after that date.

(4) Where the act is required to be done a specified number of clear days after a specified date, at least that number of days must intervene between the day on which the act is done and that date.

(5) Where the period is a period of seven days or less which would include a Saturday, Sunday or a public holiday in the place where anything which has to be done within the period falls to be done, that day shall be excluded.

In relation to England and Wales or Northern Ireland, a "public holiday" means Christmas Day, Good Friday or a day which under the Banking and Financial Dealings Act 1971 is a bank holiday.

Power of court to extend time limits relating to arbitral proceedings

79.—(1) Unless the parties otherwise agree, the court may by order extend any time limit agreed by them in relation to any matter relating to the arbitral proceedings or specified in any provision of this Part having effect in default of such agreement.

This section does not apply to a time limit to which section 12 applies (power of court to extend time for beginning arbitral proceedings, &c.).

(2) An application for an order may be made—

(a) by any party to the arbitral proceedings (upon notice to the other parties and to the tribunal), or

(b) by the arbitral tribunal (upon notice to the parties).

(3) The court shall not exercise its power to extend a time limit unless it is satisfied—

(a) that any available recourse to the tribunal, or to any arbitral or other institution or person vested by the parties with power in that regard, has first been exhausted, and

(b) that a substantial injustice would otherwise be done.

(4) The court's power under this section may be exercised whether or not the time has already expired.

(5) An order under this section may be made on such terms as the court thinks fit.

(6) The leave of the court is required for any appeal from a decision of the court under this section.

Notice and other requirements in connection with legal proceedings

80.—(1) References in this Part to an application, appeal or other step in relation to legal proceedings being taken "upon notice" to the other parties to the arbitral proceedings, or to the tribunal, are to such notice of the originating process as is required by rules of court and do not impose any separate requirement.

(2) Rules of court shall be made—

  (a) requiring such notice to be given as indicated by any provision of this Part, and

  (b) as to the manner, form and content of any such notice.

(3) Subject to any provision made by rules of court, a requirement to give notice to the tribunal of legal proceedings shall be construed—

  (a) if there is more than one arbitrator, as a requirement to give notice to each of them and

  (b) if the tribunal is not fully constituted, as a requirement to give notice to any arbitrator who has been appointed.

(4) References in this Part to making an application or appeal to the court within a specified period are to the issue within that period of the appropriate originating process in accordance with rules of court.

(5) Where any provision of this Part requires an application or appeal to be made to the court within a specified time, the rules of court relating to the reckoning of periods, the extending or abridging of periods, and the consequences of not taking a step within the period prescribed by the rules, apply in relation to that requirement.

(6) Provision may be made by rules of court amending the provisions of this Part—

  (a) with respect to the time within which any application or appeal to the court must be made,

  (b) so as to keep any provision made by this Part in relation to arbitral proceedings in step with the corresponding provision of rules of court applying in relation to proceedings in the court, or

  (c) so as to keep any provision made by this Part in relation to legal proceedings in step with the corresponding provision of rules of court applying generally in relation to proceedings in the court.

(7) Nothing in this section affects the generality of the power to make rules of court.

Saving for certain matters governed by common law

81.—(1) Nothing in this Part shall be construed as excluding the operation of any rule of law consistent with the provisions of this Part, in particular, any rule of law as to—

  (a) matters which are not capable of settlement by arbitration;

  (b) the effect of an oral arbitration agreement or

  (c) the refusal of recognition or enforcement of an arbitral award on grounds of public policy.

(2) Nothing in this Act shall be construed as reviving any jurisdiction of the court to set aside or remit an award on the ground of errors of fact or law on the face of the award.

Minor definitions

82.—(1) In this Part—

"arbitrator", unless the context otherwise requires, includes an umpire;

"available arbitral process", in relation to any matter, includes any process of appeal to or review by an arbitral or other institution or person vested by the parties with powers in relation to that matter;

"claimant", unless the context otherwise requires, includes a counterclaimant, and related expressions shall be construed accordingly;

"dispute" includes any difference;

"enactment" includes an enactment contained in Northern Ireland legislation;

"legal proceedings" means civil proceedings in the High Court or a county court;

"peremptory order" means an order made under section 41(5) or made in exercise of any corresponding power conferred by the parties;

"premises" includes land, buildings, moveable structures, vehicles, vessels, aircraft and hovercraft;

"question of law" means—

(a) for a court in England and Wales, a question of the law of England and Wales, and

(b) for a court in Northern Ireland, a question of the law of Northern Ireland;

"substantive jurisdiction", in relation to an arbitral tribunal, refers to the matters specified in section 30(1)(a) to (c), and references to the tribunal exceeding its substantive jurisdiction shall be construed accordingly.

(2) References in this Part to a party to an arbitration agreement include any person claiming under or through a party to the agreement.

Index of defined expressions: Part I

83. In this Part the expressions listed below are defined or otherwise explained by the provisions indicated—

agreement, agree and agreed	section 5(1)
agreement in writing	section 5(2) to (5)
arbitration agreement	sections 6 and 5(1)
arbitrator	section 82(1)
available arbitral process	section 82(1)
claimant	section 82(1)
commencement (in relation to arbitral proceedings)	section 14
costs of the arbitration	section 59
the court	section 105
dispute	section 82(1)
enactment	section 82(1)
legal proceedings	section 82(1)
Limitation Acts	section 13(4)
notice (or other document)	section 76(6)
party—	
— in relation to an arbitration agreement	section 82(2)
— where section 106(2) or (3) applies	section 106(4)
peremptory order	section 82(1) (and see section 41(5))
premises	section 82(1)
question of law	section 82(1)
recoverable costs	sections 63 and 64
seat of the arbitration	section 3

serve and service (of notice or other document)	section 76(6)
substantive jurisdiction (in relation to an arbitral tribunal)	section 82(1) (and see section 30(1)(a) to (c))
upon notice (to the parties or the tribunal)	section 80
written and in writing	section 5(6)

Transitional provisions

84.—(1) The provisions of this Part do not apply to arbitral proceedings commenced before the date on which this Part comes into force.

(2) They apply to arbitral proceedings commenced on or after that date under an arbitration agreement whenever made.

(3) The above provisions have effect subject to any transitional provision made by an order under section 109(2) (power to include transitional provisions in commencement order).

Modification of Part I in relation to domestic arbitration agreement

85.—(1) In the case of a domestic arbitration agreement the provisions of Part I are modified in accordance with the following sections.

(2) For this purpose a "domestic arbitration agreement" means an arbitration agreement to which none of the parties is—

    (a) an individual who is a national of, or habitually resident in, a state other than the United Kingdom, or

    (b) a body corporate which is incorporated in, or whose central control and management is exercised in, a state other than the United Kingdom,

and under which the seat of the arbitration (if the seat has been designated or determined) is in the United Kingdom.

(3) In subsection (2) "arbitration agreement" and "seat of the arbitration" have the same meaning as in Part I (see sections 3, 5(1) and 6).

Staying of legal proceedings

86.—(1) In section 9 (stay of legal proceedings), subsection (4) (stay unless the arbitration agreement is null and void, inoperative, or incapable of being performed) does not apply to a domestic arbitration agreement.

(2) On an application under that section in relation to a domestic arbitration agreement the court shall grant a stay unless satisfied—

    (a) that the arbitration agreement is null and void, inoperative, or incapable of being performed, or

    (b) that there are other sufficient grounds for not requiring the parties to abide by the arbitration agreement.

(3) The court may treat as a sufficient ground under subsection (2)(b) the fact that the applicant is or was at any material time not ready and willing to do all things necessary for the proper conduct of the arbitration or of any other dispute resolution procedures required to be exhausted before resorting to arbitration.

(4) For the purposes of this section the question whether an arbitration agreement is a domestic arbitration agreement shall be determined by reference to the facts at the time the legal proceedings are commenced.

Effectiveness of agreement to exclude court's jurisdiction

87.—(1) In the case of a domestic arbitration agreement any agreement to exclude the jurisdiction of the court under—

(a) section 45 (determination of preliminary point of law), or

(b) section 69 (challenging the award: appeal on point of law),

is not effective unless entered into after the commencement of the arbitral proceedings in which the question arises or the award is made.

(2) For this purpose the commencement of the arbitral proceedings has the same meaning as in Part I (see section 14).

(3) For the purposes of this section the question whether an arbitration agreement is a domestic arbitration agreement shall be determined by reference to the facts at the time the agreement is entered into.

Power to repeal or amend sections 85 to 87

88.—(1) The Secretary of State may by order repeal or amend the provisions of sections 85 to 87.

(2) An order under this section may contain such supplementary, incidental and transitional provisions as appear to the Secretary of State to be appropriate.

(3) An order under this section shall be made by statutory instrument and no such order shall be made unless a draft of it has been laid before and approved by a resolution of each House of Parliament.

Application of unfair terms regulations to consumer arbitration agreements

89.—(1) The following sections extend the application of the Unfair Terms in Consumer Contracts Regulations 1994 in relation to a term which constitutes an arbitration agreement.

For this purpose "arbitration agreement" means an agreement to submit to arbitration present or future disputes or differences (whether or not contractual).

(2) In those sections "the Regulations" mean those regulations and includes any regulations amending or replacing those regulations.

(3) Those sections apply whatever the law applicable to the arbitration agreement.

Regulations apply where consumer is a legal person

90. The Regulations apply where the consumer is a legal person as they apply where the consumer is a natural person.

Arbitration agreement unfair where modest amount sought

91.—(1) A term which constitutes an arbitration agreement is unfair for the purposes of the Regulations so far as it relates to a claim for a pecuniary remedy which does not exceed the amount specified by order for the purposes of this section.

(2) Orders under this section may make different provision for different cases and for different purposes.

(3) The power to make orders under this section is exercisable—

(a) for England and Wales, by the Secretary of State with the concurrence of the Lord Chancellor,

(b) for Scotland, by the Secretary of State with the concurrence of the Lord Advocate, and

(c) for Northern Ireland, by the Department of Economc Development for Northern Ireland with the concurrence of the Lord Chancellor.

(4) Any such order for England and Wales or Scotland shall be made by statutory instrument which shall be subject to annulment in pursuance of a resolution of either House of Parliament.

(5) Any such order for Northern Ireland shall be a statutory rule for the purposes of the Statutory Rules (Northern Ireland) Order 1979 and shall be subject to negative resolution, within the meaning of section 41(6) of the Interpretation Act (Northern Ireland) Order 1954.

Exclusion of Part I in relation to small claims arbitration in the county court

92. Nothing in Part I of this Act applies to arbitration under section 64 of the County Courts Act 1984.

Appointment of judges as arbitrators

93.—(1) A judge of the Commercial Court or an official referee may, if in all the circumstances he thinks fit, accept appointment as a sole arbitrator or as umpire by or by virtue of an arbitration agreement.

(2) A judge of the Commercial Court shall not do so unless the Lord Chief Justice has informed him that, having regard to the state of business in the High Court and the Crown Court, he can be made available.

(3) An official referee shall not do so unless the Lord Chief Justice has informed him that, having regard to the state of official referees' business, he can be made available.

(4) The fees payable for the services of a judge of the Commercial Court or official referee as arbitrator or umpire shall be taken in the High Court.

(5) In this section—
"arbitration agreement" has the same meaning as in Part I and
"official referee" means a person nominated under section 68(1)(a) of the Supreme Court Act 1981 to deal with official referees' business.

(6) The provisions of Part I of this Act apply to arbitration before a person appointed under this section with the modifications specified in Schedule 2.

Application of Part I to statutory arbitrations

94.—(1) The provisions of Part I apply to every arbitration under an enactment (a "statutory arbitration"), whether the enactment was passed or made before or after the commencement of this Act, subject to the adaptations and exclusions specified in sections 95 to 98.

(2) The provisions of Part I do not apply to a statutory arbitration if or to the extent that their application—
    (a) is inconsistent with the provisions of the enactment concerned, with any rules or procedure authorised or recognised by it, or
    (b) is excluded by any other enactment.

(3) In this section and the following provisions of this Part "enactment"—
    (a) in England and Wales, includes an enactment contained in subordinate legislation within the meaning of the Interpretation Act 1978;
    (b) in Northern Ireland, means a statutory provision within the meaning of section 1(f) of the Interpretation Act (Northern Ireland) 1954.

General adaptation of provisions in relation to statutory arbitrations

95.—(1) The provisions of Part I apply to a statutory arbitration—
    (a) as if the arbitration were pursuant to an arbitration agreement and as if the enactment were that agreement, and

(b) as if the persons by and against whom a claim subject to arbitration in pursuance of the enactment may be or has been made were parties to that agreement.

(2) Every statutory arbitration shall be taken to have its seat in England and Wales or, as the case may be, in Northern Ireland.

Specific adaptations of provisions in relation to statutory arbitrations

96.—(1) The following provisions of Part I apply to a statutory arbitration with the following adaptations.

(2) In section 30(1) (competence of tribunal to rule on its own jurisdiction), the reference in paragraph (a) to whether there is a valid arbitration agreement shall be construed as a reference to whether the enactment applies to the dispute or difference in question.

(3) Section 35 (consolidation of proceedings and concurrent hearings) applies only so as to authorise the consolidation of proceedings, or concurrent hearings in proceedings, under the same enactment.

(4) Section 46 (rules applicable to substance of dispute) applies with the omission of subsection (1)(b) (determination in accordance with considerations agreed by parties).

Provisions excluded from applying to statutory arbitrations

97. The following provisions of Part I do not apply in relation to a statutory arbitration—
   (a) section 8 (whether agreement discharged by death of a party);
   (b) section 12 (power of court to extend agreed time limits);
   (c) sections 9(5), 10(2) and 71(4) (restrictions on effect of provision that award condition precedent to right to bring legal proceedings).

Power to make further provision by regulations

98.—(1) The Secretary of State may make provision by regulations for adapting or excluding any provision of Part I in relation to statutory arbitrations in general or statutory arbitrations of any particular description.

(2) The power is exercisable whether the enactment concerned is passed or made before or after the commencement of this Act.

(3) Regulations under this section shall be made by statutory instrument which shall be subject to annulment in pursuance of a resolution of either House of Parliament.

Continuation of Part II of the Arbitration Act 1950

99. Part II of the Arbitration Act 1950 (enforcement of certain foreign awards) continues to apply in relation to foreign awards within the meaning of that Part which are not also New York Convention awards.

New York Convention awards

100.—(1) In this Part a "New York Convention award" means an award made, in pursuance of an arbitration agreement, in the territory of a state (other than the United Kingdom) which is a party to the New York Convention.

(2) For the purposes of subsection (1) and of the provisions of this Part relating to such awards—
   (a) "arbitration agreement" means an arbitration agreement in writing, and

(b) an award shall be treated as made at the seat of the arbitration, regardless of where it was signed, despatched or delivered to any of the parties.

In this subsection "agreement in writing" and "seat of the arbitration" have the same meaning as in Part I.

(3) If Her Majesty by Order in Council declares that a state specified in the Order is a party to the New York Convention, or is a party in respect of any territory so specified, the Order shall, while in force, be conclusive evidence of that fact.

(4) In this section "the New York Convention" means the Convention on the Recognition and Enforcement of Foreign Arbitral Awards adopted by the United Nations Conference on International Commercial Arbitration on 10th June 1958.

Recognition and enforcement of awards

101.—(1) A New York Convention award shall be recognised as binding on the persons as between whom it was made, and may accordingly be relied on by those persons by way of defence, set-off or otherwise in any legal proceedings in England and Wales or Northern Ireland.

(2) A New York Convention award may, by leave of the court, be enforced in the same manner as a judgment or order of the court to the same effect.

As to the meaning of "the court" see section 105.

(3) Where leave is so given, judgment may be entered in terms of the award.

Evidence to be produced by party seeking recognition or enforcement

102.—(1) A party seeking the recognition or enforcement of a New York Convention award must produce—

(a) the duly authenticated original award or a duly certified copy of it, and

(b) the original arbitration agreement or a duly certified copy of it.

(2) If the award or agreement is in a foreign language, the party must also produce a translation of it certified by an official or sworn translator or by a diplomatic or consular agent.

Refusal of recognition or enforcement

103.—(1) Recognition or enforcement of a New York Convention award shall not be refused except in the following cases.

(2) Recognition or enforcement of the award may be refused if the person against whom it is invoked proves—

(a) that a party to the arbitration agreement was (under the law applicable to him) under some incapacity;

(b) that the arbitration agreement was not valid under the law to which the parties subjected it or, failing any indication thereon, under the law of the country where the award was made;

(c) that he was not given proper notice of the appointment of the arbitrator or of the arbitration proceedings or was otherwise unable to present his case;

(d) that the award deals with a difference not contemplated by or not falling within the terms of the submission to arbitration or contains decisions on matters beyond the scope of the submission to arbitration (but see subsection (4));

(e) that the composition of the arbitral tribunal or the arbitral procedure was not in accordance with the agreement of the parties or, failing such agreement, with the law of the country in which the arbitration took place;

(f) that the award has not yet become binding on the parties, or has been set aside or suspended by a competent authority of the country in which, or under the law of which, it was made.

(3) Recognition or enforcement of the award may also be refused if the award is in respect of a matter which is not capable of settlement by arbitration, or if it would be contrary to public policy to recognise or enforce the award.

(4) An award which contains decisions on matters not submitted to arbitration may be recognised or enforced to the extent that it contains decisions on matters submitted to arbitration which can be separated from those on matters not so submitted.

(5) Where an application for the setting aside or suspension of the award has been made to such a competent authority as is mentioned in subsection (2)(f), the court before which the award is sought to be relied upon may, if it considers it proper, adjourn the decision on the recognition or enforcement of the award.

It may also on the application of the party claiming recognition or enforcement of the award order the other party to give suitable security.

Saving for other bases of recognition or enforcement

104. Nothing in the preceding provisions of this Part affects any right to rely upon or enforce a New York Convention award at common law or under section 66.

Meaning of "the court": jurisdiction of High Court and county court

105.—(1) In this Act "the court" means the High Court or a county court, subject to the following provisions.

(2) The Lord Chancellor may by order make provision—
- (a) allocating proceedings under this Act to the High Court or to county courts or
- (b) specifying proceedings under this Act which may be commenced or taken only in the High Court or in a county court.

(3) The Lord Chancellor may by order make provision requiring proceedings of any specified description under this Act in relation to which a county court has jurisdiction to be commenced or taken in one or more specified county courts.

Any jurisdiction so exercisable by a specified county court is exercisable throughout England and Wales or, as the case may be, Northern Ireland.

(4) An order under this section—
- (a) may differentiate between categories of proceedings by reference to such criteria as the Lord Chancellor sees fit to specify, and
- (b) may make such incidental or transitional provision as the Lord Chancellor considers necessary or expedient.

(5) An order under this section for England and Wales shall be made by statutory instrument which shall be subject to annulment in pursuance of a resolution of either House of Parliament.

(6) An order under this section for Northern Ireland shall be a statutory rule for the purposes of the Statutory Rules (Northern Ireland) Order 1979 which shall be subject to annulment in pursuance of a resolution of either House of Parliament in like manner as a statutory instrument and section 5 of the Statutory Instruments Act 1946 shall apply accordingly.

Crown application

106.—(1) Part I of this Act applies to any arbitration agreement to which Her Majesty, either in right of the Crown or of the Duchy of Lancaster or otherwise, or the Duke of Cornwall, is a party.

(2) Where Her Majesty is party to an arbitration agreement otherwise than in right of the Crown, Her Majesty shall be represented for the purposes of any arbitral proceedings—

(a) where the agreement was entered into by Her Majesty in right of the Duchy of Lancaster, by the Chancellor of the Duchy or such person as he may appoint, and

(b) in any other case, by such person as Her Majesty may appoint in writing under the Royal Sign Manual.

(3) Where the Duke of Cornwall is party to an arbitration agreement, he shall be represented for the purposes of any arbitral proceedings by such person as he may appoint.

(4) References in Part I to a party or the parties to the arbitration agreement or to arbitral proceedings shall be construed, where subsection (2) or (3) applies, as references to the person representing Her Majesty or the Duke of Cornwall.

Consequential amendments and repeals

107.—(1) The enactments specified in Schedule 3 are amended in accordance with that Schedule, the amendments being consequential on the provisions of this Act.

(2) The enactments specified in Schedule 4 are repealed to the extent specified.

Extent

108.—(1) The provisions of this Act extend to England and Wales and, except as mentioned below, to Northern Ireland.

(2) The following provisions of Part II do not extend to Northern Ireland—
section 92 (exclusion of Part I in relation to small claims arbitration in the county court), and
section 93 and Schedule 2 (appointment of judges as arbitrators).

(3) Sections 89, 90 and 91 (consumer arbitration agreements), extend to Scotland and the provisions of Schedules 3 and 4 (consequential amendments and repeals) extend to Scotland as far as they relate to enactments which so extend, subject as follows.

(4) The repeal of the Arbitration Act 1975 extends only to England and Wales and Northern Ireland.

Commencement

109.—(1) The provisions of this Act come into force on such day as the Secretary of State may appoint by order made by statutory instrument, and different days may be appointed for different purposes.

(2) An order under subsection (1) may contain such transitional provisions as appear to the Secretary of State to be appropriate.

Short title

110. This Act may be cited as the Arbitration Act 1996.

SCHEDULE 1: MANDATORY PROVISIONS OF PART I (SECTION 4(1))

sections 9 to 11 (stay of legal proceedings);
section 12 (power of court to extend agreed time limits);
section 13 (application of Limitation Acts);
section 24 (power of court to remove arbitrator);
section 26(1) (effect of death of arbitrator);
section 28 (liability of parties for fees and expenses of arbitrators);
section 29 (immunity of arbitrator);
section 31 (objection to substantive jurisdiction of tribunal);

section 32 (determination of preliminary point of jurisdiction);

section 33 (general duty of tribunal);

section 37(2) (items to be treated as expenses of arbitrators);

section 40 (general duty of parties);

section 43 (securing the attendance of witnesses);

section 56 (power to withhold award in case of non-payment);

section 60 (effectiveness of agreement for payment of costs in any event);

section 66 (enforcement of award);

sections 67 and 68 (challenging the award: substantive jurisdiction and serious irregularity), and sections 70 and 71 (supplementary provisions effect of order of court) so far as relating to those sections;

section 72 (saving for rights of person who takes no part in proceedings);

section 73 (loss of right to object);

section 74 (immunity of arbitral institutions, &c.);

section 75 (charge to secure payment of solicitors' costs).

SCHEDULE 2: MODIFICATIONS OF PART I IN RELATION TO JUDGE-ARBITRATORS (SECTION 93(6))

Introductory

1. In this Schedule "judge-arbitrator" means a judge of the Commercial Court or official referee appointed as arbitrator or umpire under section 93.

General

2.—(1) Subject to the following provisions of this Schedule, references in Part I to the court shall be construed in relation to a judge-arbitrator, or in relation to the appointment of a judge-arbitrator, as references to the Court of Appeal.

(2) The references in sections 32(6), 45(6) and 69(8) to the Court of Appeal shall in such a case be construed as references to the House of Lords.

Arbitrator's fees

3.—(1) The power of the court in section 28(2) to order consideration and adjustment of the liability of a party for the fees of an arbitrator may be exercised by a judge-arbitrator.

(2) Any such exercise of the power is subject to the powers of the Court of Appeal under sections 24(4) and 25(3)(b) (directions as to entitlement to fees or expenses in case of removal or resignation).

Exercise of court powers in support of arbitration

4.—(1) Where the arbitral tribunal consists of or includes a judge-arbitrator the powers of the court under sections 42 to 44 (enforcement of peremptory orders, summoning witnesses, and other court powers) are exercisable by the High Court and also by the judge-arbitrator himself.

(2) Anything done by a judge-arbitrator in the exercise of those powers shall be regarded as done by him in his capacity as judge of the High Court and have effect as if done by that court.

Nothing in this sub-paragraph prejudices any power vested in him as arbitrator or umpire.

Extension of time for making award

5.—(1) The power conferred by section 50 (extension of time for making award) is exercisable by the judge-arbitrator himself.

(2) Any appeal from a decision of a judge-arbitrator under that section lies to the Court of Appeal with the leave of that court.

Withholding award in case of non-payment

6.—(1) The provisions of paragraph 7 apply in place of the provisions of section 56 (power to withhold award in the case of non-payment) in relation to the withholding of an award for non-payment of the fees and expenses of a judge-arbitrator.

(2) This does not affect the application of section 56 in relation to the delivery of such an award by an arbitral or other institution or person vested by the parties with powers in relation to the delivery of the award.

7.—(1) A judge-arbitrator may refuse to deliver an award except upon payment of the fees and expenses mentioned in section 56(1).

(2) The judge-arbitrator may, on an application by a party to the arbitral proceedings, order that if he pays into the High Court the fees and expenses demanded, or such lesser amount as the judge-arbitrator may specify—

(a) the award shall be delivered,
(b) the amount of the fees and expenses properly payable shall be determined by such means and upon such terms as he may direct, and
(c) out of the money paid into court there shall be paid out such fees and expenses as may be found to be properly payable and the balance of the money (if any) shall be paid out to the applicant.

(3) For this purpose the amount of fees and expenses properly payable is the amount the applicant is liable to pay under section 28 or any agreement relating to the payment of the arbitrator.

(4) No application to the judge-arbitrator under this paragraph may be made where there is any available arbitral process for appeal or review of the amount of the fees or expenses demanded.

(5) Any appeal from a decision of a judge-arbitrator under this paragraph lies to the Court of Appeal with the leave of that court.

(6) Where a party to arbitral proceedings appeals under sub-paragraph (5), an arbitrator is entitled to appear and be heard.

Correction of award or additional award

8. Subsections (4) to (6) of section 57 (correction of award or additional award: time limit for application or exercise of power) do not apply to a judge-arbitrator.

Costs

9. Where the arbitral tribunal consists of or includes a judge-arbitrator the powers of the court under section 63(4) (determination of recoverable costs) shall be exercised by the High Court.

10.—(1) The power of the court under section 64 to determine an arbitrator's reasonable fees and expenses may be exercised by a judge-arbitrator.

(2) Any such exercise of the power is subject to the powers of the Court of Appeal under sections 24(4) and 25(3)(b) (directions as to entitlement to fees or expenses in case of removal or resignation).

Enforcement of award

11. The leave of the court required by section 66 (enforcement of award) may in the case of an award of a judge-arbitrator be given by the judge-arbitrator himself.

Solicitor's costs

12. The powers of the court to make declarations and orders under the provisions applied by section 75 (power to charge property recovered in arbitral proceedings with the payment of solicitors' costs) may be exercised by the judge-arbitrator.

Powers of court in relation to service of documents

13.—(1) The power of the court under section 77(2) (powers of court in relation to service of documents) is exercisable by the judge-arbitrator.

(2) Any appeal from a decision of a judge-arbitrator under that section lies to the Court of Appeal with the leave of that court.

Powers of court to extend time limits relating to arbitral proceedings

14.—(1) The power conferred by section 79 (power of court to extend time limits relating to arbitral proceedings) is exercisable by the judge-arbitrator himself.

(2) Any appeal from a decision of a judge-arbitrator under that section lies to the Court of Appeal with the leave of that court.

THE DAC REPORT: EXTRACTS RELATING TO COSTS

The Departmental Advisory Committee on Arbitration Law published a report on the Arbitration Bill in February 1996. This committee was responsible for the text of the Bill which, with amendments, is now the Arbitration Act 1996. Extracts from the report relating specifically to the subject matter of this book are given below.

Clause 28. Joint and several liability of parties to arbitrators for fees and expenses

120. Arbitration proceedings necessarily involve the incurring of expenditure. The arbitrators have to be paid, and the parties incur expense in presenting their cases to the tribunal. The issue of costs involves at least three quite discrete elements:

(i) As a matter of general contract law, arbitrators, experts, institutions and any other payees whatsoever are entitled to be paid what has been agreed with them by any of the parties. Therefore, for example, if a party appoints an arbitrator for an agreed fee, as a matter of general contract law (rather than anything in this Bill), that arbitrator is entitled to that fee.

(ii) It is generally accepted that all parties are jointly and severally liable for the fees of an arbitrator. This is an issue as to the entitlement of arbitrators, and as such is quite distinct from the third element.

(iii) As in court litigation, when one party is successful, that party should normally recover at least a proportion of his costs. This issue, being where the burden of costs should lie, is an issue as between the parties.

121. The Bill contains provisions as to costs and fees in two separate parts: the joint and several liability owed by the parties to the arbitrators (the second element) is addressed in this clause, whilst the third element (i.e. the responsibility for costs as between the parties) is addressed in Clauses 59–65. The first element, being a matter of general contract law, is not specifically addressed by either set of provisions, but is preserved in both. It is extremely important to distinguish between these provisions.

122. Clause 28 is concerned with the rights of the arbitrators in respect of fees and expenses. As subsection (5) makes clear, and as explained above, this provision is not concerned with which of the parties should (as between themselves) bear these costs as the result of the arbitration, which is dealt with later in the Bill, nor with any contractual right an arbitrator may have in respect of fees and expenses.

123. As we understand the present law, the parties are jointly and severally liable to the arbitrator for his fees and expenses. The present position seems to be that if these are agreed by one party, the other party becomes liable, even if he played no part in making that agreement; and circumstances may arise in which that party is unable to obtain a reduction of the amount by taxation. It seems to us that whilst arbitrators should be protected by this joint and several liability of the parties, a potentially unfair result must be avoided: a party who never agreed to the appointment by another party of an exceptionally expensive arbitrator should not be held jointly and severally liable

187

for that arbitrator's exceptional fees. To this end, we have stipulated, in Clause 28(1), that a party's joint and several liability to an arbitrator only extends to "reasonable fees". Of course, if a party has agreed an exceptional fee with an arbitrator, that party may still be pursued by that arbitrator, under general contract law, which is preserved in Clause 28(5).

124. We have proposed a mechanism to allow a party to go to the Court if any question arises as to the reasonableness of the arbitrator's charges. The Court is empowered to adjust fees and expenses even after they have been paid, since circumstances may well arise in which a question about the level of fees and expenses only arises after payment has been made. For example, a large advance payment may be made at a time when it is considered that the arbitration will take a long time, but this does not turn out to be the case. However, the Court must be satisfied that it is reasonable in the circumstances to order repayment. Thus an applicant who delays in making an application is likely to receive short shrift from the Court, nor is the Court likely to order repayment where the arbitrator has in good faith acted in such a way that it would be unjust to order repayment. It seems to us that it is necessary to set out expressly in the Bill that the power of the Court extends to dealing with fees and expenses aleady paid since otherwise there could be an argument that this power is confined to fees and expenses yet to be paid.

125. These provisions are extended by subsection (6) to include an arbitrator who has ceased to act and an umpire who has not replaced the other arbitrators. An arbitrator may cease to act through the operation of Clauses 23 to 26, or if an umpire takes over following a disagreement.

126. The liability in Clause 28(1) is to "the parties". It seems to us to follow that a person who has not participated at all, and in respect of whom it is determined that the arbitral tribunal has no jurisdiction, would not be a "party" for the purposes of this clause (*cf.* Clause 72). More difficult questions may well arise in respect of persons who have participated, for there the doctrine of Kompetenz-Kompetenz (Clauses 30 and 31) may have to be weighed against the proposition that a party can hardly be under any liability in respect of the fees and expenses of the tribunal which he has successfully established should not have been acting at all on the merits of the dispute.

127. It is to be noted that arbitrators' fees and expenses include, by virtue of Clause 37(2), the fees and expenses of tribunal appointed experts, etc.

128. It seems that the present joint and several liability of the parties to an arbitrator for his fees may rest on some implied contract said to exist between them. Be this as it may, such an implied contract (in so far as it related to fees and expenses) would not survive by virtue of Clause 81 of this Bill, because this only saves rules of law which are consistent with Part I. Any implied contract imposing a liability for more than reasonable fees and expenses would clearly be inconsistent with Clause 28(1). Furthermore, since Clause 28(1) gives a statutory right there remains no good reason for any implied contractual right. As stated above, any specific contract would, however, of course be preserved by Clause 28(5).

129. Contrary to some suggestions made to us, it seems to us that rights of contribution between the parties in relation to their statutory liability under Clause 28(1) can best be left to the ordinary rules which relate to joint and several liability generally.

130. Clause 28 is made mandatory, since otherwise the parties could by agreement between themselves deprive the arbitrators of what seems to us to be a very necessary protection.

THE ARBITRAL PROCEEDINGS

Clause 33. General duty of the tribunal

150. This is one of the central proposals in our Bill (grounded on Article 18 of the Model Law). It is a mandatory provision, since, as is explained below, we fail to see how a proceeding which departed from the stipulated duties could properly be described as an arbitration. We endeavour to set out, in the simplest, clearest terms we have been able to devise, how the tribunal should approach and deal with its task, which is to do full justice to the parties. In the following Clauses we set out in detail the powers available to the tribunal for this purpose.

151. It has been suggested that the generality of Clause 33 may be problematic: that it may be an invitation to recalcitrant parties to launch challenges, or that vagueness will give rise to arguments. The advantage of arbitration is that it offers a dispute resolution system which can be tailored to the particular dispute to an extent which litigation finds it difficult to do. Thus depending on the nature of the dispute, there will be numerous ways in which the arbitration can be conducted. It is quite impossible to list all the possible variants and to set out what may or may not be done. Indeed any attempt to do so would defeat one of the main purposes of the Bill, which is to encourage arbitral tribunals not slavishly to follow court or other set procedures. It follows that the only limits can be those set out in the present clause. It is to be hoped that the Courts will take a dim view of those who try to attack awards because of suggested breaches of this clause which have no real substance. At the same time, it can hardly be suggested that awards should not be open to attack when the tribunal has not acted in accordance with the principles stated.

152. It has further been suggested that this part of the Bill will cause the demise of the amateur arbitrator. If by this is meant the demise of people who purport to act as arbitrators but who are either unable or unwilling (or both) to conduct the proceedings in accordance with what most would regard as self-evident rules of justice, then we indeed hope that this will be one of the results. But since these rules of justice are generally accepted in our democratic society, and are not merely theoretical considerations that concern lawyers alone, we can see no reason why the Bill should discourage anyone who is ready willing and able to apply them. Indeed we consider that the Bill will encourage and support all such people.

153. Sometimes the parties to an arbitration employ lawyers who seek, in effect, to bully a non-legal arbitrator into taking a course of action which is against his better instincts, by seeking to blind him with legal "science" to get their way. Again, in some circles it is thought that somehow the procedures in an arbitration should be modelled on Court procedures, and that to adopt other methods would be "misconduct" (an expression that the Bill does not use) on the part of the arbitrator. This part of the Bill is designed to prevent such bullying and to explode the theory that an arbitration has always to follow Court procedures. If an arbitrator is satisfied that the way he wants to proceed fulfils his duty under this Clause and that the powers he wants to exercise are available to him under the following Clauses, then he should have the courage of his own convictions and proceed accordingly, unless the parties are agreed that he should adopt some other course.

The relationship between Clauses 1(b), 33 and 34(1)

154. It has been suggested to us there could be a conflict between:
(i) the mandatory duty cast on arbitrators by Clause 33 and
(ii) the principle of party autonomy in Clause 1(b) and the proviso in Clause 34(1). As we explain below, the DAC does not consider that there is any inconsistency between these two principles.

155. Under the principle of party autonomy, the parties are free to agree upon

anything to do with the arbitration, subject only to such safeguards as are necessary in the public interest (Clause 1(b)). The mandatory provisions set out those matters which have effect notwithstanding any agreement to the contrary: see Clause 4. It seems to us that the public interest dictates that Clause 33 must be mandatory, i.e. that the parties cannot effectively agree to dispense with the duty laid on arbitrators under Clause 33. In other words, they cannot effectively agree that the arbitrators can act unfairly, or that the arbitrators can be partial, or that the arbitrators can decide that the parties (or one of them) should not have a reasonable opportunity of putting his case or answering that of his opponent, or indeed that the arbitrators can adopt procedures that are unsuitable for the particular circumstances of the case or are unnecessarily slow or expensive, so that the means for resolving the matters to be determined is unfair. It is, of course, extremely unlikely in the nature of things that the parties would wish deliberately to make such bizarre agreements, but were this to happen, then it seems to us that such agreements should be ineffective for the purposes of this Bill, i.e not binding on the parties or the tribunal.

156. However, a situation could well arise in practice in cases where the parties are agreed on a method of proceeding which they consider complies with the first of the general principles set out in Clause 1 (and which therefore the tribunal could adopt consistently with its duty under Clause 33) but the tribunal takes a different view, or where they are agreed in their opposition to a method of proceeding which the tribunal considers should be adopted in order to perform its Clause 33 duty.

157. In our view it is neither desirable nor practicable to stipulate that the tribunal can override the agreement of the parties. It is not desirable, because the type of arbitration we are discussing is a consensual process which depends on the agreement of the parties who are surely entitled (if they can agree) to have the final say on how they wish their dispute to be resolved. It is not practicable, since there is no way in which the parties can be forced to adopt a method of proceeding if they are agreed that this is not the way they wish to proceed. The latter is the case even if it could be established that their agreement was ineffective since it undermined or prevented performance of the duty made mandatory by Clause 33.

158. A party would be unable to enforce an ineffective agreement against the other parties, nor would such an agreement bind the tribunal, but the problem under discussion only exists while the parties are in fact at one, whether or not their agreement is legally effective.

159. In circumstances such as these, the tribunal (assuming it has failed to persuade the parties to take a different course) has the choice of adopting the course preferred by the parties or of resigning. Indeed, resignation would be the only course if the parties were in agreement in rejecting the method preferred by the tribunal, and no other way of proceeding was agreed by them or considered suitable by the tribunal.

160. We have stipulated elsewhere in the Bill that the immunity we propose for arbitrators does not extend to any liability they may be under for resigning (Clause 29) though under Clause 25 they may seek relief in respect of such liability from the Court. The reason for the limitation on immunity is that cases may arise where the resignation of the arbitrator is wholly indefensible and has caused great delay and loss. In our view Clause 25 would suffice to protect arbitrators who resigned because they reasonably believed that the agreement of the parties prevented them from properly performing their Clause 33 duty. Furthermore, arbitrators could always stipulate for a right to resign in such circumstances as a term of their appointment.

161. If, on the other hand, the tribunal adopted a method of proceeding agreed by the parties, it seems to us that none of the parties could afterwards validly complain that the tribunal had failed in its Clause 33 duty, since the tribunal would only have done what the parties had asked it to do. Again, the fact that as between the parties such an agreement may have been ineffective as undermining or preventing performance of the Clause 33 duties seems to us to be wholly irrelevant. It could of course be said

that the tribunal had breached its Clause 33 duty, but this would have no practical consequences since the parties themselves would have brought about this state of affairs, and would therefore be unable to seek any relief in respect of it.

162. Some people have expressed concern that there is a danger that lawyers will agree between themselves a method of proceeding which the tribunal consider to be unnecessarily long or expensive. However, if a tribunal considered, for example, that lawyers were trying either deliberately to "churn" the case for their own private advantage or were simply but misguidedly seeking to adopt unnecessary procedures etc, the obvious solution would be to ask them to confirm that their respective clients had been made aware of the views of the tribunal but were nevertheless in agreement that the course proposed by their lawyers should be adopted. At the end of the day, however, the fact remains that the only sanction the arbitrators have is to resign.

163. In summary, therefore, we consider that the duty of the arbitrators under Clause 33 and the right of the parties to agree how the arbitration should be conducted do fit together. Under Clause 33 the tribunal have the specified duties. Under Clause 34 therefore, the tribunal must decide all procedural and evidential matters, subject to the right of the parties to agree any matter. If the parties reach an agreement on how to proceed which clashes with the duty of the tribunal or which the tribunal reasonably considers does so, then the arbitrators can either resign and have the protection of Clause 25, or can adopt what the parties want and will not afterwards be liable to the parties for doing so.

Further points

164. In this Clause we have provided that the tribunal shall give each party a "reasonable opportunity" of putting his case and dealing with that of his opponent. Article 18 of the Model Law uses the expression "full opportunity".

165. We prefer the word "reasonable" because it removes any suggestion that a party is entitled to take as long as he likes, however objectively unreasonable this may be. We are sure that this was not intended by those who framed the Model Law, for it would entail that a party is entitled to an unreasonable time, which justice can hardly require. Indeed the contrary is the case, for an unreasonable time would *ex hypothesi* mean unnecessary delay and expense, things which produce injustice and which accordingly would offend the first principle of Clause 1, as well as Clauses 33 and 40.

Clause 38 General powers exercisable by the tribunal

189. These provisions represent a significant re-drawing of the relationship between arbitration and the Court. Wherever a power could properly be exercised by a tribunal rather than the Court, provision has been made for this, thereby reducing the need to insur the expense and inconvenience of making applications to Court during arbitral proceedings.

190. The first of the powers in this Clause is one which enables the tribunal to order security for costs. The power presently given to the Court to order security for costs in arbitrations is removed in its entirety.

191. This is a major change from the present position where only the Court can order security for costs. The theory which lay behind the present law is that it is the duty of an arbitral tribunal to decide the substantive merits of the dispute referred to it and that it would not be performing this duty if it stayed or struck out the proceedings pending the provision of security: see for example, *Re Unione Stearinerie Lanza and Weiner* [1917] 2 KB 558.

192. We do not subscribe to this theory, which Parliament has already abandoned in the context of striking out a claim for want of prosecution. In our view, when the parties agree to arbitrate, they are agreeing that their dispute will be resolved by this means. To our minds (in the absence of express stipulations to the contrary) this does

not mean that the dispute is necessarily to be decided on its substantive merits. It is in truth an agreement that it will be resolved by the application of the agreed arbitral process. If one party then fails to comply with that process, then it seems to us that it is entirely within what the parties have agreed that the tribunal can resolve the dispute on this ground.

193. Apart from this, the proposition that the Court should involve itself in such matters as deciding whether a claimant in an arbitration should provide security for costs has received universal condemnation in the context of international arbitrations. It is no exaggeration to say that the recent decision of the House of Lords in *S.A. Coppee Lavalin NV* v. *Ken-Renn Chemicals and Fertilisers* [1994] 2 WLR 631 was greeted with dismay by those in the international arbitration community who have at heart the desire to promote our country as a world centre for arbitration. We share those concerns.

194. It has been suggested to the DAC that the court should retain a power to order security for costs that may be incurred up to the appointment of the tribunal. We have not been persuaded, however, that this is really necessary.

195. It has been pointed out that in some cases an application for security before an arbitral tribunal might involve disclosing to that tribunal the fact that an offer of settlement had been or was about to be made. Under the court system, such disclosure can be made to a court other than that which will try the merits of the case.

196. We are not disturbed by this. It seems to us that a tribunal, properly performing its duty under Clause 33, could and should not be influenced by such matters, if the case proceeds to a hearing on the merits, nor do we accept that the disclosure of such information could somehow disqualify the tribunal from acting.

197. Clause 38(3) has been the subject of significant criticism since the Bill was introduced. In the light of this, we have concluded that it must be redrawn. Chapter 6, to which reference should be made, contains a full discussion of the problems with this provision as currently drafted, and our recommendations for its amendment.

198. Whilst the sanction in court for a failure to provide security for costs is normally a stay of the action, this is inappropriate in arbitration: if an arbitrator stayed proceedings, the arbitration would come to a halt without there necessarily being an award which could be challenged (e.g. if a party seeks to continue the proceedings). We have therefore included a specific sanction with respect to a failure to provide security for costs, which is to be found in Clause 41(6). This provision also follows the practice of the English Commercial Court, which changed from the old practice of ordering a stay of proceedings if security was not provided. The disadvantage of the latter course was that it left the proceedings dormant but alive, so that years later they could be revived by the provision of security.

199. Clause 38 provides the tribunal with other powers in relation to the arbitration proceedings. We trust that these are self-explanatory.

COSTS OF THE ARBITRATION

Clause 59. Costs of the arbitration
Clause 60. Agreement to pay costs in any event
Clause 61. Award of costs
Clause 62. Effect of agreement or award about costs
Clause 63. The recoverable costs of the arbitration
Clause 64. Recoverable fees and expenses of arbitrators
Clause 65. Power to limit recoverable costs

265. In these Clauses we have attempted to provide a code dealing with how the costs of an arbitration should be attributed between the parties. The question of the

right of the arbitrators to fees and expenses is dealt with earlier in that part of the Bill concerned with the arbitral tribunal: see Clause 28.

266. Clause 59 defines costs.

267. Clause 60 is a mandatory provision preventing effective agreements to pay the whole or part of the costs in any event unless made after the dispute has arisen. The Clause is based on section 18(3) of the Arbitration Act 1950. The Committee are of the view that public policy continues to dictate that such a provision should remain.

268. Clause 62 empowers the arbitrators to make an award in relation to costs. Subsection (2) sets out the general principle to be applied, which is the same principle that is applicable in Court.

269. It has been suggested that arbitral tribunals should not be fettered in this way, but to our minds it is helpful to state the principle, especially for those who may not be lawyers and who otherwise might not know how to proceed. Furthermore, it seems to us that there is no reason why the general principle should not apply to arbitrations: it certainly does under the present law. The parties are, of course, free to agree on other principles, subject to Clause 60.

270. Clauses 63 and 64 are we hope more or less self-explanatory. Clearly there has to be a special regime for the fees and expenses of the arbitrators, for otherwise they would be left with the power to decide for themselves whether or not they had overcharged!

271. Clause 64(4) presents any contractual right an arbitrator may have to payment of his fees and expenses. If a party has agreed these, then it would in our view be wrong to allow the Court to adjust the amount, i.e. to rewrite that agreement.

272. Clause 65 contains a new proposal. It gives the tribunal power to limit in advance the amount of recoverable costs. We consider that such a power, properly used, could prove to be extremely valuable as set out in Clause 33. The Clause enables the tribunal to put a ceiling on the costs, so that while a party can continue to spend as much as it likes on an arbitration it will not be able to recover more than the ceiling limit from the other party. This will have the added virtue of discouraging those who wish to use their financial muscle to intimidate their opponents into giving up through fear that by going on they might be subject to a costs order which they could not sustain.

SUPPLEMENTARY RECOMMENDATIONS

356. The foregoing discussion is based on the text of the Bill as it was introduced in December 1995. Since that date we have had the advantage of considering the speeches made in the House of Lords on the Second Reading and some comments and suggestions from others, as well as looking once against the text of the Bill in the course of preparing this Report. In consequence, we make the following recommendations.

Clause 38(3). Security for costs

364. In the draft Clauses published in July 1995, the power to order security for costs was expressed in very general terms. This elicited a number of responses which expressed concern that there were no principles or guidelines for the exercise of this power. It is certainly the case that the power to order security for costs, unless exercised with great care, can all too easily work injustice rather than justice.

365. The rules and principles applied by the Courts with respect to security for costs have been carefully worked out over many years, and are contained in a large amount of case law that has developed alongside Order 23 of the Rules of the Supreme Court. Given the concerns referred to above, the DAC considered whether to set out these rules and principles in the Bill. In the end we decided that this would be simply

impracticable: a codification of all the relevant case law would be extremely difficult, would result in very lengthy and complicated provisions, and may well have an unintended impact on how this area is approached by the Courts.

366. Clause 38(3) of the current draft of the Bill reflects what we initially concluded was the only solution to this difficulty: it provides that arbitrators are to have power to order a party to provide security for costs "wherever the court would have power ..." and that this power is to be exercised: "on the same principles as the court." In the light of many comments received since the Bill was introduced (including a significant number of criticisms of this subsection from foreign arbitration specialists and institutions), we have had to reconsider this area, and, after much careful thought, we have concluded that Clause 38(3) requires amendment for the following reasons:

(i) As drafted, this subsection is very far from being "user-friendly". Without referring to the Rules of the Supreme Court, and the case law referred to in the relevant part of the White Book, it would be impossible for any domestic or foreign user to determine what the nature and scope of the power conferred here is. Lay arbitrators may have difficulty locating or even, perhaps, understanding the relevant law (any error of law, of course, being a potential ground for appeal). In the case of a foreign arbitration that has its seat in this country for the sole reason that this is a neutral forum, it would be extremely undesirable for parties to have to instruct English lawyers in order to make sense of this provision. This alone could constitute a powerful disincentive to selecting this country as an arbitral seat. Indeed, throughout the Bill, we have been very careful to avoid any such express cross-references to other legal sources.

(ii) One of the grounds on which an order for security for costs may be made in Court is that the plaintiff is ordinarily resident out of the jurisdiction: see Order 23, Rule 1(1)(a) of the Rules of the Supreme Court. On further consideration of the matter, we have concluded that it would be very damaging to this country's position as the leading centre for international arbitrations to make this ground available to arbitral tribunals. It would reasonably appear to those abroad who are minded to arbitrate their claims here that foreigners were being singled out for special and undeserved treatment. (Of course if the parties agree to invest their tribunal with power to order security for costs on this ground, they are free to do so.)

(iii) On reflection, the concerns expressed above as to the potential scope of the power conferred by Clause 38(3) and the possibilities of injustice may be overstated. The other provisions of the Bill confer very far-reaching powers on arbitrators, and it has been made clear throughout that this is tempered, for example, by the mandatory duty in Clause 33. The same would be true of the power to order security for costs: in exercising the power, the tribunal would have to comply with Clause 33, and any serious irregularity could form the basis of a challenge. In agreeing to arbitration, parties in effect agree that their disputes could be decided differently from a Court, although in accordance with principles of justice. The fact that arbitrators may decide an issue as to security for costs differently from a judge appears to be no more than an aspect of this. It is true that if this power is improperly exercised, a claim could, for example, be stifled without justification. It is equally true, however, that the Bill contains mechanisms for parties to challenge any such injustice or improper conduct, and sufficient warnings to arbitrators as to their mandatory duties.

367. We remain of the view that the power to order security for costs is an important one, and should be given to arbitrators, and also that some basic restrictions should be set out in this Clause, in the light of the points made above. To this end, we recommend that Clause 38(3) be deleted, and replaced with a new provision along the following lines:

"(3) The tribunal may order a claimant to provide security for the costs of the arbitration.

Such power shall not be exercised on the grounds only that such party is

(a) an individual ordinarily resident in a state other than the United Kingdom,

(b) a body corporate which was incorporated in or has its central management and control exercised in a state other than the United Kingdom."

368. Such a provision would allow arbitrators a flexibility in exercising this power, within the confines of their strict duty in Clause 33. The risk of an order on the sole ground that a party is from abroad, would be removed. Similarly, there would be no need for an arbitrator, whether domestic or foreign, to discern the English or Northern Irish law in this area, or, indeed, to instruct local lawyers in this respect. An arbitrator may well exercise this power differently from a Court (as with many other powers conferred by the Bill), but any misuse could be corrected under the other provisions of the Bill.

369. It is of course the case that orders for security are not to be made automatically, but only when the justice of the case so requires. We appreciate that cases are likely to arise when deciding what is just may be very difficult. For example, a claimant may contend that he might be prevented from continuing if he has to put up security, whilst at the same time a respondent is contending that unless security is provided, he is likely to be ruined. However, to our minds, this is merely an example of the balancing of factors in order to achieve the most just result possible which is part of the essential function of arbitrators.

370. The power to award security for costs under the proposed provision could be exercised against counter-claimants as well as claimants. This we have covered in the definition Clause (see Clause 82(1)).

INDEX

Index

Index

ARBITRATION PRACTICE AND PROCEDURE
Interlocutary and Hearing Problems, 2nd Edition
by D Mark Cato
Foreword by Lord Mustill, President, Chartered Institute of Arbitrators
Lloyd's Commercial Law Library

Commenting on the first edition, Rowen Planterose, leading construction barrister, said:

'The test of any work of reference is the frequency of its use. This volume will not gather dust. Most will regard it as an essential source of information' **Arbitration**
Journal of the Chartered Institute of Arbitrators

Cato has extensively re-written and expanded his classic and invaluable practical guide to arbitration, to reflect the provisions of the 1996 Arbitration Act and to discuss and explore potential problems which might arise from that act.

Taking his lead from the experience of practising arbitrators, Cato examines the very problems encountered on a day to day basis by professional advisers, lawyers, arbitrators, expert witnesses and parties to arbitration.

Alphabetically arranged from *Appointments* to *Witnesses*, each problem is listed with the facts of the case, questions arising and a suggested course of action to take, making this an essential and accessible work of reference for all involved in arbitration. *Arbitration Practice and Procedure* has secured its position, for years to come, as the leading and most authoritative textbook of its kind on the subject.

ORDER FORM

Please complete and return this form today by mail or fax to:

LLP Limited,
Customer Services Dept., Sheepen Place,
Colchester, Essex CO3 3LP, UK.
Fax: +44 (0) 1206 772 771
OR phone your order and pay by credit card
AND CLAIM A 5% DISCOUNT
Tel: +44 (0) 1206 772 866

Please supply___copy(ies) of:
Arbitration Practice and Procedure   £150 / US$285
Please add Postage and Packing of £5/$8 per book
(Free on 4 or more copies) £/$_____

Total value of order   £/$_____

|L|L|P|

Payment details

❑ I enclose a cheque for £/$ _____
made payable to LLP Limited

❑ Please charge my credit card:
Access/Visa/Diners/Amex/Mastercard
No._____Exp_____

❑ Please send me a prepayment invoice
(your books will be sent when your
payment is received)

Name _____
Company_____
Address _____
_____
_____
Tel _____ Fax _____
Nature of business _____

ARBITRATION LAW

THE DEFINITIVE WORK

Professor R. M. Merkin

Concentrating on modern trends in arbitration law for maximum practical use, *Arbitration Law* is indispensable to the work of lawyers, arbitrators, trade associations, bankers and insurers.

Clear subject headings and comprehensive coverage provide both informative discussion of the principles and a reliable reference to the relevant source materials, whilst comprehensive appendices set out the UK legislation. The facts of leading cases and their implications are explained, covering both commercial and consumer arbitrations and referring to international arbitrations where these have significance for English law and the Arbitration Act 1996.

Regular supplements and new chapters on procedure and the Arbitration Act 1996 - with annotations and clause-by-clause commentary - ensure that you are always kept informed of the latest cases and decisions.

185044367X Looseleaf 2 Volumes Updated Work

ORDER FORM

AN ARBITRATION WORKBOOK
THE SANCTUARY HOUSE CASE
by D. Mark Cato

The Sanctuary House Case, published in two easily accessible volumes, is an innovative and unique practice manual.

In two volumes

Volume One outlines a hypothetical situation based on real life cases addressing the entire arbitral process from appointment of arbitrator to award. Volume Two leads the practitioner through many practice suggestions and solutions substantiated by appropriate/accompanying documentation including invaluable in-depth commentary on each clause of the Arbitration Act 1996. Through extensive cross-referencing between volumes, the reader is encouraged to work through both common and complex arbitral issues.

The author has succeeded in closing the gap between the theory of arbitration law, substantive law and procedural law and the practical management of the arbitral process.

1850448531 Hard Cover £136/US$258 1996